Table of Contents

vii List of Reviewers

ix Editors' Note

ARTICLES

1 **The National Association for Women in Education: An Enduring Legacy**
by Lynn M. Gangone

23 **Gender Differences Over the Span of College: Challenges to Achieving Equity**
by Linda J. Sax, Emily Arms

49 **Leadership in a World of Divided Feminism**
by Adrianna Kezar, Jamie Lester

74 **A Window Into the Culture of Leadership Within Higher Education Through the Leadership Definitions of Women Faculty: A Case Study of ELAM Women Faculty Alumnae**
by Sharon A. McDade, Kirk A. Nooks, Phillip J. King, Lorraine Sloma-Williams, Yu-Chuan Chuang, Rosalyn C. Richman, Page S. Morahan

103 **Welfare Women Go Elite: The Ada Comstock Scholars Program**
by Auden D. Thomas

123 **Communities of Exclusion: Women Student Experiences in Information Technology Classrooms**
by Julia Colyar

143 **The Impact of Childhood Abuse on University Women's Career Choice**
by Rosemary C. Reilly, Miranda D'Amico

164 **She Fears You: Teaching College Men to End Rape**
by Keith E. Edwards, Troy Headrick

181 **A Man's Academy? The Dissertation Process as Feminist Resistance**
by Jennifer R. Wolgemuth, Clifford P. Harbour

202 **American Indian Women in Academia: The Joys and Challenges**
by Mary Jo Tippeconnic Fox

PROGRAM DESCRIPTIONS

222 **Virtual Women's Center**
by Karyn Benner, Ferris State University, Michigan

223 **Pilot Women's Empowerment Program**
by Claudia F. Curry, Community College of Philadelphia

225 **Professional Peer Clinical Supervision: A Model for the Professional Development of Counselor Educators**
by Jody B. Gallagher, Edinboro University of Pennsylvania

227 **Benefiting Female Students in Science, Math, and Engineering: Establishing a WISE Learning Community**
by Laurie A. Witucki, Diana G. Pace,
Kathleen M. Blumreich, Grand Valley State University, Michigan

229 **Mentoring-for-Leadership Lunch Series for Women SEM Faculty**
by Joyce Yen, University of Washington

BOOK REVIEWS

231 ***The Balancing Act: Gender Perspectives in Faculty Roles and Work Lives***
Reviewed by Jennifer O. Duffy, Suffolk University, Massachusetts

Journal About

Women in Higher Education

VOLUME 1 ◆ WWW.NASPA.ORG/JAWHE

Scholarship about women faculty, students, and administrators in higher education

Published by
NASPA–Student Affairs Administrators in Higher Education

About the *Journal*

Published annually, the *Journal About Women in Higher Education* is a blind peer-reviewed scholarly journal that aims to deepen understanding of issues facing women faculty, students, and administrators. The *Journal About Women in Higher Education* publishes articles that focus on empirical research, pedagogy and administrative practice. Intended for both practitioners and researchers, the *Journal* is designed to increase interest in research about women faculty, students, and administrators in higher education and to highlight current examples of this research. The *Journal About Women in Higher Education* offers research reflecting a variety of paradigms and issues affecting women in higher education in all their diversity.

The *Journal About Women in Higher Education* is sponsored by NASPA's Center for Scholarship, Research, and Professional Development for Women. Financial support for the inaugural issue provided by *Diverse: Issues in Higher Education.*

Membership and Subscriptions

Information concerning application for membership in NASPA and subscriptions to the *Journal About Women in Higher Education* may be obtained from

NASPA
1875 Connecticut Ave., NW, Suite 418
Washington, DC 20009
telephone 202-265-7500 • www.naspa.org

Manuscripts

Manuscripts submitted for publication should meet the requirements of the *Journal About Women in Higher Education's* "Guidelines for Authors." Visit www.naspa.org/jawhe for complete submission information.

Ownership

The *Journal About Women in Higher Education* is published annually by the National Association of Student Personnel Administrators (NASPA), 1875 Connecticut Ave., NW, Suite 418, Washington, DC 20009.

POSTMASTER: Send address changes to: *Journal About Women in Higher Education,* National Association of Student Personnel Administrators, 1875 Connecticut Ave., NW, Suite 418, Washington, DC 20009

Permissions, Reprints, and Single Issues

NASPA does not discriminate on the basis of race, color, national origin, religion, sex, age, gender identity, gender expression, affectional or sexual orientation, or disability in any of its policies, programs, and services.

Additional copies may be purchased by contacting the NASPA publications department at 301-638-1749 or visiting http://bookstore.naspa.org

ISSN 1940-7882

ISBN 0-931654-54-8

234 *The Doctor's Complete College Girls' Health Guide: From Sex to Drugs to the Freshmen Fifteen*
Reviewed by M.E. Yeager, Kansas State University

236 *"Strangers" of the Academy: Asian Women Scholars in Higher Education*
Reviewed by Yuanting Zhang, Bowling Green University, Ohio

239 *Removing Barriers: Women in Academic Science, Technology, Engineering, and Mathematics*
Reviewed by Shaki Asgari, Fordham University, New York

242 *College Girls: Bluestockings, Sex Kittens, and Coeds, Then and Now*
Reviewed by Amy Thompson McCandless, College of Charleston, South Carolina

List of Reviewrs

Editors

Barbara K. Townsend	University of Missouri – Columbia
Susan B. Twombly	University of Kansas

Editorial Board

Ann Blackhurst	Minnesota State University
Jill Carnaghi	Washington University in St. Louis
Johnetta Cross Brazzell	University of Arkansas – Fayetteville
Jeni Hart	University of Missouri
Susan Jones	University of Maryland
Sarah Marshall	Central Michigan University
Sharon McDade	George Washington University
Laura Perna	University of Pennsylvania
Robert Schwartz	Florida State University
Gail Short Hansen	American University
Bette Simmons	County College of Morris
Kathryn Tuttle	University of Kansas
Ed Whipple	Bowling Green State University

Other Reviewers

Marilyn Amey	Michigan State University
Karen Cockrell	University of Missouri
Brad Curs	University of Missouri
Zaneeta Daver	NASPA
Patrick Dilley	Southern Illinois University
Joe Donaldson	University of Missouri
Pam Eddy	Central Michigan University
Gail Fitzgerald	University of Missouri

Editors' Note

We welcome you to the inaugural issue of the *Journal About Women in Higher Education*. Sponsored by NASPA's Center for Scholarship, Research, and Professional Development for Women, the *Journal* focuses on women in higher education: students, student affairs staff, other staff and administrative groups, and faculty. The intended audience is anyone who cares about highlighting and improving the experiences of women in higher education.

In the 2007 call for manuscripts, the *Journal* editors sought scholarly essays and research-based manuscripts that illuminate important issues related to women in higher education and that make an original contribution to the knowledge base about these women. In response to this call, we received 67 articles indicating, as the NASPA Center for Women thought, that there is an interest in scholarly writing and publication about women in higher education. The bulk of the manuscripts were about college students, primarily undergraduates; as a consequence, the majority of the articles in this issue are about students. Other topics among the submitted manuscripts were articles about women faculty; women leaders, especially deans of women; and curriculum and pedagogy that supported women. We also received a few articles about women in other countries. Although none of those articles appear in this issue, we look forward to publishing comparative articles in future issues of the *Journal About Women in Higher Education*. In terms of institutional settings, the majority of the articles focused on women in research universities or more generically women, especially students, in 4-year institutions. Since our intent is to represent all of higher education in this *Journal,* including community colleges, we were disappointed to receive almost no manuscripts addressing women in this important sector.

Among the 67 manuscripts we received, several described and sometimes evaluated a specific institutional program that benefited women students or faculty. We selected to spotlight these programs by asking the authors to write a 500-word description of the programs and provide contact information so that others could learn more about the programs. Additionally, we sought to include more authors in the *Journal* by including reviews of books that focused on some aspect of women in higher education.

The next volume of the *Journal About Women in Higher Education* will also include book reviews as well as spotlighted programs.

Finally, we believe that collectively the articles selected for the inaugural issue of JAWHE illustrate the variety of methods currently used to look at women in higher education and provide a view of some of the current research about these women. In most instances the articles reflect, either explicitly or implicitly, the perspective that gender relations are still problematic for women in higher education. It is our hope that this *Journal* will serve to highlight these relations and illustrate ways to improve them so that all participants in higher education can enjoy and benefit from an academy relatively free of gender discrimination.

Barbara K. Townsend
University of Missouri – Columbia

Susan B. Twombly
University of Kansas

January 2008

The National Association for Women in Education: An Enduring Legacy

Lynn M. Gangone
Dean, The Women's College of the University of Denver
Chambers Center for the Advancement of Women

This chronicle of the National Association for Women in Education (NAWE) from 1916–2000 examines the contributions the association and its leaders made to the advancement of women administrators, faculty, and students during its 84-year history. Established at the turn of the 20th century when women still lacked the right to vote, the association's founding members, the deans of women, set a high standard for their profession and their students, placing advocacy for women front and center. Although NAWE came to an end at the turn of the 21st century, the association left a significant legacy worthy of its original mission and intent.

INTRODUCTION

In September 2000, the higher education community lost one of its most venerable associations. After many years of effort to turn around declines in its revenues, members, and conference attendance, the National Association for Women in Education (NAWE) membership voted on August 13, 2000, to dissolve the Association; the vote also included a decision to distribute its remaining assets to other 501(c)(3) organizations that best reflected NAWE's mission and core values (L.M. Gangone, personal communication to NAWE members, August 30, 2000). The NAWE membership approved the transfer of the NAWE database and copyrights for the Institute for Emerging Women Leaders in Higher Education (IEWL) and the International Conference on Women in Higher Education (ICWIHE) to Higher Education Resource Services

(HERS); a request for proposals was distributed in September 2000 inviting 501(c)(3) organizations to seek ownership of the National Conference for College Women Student Leaders (NCCWSL) (L.M. Gangone, personal communication to 501(c)(3) organizations, August 21, 2000). Ultimately, ownership of NCCWSL was granted to the American Association of University Women (AAUW), a partner of the Association since the early 1900s. The Association's journal, *Initiatives: The Journal of NAWE,* a highly regarded journal dedicated to women, was retired with the Association's closure. NAWE, founded in 1916 as the National Association of Deans of Women (NADW), a pioneering guidance and personnel association dedicated to the advancement of women, was no longer.

Founded when Margaret Sanger first tested the validity of anticontraception laws, when the 19th amendment of the U.S. Constitution was ratified, during an era when the Equal Rights Amendment (ERA) was first introduced (The National Women's History Project, 2007), and when women's education was a topic of controversy (Schwartz, 1997), NAWE preserved its separatism as a women's organization and maintained an unwavering commitment to women throughout its 84 years of existence. NAWE was one of the first higher education associations in America, one of the first personnel and guidance associations, and one of the first educational associations dedicated to women. The deans of women, and their successors, opened doors and opportunities for women students, faculty, and administrators throughout American campuses (Sayre, 1950; Strang, 1966; Gangone, 1999). The scholarly journal, research monographs, symposia, and conferences provide evidence of the vast contributions that the association and its members made to the higher education community. Yet, despite these facts, there is little research or mention of the association in the history and literature of higher education and higher education associations (Gangone, 1999).

Utilizing previously understudied archives including personal correspondence, association resolutions, and other documents, as well as interorganizational records, the scholarly journal, and conference programs, this article celebrates the history of NAWE and its contributions to the advancement of women in education, from its founding in 1916 to its closing in 2000; this work is part of two larger studies, one that examines the history and organizational life cycle of NAWE, and the other that focuses on the organization's efforts during the feminist movement of the 1960s and 1970s. While NAWE as an organization is gone, its legacy and contributions to women in education live on.

THE NATIONAL ASSOCIATION OF WOMEN DEANS (NADW)

THE FORMATION OF NADW 1916–30: ADVANCING WOMEN DEANS AND THEIR STUDENTS

In 1870 only 30% of colleges were coeducational, but by the turn of the century that figure had risen to 70%; women constituted 30% of the students in higher education (Chamberlain, 1988), and the rising tide of women in the academy buoyed the creation of the position of dean of women. "Deans of women arrived on coeducational campuses at the turn of the century partly to 'defend the position of women' but primarily to help disconcerted presidents deal with increasing numbers of female students and their housing, health, counseling, and social needs" (Tuttle, 1996, pp. 1–2). The first dean of women was Alice Freeman Palmer, former president of Wellesley College, appointed in 1892 to the University of Chicago by William Raney Harper who "envisaged a free, open, academic environment and recruited women as undergraduates, graduates, and faculty members" (Solomon, 1985, p. 57); Palmer brought Marion Talbot to be her assistant and Talbot ultimately became her successor there (Nidiffer in Eisenmann, 1998). Both Palmer and Talbot were academic scholars and faculty members before moving into the position of dean of women. The position of dean of women allowed academic women, many educated at women's colleges, entree into leadership positions at coeducational institutions.

In 1913, Anne Dudley Blitz, then a graduate student at Teachers College, Columbia University, helped initiate a program of graduate study for deans of women (Potter, 1926). The women at Teachers College believed that prestige and respect would come through professional training and academic credentialing specific to the dean's position. The formation of the graduate study program for deans of women was the beginning of the professionalization of the position as a unique occupation that merited professional study and preparation; it established the roots of future counseling and student personnel degree programs. By 1914, Teachers College was awarding a professional diploma for deans of women in colleges and normal schools along with the master's degree (Schetlin, 1966).

By 1915 the 26 women studying at Teachers College had begun meeting for informal discussions. Kathryn Sisson Phillips, dean of women at Ohio Wesleyan, wrote, "They were all comparatively new at the work so what to do and how to do it, the technique of deaning, so to speak, was the absorbing thing" (Phillips, Kerr, & Wells, 1926, p. 17). Sisson Phillips had initiated the informal meetings and, knowing that the group members were to return the next summer to continue their studies, decided to have a more formal meeting to coincide with a meeting of the National Education Association (NEA). The NEA agreed, and the first program for the deans of women was held at the Horace Mann Auditorium at Teachers College on July 6, 1916. By 1923, the association began publication of a yearbook; in 1938 the association began publishing a scholarly journal edited by Ruth Strang (Sayre, 1950; Catton, 1956). "The deans of women were diligent in building their profession on the bedrock of academic discipline, research, and publication" (Schwartz, 1997, p. 507).

In January 1919, the first meeting of what was to become the National Association of Deans and Advisers of Men (NADAM) was held at the University of Wisconsin (NASPA, 2007). As a contrast to the development of graduate study, scholarship, and research promoted by NADW and its members, Schwartz (2002) notes:

> Deans of men saw the deanship as a calling, as a minister or priest might be called to the pulpit. Unlike deans of women, deans of men eschewed graduate study, research, and publication. Instead, they championed the notion that the best deans of men were "born, not made." For a man called to be a dean, graduate training was superfluous. For those men not destined to be a dean, any effort to teach the work of "deaning" through graduate study was a sham; a man cut out to be a dean carried the inherent skills he needed in his genes. (p. 219)

It was "1925 when the first piece of 'research' was offered at a NADAM meeting . . . presented by John Bennett of Teacher's College" (NASPA, ¶ 5, 2007) and the *NASPA Journal* was not introduced until 1963.

The development of the deans of women as professionals in higher education was obvious as their discussions turned from routine topics to issues that were on the "cutting edge" of higher education: vocations for women and the adaptation of the curriculum to suit college women learners (Gangone, 1999). "The deans of women were early champions of the new scientific methods of guidance for students. They often challenged each other and their campuses to 'do the right thing' by women" (Schwartz, 1997, p. 507). While tensions between deans of women schooled in traditional academic disciplines and those educated in the newer professional degree programs would arise (Nidiffer, 2000), the development of the deans of women as professionals would continue into the latter half of the 20th century. Even as each dean sought on her campus to create job duties and determine roles, she established early on her credibility with the faculty, president, and students. So, too, that credibility extended to the organized group of deans of women and the women students they served.

NADW 1930–47: Putting the Needs of Women in Education on the National Agenda

By the 1930s, women in all professions were becoming casualties of the severe economic downturn that overwhelmed the country. Chafe (1972), Strickler (1984), and Cott (1987) all documented the gradual constriction of women's opportunities during and after the Great Depression (Schwartz, 1998). In higher education, the number of women faculty peaked in the early 1930s but then declined for years, while the number of women earning college degrees began a decline that did not end until the mid-1960s (Schwartz). The Depression affected the association specifically, and women in higher education generally, by precipitating a backlash against women's educational and professional development. NADW members witnessed the personal agony of those deans who lost their jobs during the 1930s (Brown, 1963; Fley, 1978; Tuttle, 1996; Schwartz, 1998).

Not to be deterred, the association and its members conducted research and produced scholarship on women deans and women students specifically, and personnel services in general. Published by NADW in 1938 were two pamphlets, "The Dean of Girls in the High School" and "The Dean of Women in the Institution of Higher Learning," and in 1940, "The Head Resident on College and University Campuses." Additionally, NADW published "Orientation of Freshmen in Colleges and Universities" (1942), "Residence Halls for Women Students" (1947), and "Administrative Principles and Procedures" (1947). Through scholars at Teachers College, additional research on and by the deans of women was disseminated (Holmes, 1939; Gilroy, 1987). These efforts, as well as the scholarly work disseminated through the association's scholarly journal and its annual meetings, placed the association at the forefront of advocacy for women students.

During this time, African American deans of women continued to fight for equitable participation in NADW. Lucy Diggs Slowe, dean of women at Howard University, became the first African American member of NADW in the 1920s (Brett, Calhoun, Piggott, Davis, & Scott, 1979). Beginning in 1929, Slowe began an effort to meet with colleagues who, like her, worked with African American students; by 1935, the Association of Deans of Women and Advisers to Girls in Negro Colleges and Schools was formed (Eisenmann, 2006). Despite the creation of the Negro college group, Slowe remained committed to improving the circumstances under which African American deans participated in NADW. "Several years before she died in 1937, Dean Slowe had publicly deplored the conditions under which the Negro members could participate in NADW's national conventions" (Brett et al., 1979, p. 10). Ruth Brett, former director of counseling and academic advising at Morgan State University, recalled her experience at the 1940 NADW convention saying, "I 'wept inside' when a black woman who was planning to stay in the only hotel where blacks could live . . . left and never returned to NADW" (Brett, p. 3). In the association's early years it was a common occurrence to hold its national conventions in segregated settings. It was not until the 1950s that the association adopted a "policy that it would not hold its meetings in a city or in a hotel in which all of its members could not fully participate" (Brett et al., p. 11); by 1954, NADW was the only guidance association to openly support the U.S. Supreme Court decision in *Brown v. Board of Education of Topeka* (Eisenmann, 2006). While NADW's efforts in the 1950s were a marked, positive shift in its support of African American members, it was not until the 1970s that the association created a minority member-at-large position on the board, undertook significant efforts to address racism, and had minority members visible in its programs and as major speakers (Brett et al., 1979).

The onset of World War II temporarily placed the backlash against women, and against the deans of women, on hold. As men entered the military, women entered the workforce, filled campus classrooms, and took on employment positions previously held by men. Although opportunities for women expanded, the situation for women in general during World War II, and women students on campus, "was a complicated tangle of restriction and opportunity" (Tuttle, 1996, p. 111). Indicators that signaled continuing threats to the position of dean of women included calls for centralization of the student personnel function, the growing prominence of the deans of men, and societal mores that placed men in superior roles. During this time, NADW and AAUW continued to monitor the dean of women positions around the country, with AAUW taking the lead in advocating for women. Leaders in both organizations understood the critical role of the dean of women in the support for and advocacy of women students in coeducational institutions. The AAUW decried the situation for deans of women, not only for women students who lost personal contact with a "highly qualified woman in a position of administrative significance," but also for the women faculty and staff who lost "one of the few channels of expression in the administration" (Tuttle, p. 190). An AAUW-commissioned study of the deans of women at AAUW-approved institutions confirmed that of nearly 170 colleges and universities surveyed, 69 had no woman administrators (Tuttle).

NADW 1947–56: Perseverance and Renewed Commitment to a Single-Gender Association

The late 1940s and early 1950s were years of severe strain and stress for the deans of women and for women students in general. Environmental pressures such as the return of veterans to the workforce, most of whom were men, caused a shift in society from encouraging women to work to encouraging women to go back to the home. Fley (1978) noted that "the post war period brought problems . . . the Association became acutely aware of diminished opportunities for women students and women professionals as well as a Freudian theory to rationalize discrimination" (p. 46).

For the deans of women, continued professional pressure to centralize student personnel functions, combined with societal pressure for women to return to the home, contributed to diminishing prospects for women in academe. NADW worked to protect the dean of women position in its own ways. In 1950 the Association mailed a second edition of a pamphlet "The Dean of Women in the Institution of Higher Learning" to presidents, particularly those presidents whose institutions had eliminated the position of dean of women (Tuttle, 1996). Several committees of the association, including the Committee on the Dean and the Committee on the Status of Women in Higher Education continued to advocate in more subtle ways. NADW also lobbied its organizational colleagues such as the Federation of Women's Clubs and the Business and Professional Women's Club to assist in retaining women in policy-making positions (Tuttle).

Despite their efforts, NADW members watched as the deans of men gained a distinct advantage with the new campus population of G.I. Bill veterans, the vast majority of whom were male, crowding campuses all across the country. Tuttle (1996) notes that a 1948 NADAM "Functional Survey of the Association" showed that "for institutions that retained deans of men, which included 27% of the centralized programs and 74% of the noncentralized programs, not one dean of men reported a loss of prestige for his office" (p. 210). It was ironic that the deans of men, who had "eschewed graduate study, research, and publication" (Schwartz, 2002, p. 219) became deans of students, while deans of women were fired or demoted. Schwartz further notes:

> On first glance, it appears that the deans of women paralleled the values of the academic world—research, data, graduate preparation, and advanced degrees. But when the positions of dean of women and dean of men were dismantled after World War II, it was the deans of men, not the deans of women, who survived the organizational changes. (p. 219)

Former deans of women became counselors and senior counselors, or assistant and associate deans. Often, these women were reporting to men who were far less qualified and credentialed. "The percentage of women faculty fell to 24.5% . . . in 1940, 86% of the deans of women reported directly to the president; in 1962, that figure decreased to 29.5%" (Tuttle, pp. 172–3). In these difficult times, the "deans of women turned increasingly to NADW for personal support and corporate response" (Bashaw, 2001, p. 263).

The diminishment of women as faculty and deans in the academy was mirrored by the decline in women students, who "were increasingly turned down for admission to graduate and professional schools to make way for the bulge of veterans who were returning to or entering colleges and universities with financial assistance from the G.I. Bill" (Fley, 1978, p. 46). Tuttle (1996) notes a 1947 NADW survey of colleges that found that 26 institutions had quotas for women students, primarily because of housing shortages and efforts to restore pre-war ratios of male and female students. "Women suffered a large setback when the operation of the G.I. Bill reduced female access to higher education" (Solomon, 1985, p. 189). Post-war America saw the presence and influence of women at all levels of the academy deeply compromised.

Once again, the women of NADW would not be deterred. In the early 1950s the association's leaders made two important decisions. First, in 1951 the membership voted to maintain NADW's autonomy and its commitment to women. There was recognition among the deans of women, and other NADW members, that NADW's single-gender environment provided them with opportunities they would not have in other gender-integrated personnel and guidance associations. NADW women knew that their ability to gain significant leadership skills was more likely in an all-women environment. Although it was a financial and professional risk to not merge with its sister guidance and personnel associations, the women of NADW remained committed to women (Gangone, 1999). The second decision was the association's choice to engage the American Council on Education (ACE) in women's advocacy efforts.

In 1953, with generous funding from NADW founder Kathryn Sisson Phillips and her husband Ellis L. Phillips' family foundation, NADW agreed to work with ACE and facilitated the Phillips' $50,000 gift to ACE to establish a Commission on the Education of Women (CEW). According to Eisenmann:

> These deans thought that citizenship would be served by improving the educational experience of women students . . . providing better statistics on colleges women, and enhancing the status of women leaders in higher education. Applying the Phillips gift to this agenda, they reasoned, could further both groups' interests. (2005, p. 90)

Esteemed NADW members such as Esther Lloyd-Jones from Teachers College, Althea Hottel from University of Pennsylvania, Lucile Allen from Chatham College, and Ruth Brett Quarles from Dillard University, the only African American member, served on the CEW (Eisenmann). Although the CEW was disbanded in 1962, "by fostering research on women, they created a knowledge base that supported later work in women's studies, women's centers, and support programs for women's needs" (Eisenmann, p. 233).

At the 1956 Annual Conference in Cincinnati, Ohio, President Eunice Hilton declared the name of the organization to be the National Association of Women Deans and Counselors (NAWDC) (Brown, 1963). Despite less-than-favorable attitudes toward women, many in the NAWDC leadership remained steadfast. Bashaw (2001) notes that Hilton, director of the prestigious Syracuse University graduate student personnel program, gave a rousing speech at the association's 1957 convention, when she argued that the deans of women were needed as advocates for women students more than ever before and that challenges to women's higher education reinforced the need for single-sex professional associations like NAWDC.

THE NATIONAL ASSOCIATION OF WOMEN DEANS AND COUNSELORS (NAWDC)

NAWDC 1957–73: Engaging in Collaborative Work on Behalf of All Women

As the association embraced its new name, the external environment in higher education and in the broader society continued to devalue women and their contributions. Women were still discouraged from higher education and encouraged to limit their ambitions to the domestic arena. In 1957 the average woman in the United States married at the age of 20; the typical college woman, if she graduated, married somewhat later, at the age of 22 or 23 (Solomon, 1985). This trend for women was often used as an excuse to deny women admission into graduate programs or not to hire them for professional positions. However, societal change was brewing as the decade of the 1960s approached. This would ultimately affect women and their participation in all facets of American society.

Higher education was influenced profoundly by the social, political, and economic changes in the late 1950s and early 1960s. Increasing global competition in the sciences and technologies provided the impetus for the United States to invest human and fiscal resources to open up higher education to a broader audience, including women (Solomon, 1985). The greater availability of student aid, the growth of the community college sector, and increased efforts to recruit more students to fill new positions in the sciences and technologies fueled an overall movement of greater access to higher education (Thelin, 2004). In this environment of growth and expansion in higher education, more faculty, staff, and administrators were necessary to meet the needs of a growing student population. These shifts affected the growth of the personnel and guidance movement as more and more students required care and attention.

In support of civil and women's rights, federal legislation and a series of federal appointments strengthened the beginning efforts to promote equality for women. The first sign of new life came with the establishment of the Commission on the Status of Women by President Kennedy in 1961 and chaired by former First Lady Eleanor Roosevelt. The year 1963 witnessed the passage of the Equal Pay Act; 1964 brought the inclusion of Title VII of the Civil Rights Act, making sexual, racial, and religious discrimination illegal; and in 1965 Betty Friedan founded the National Organization for Women (NOW) (The National Women's History Project, 2007).

During this period the inimitable Helen B. Schleman led NAWDC as its president. A World War II commander and assistant director of the Women's Reserve of the U.S. Coast Guard, more commonly known by the term "SPARs" (Purdue University Office of the Dean of Students, 2007), Schleman returned to Purdue as dean of women in 1947 and remained in the dean's position until 1968 (Purdue University, 2006). Schleman also had a national reputation as an administrator and educator and served, at Eleanor Roosevelt's request, as a member of the education committee for the President's Commission on the Status of Women. As NAWDC president, Schleman used her influence to effect change for students in general and women students in particular. Her speeches and writings as association president were illustrative of the association's recognition of broader systemic discrimination against women (Gangone, 2007).

As the association's leaders and members began to reconsider what collective action on behalf of women and girls in education meant, a strategy employed by the association was to more effectively use its resolutions process to effect change and to have a broad impact on education. In her 1964 annual report, Schleman rallied members to consider ways to turn association concerns and interests into action. She placed primacy on group or organizational action and pushed the membership to think of ways to effect change. Beyond "going on record," Schleman called the NAWDC members to conscious action through personal networks of influence, through conversation with elected officials, through testimony before government entities, and through participation in interorganizational activities. In its resolutions of 1964, the association reiterated its concern, from its founding, with the status and education of women and urged the association's members to take action in ways such as working to create statewide commissions on women, and to use the study as an aid in their work (NAWDC, 1964).

In 1965 Schleman reflected on the association's brave and far-sighted decision to recommend the funding of the CEW, which had disbanded in 1962:

> one would also have difficulty identifying any other efforts, that has greater claim to distinction of being the starting point of the revolution, than NAWDC's deliberate choice to recommend, with an irresistible accompanying bonus of $50,000, the creation of the Commission on the Education of Women with the established and educationally accepted framework of the American Council on Education. *If we had not been an all-women's organization, I doubt if we could have made this*

> *choice* (italics added) . . . that we could see the need for special attention to the education of girls and women and could say so convincingly . . . it seems imperative to me that both our organization and we ourselves should continue to function in this educational area of the particular and special needs of girls and women. (Schleman in Eisenmann, 2005, p. 3)

Schleman articulated the link between the "valiant service" (Eisenmann, p. 4) of the CEW to subsequent events such as the President's Commission on the Status of Women, as well as Governors Commissions on the state level. Furthermore, she explicated the attention to the special educational issues of women and girls extended to all areas of women's activities, and that NAWDC had been "a part of significant development" (Eisenmann, p. 4) of the growing second wave of the women's movement. Hartmann (1994), writing about the CEW near the turn of the 21st century, supports Schleman's view, noting that the CEW's work "foreshadowed elements of the feminist movement that would emerge a decade later" (p. 90). In its 1965 resolutions, NAWDC reaffirmed its particular interest in the education of women and its inherent belief in the value to an institution in employing in administrative positions women who are educationally qualified and professionally competent (Gangone, 2007).

By the late 1960s women of all ages and circumstances had become increasingly involved in debates about gender, discrimination, and the nature of equality; and they were beginning to look beyond their own perceptions of self to the radical possibility that the broader society was inherently opposed to their equality. The women of NAWDC were no exception. While the association had "long experience in downplaying or disavowing the explicit feminist implications of their activities and interests" (Eisenmann, 2005, p. 138), there were signs that NAWDC members were beginning to blame "their own lack of protest rather than their insufficient preparation or poor training" (Eisenmann, p. 139). This shift was evidenced in the association's resolutions, which, with each subsequent year, made more explicit reference to the specific needs of women administrators and students; and resolutions for both traditional and nontraditional women students, for equal educational opportunity, for women appointees in key government positions, and for the formations of commissions on the status of women all emerged at this time (Gangone, 2007).

Membership numbers were at their highest levels in the association's history during the 1960s. The strong presence of the association within the personnel and guidance profession, the continued role of the association as the professional home for women in personnel and guidance, and the growing women's movement all combined to make the 1960s a banner decade for NAWDC (Gangone, 1999). In 1970, NAWDC again considered the possible merger of NAWDC with the National Association of Student Personnel Administrators (NASPA) and the American Personnel and Guidance Association (APGA) (Fley, 1978). During the 1971 NAWDC conference, members voted to remain a single-gender association and "broaden its role to include all professional women in education and those allied fields which promote learning and human development" (Fley, 1978, pp. 85–86).

NAWDC members voted down the merger proposal and affirmed the Association's intention to maintain a unique focus on gender and equity issues in education. At the same time, NAWDC pledged to engage in cooperative ventures with those related professional associations with whom it shared interests in the training and development of student affairs professionals, in policy formation, and in the development and delivery of extracurricular and co-curricular programs and services (Gangone, 1999). The association's guiding assumption in this phase of its development held that while women's and men's educational spheres had been integrated, continuing sex discrimination and inequities in educational opportunity justified maintaining an autonomous organization for women student affairs professionals (Hanson, 1995a). There was still a reason to "be a feminist organization with a ladylike emphasis" (Truex, 1971, p. 13). By 1973, the name of the association changed to the National Association of Women Deans, Administrators, and Counselors (NAWDAC), a name it would maintain until 1991.

THE NATIONAL ASSOCIATION OF/FOR WOMEN DEANS, ADMINISTRATORS, AND COUNSELORS (NAWDAC)

NAWDAC 1973–80: Asserting its Role as an Organization of and for Women

The association added "Administrators" to its name at a time of great positive change for women. The legislation passed in the 1960s provided the foundation for the creation of Title IX; the impact of that piece of legislation on equity for girls and women in education has been unmatched. The desire to embrace the spirit of Title IX moved NAWDAC to change from an organization "of women" to an organization "for women," opening the door for men to join (Hanson, 1995a).

As the decade of the 1970s progressed, the association's resolutions continued to define its stance on gender equity and women's advancement, both within and outside of education, and provided a means of influence with college and university leaders, elected officials, and others in positions of authority in and outside of higher education. NAWDAC reconfirmed that a primary goal was as an active supporter of the concerns of women (Thrash, 1973) and its leaders were determined to be "front and center" in the quest for women's equity. Executive Director Joan McCall, writing in the winter 1973 issue of the *Journal,* reported the association's involvement in government departmental briefings on legislation such as the Equal Pay Act and Title IX, participation in the drafting of the "Joint Statement on Women in Higher Education" with AAUW, facilitation of meetings between members and representatives of the U.S. Department of Labor, participation in the formation of the Federation of Organizations of Professional Women, and other similar ventures. The NAWDAC Position Paper on Title IX was distributed to all members, sent to the Secretary of Health, Education, and Welfare, and endorsed by the AAUW. By 1975, at its 59th annual conference in Philadelphia, NAWDAC became the first organization in the nation to pass a resolution refusing to hold its conferences in states that had not ratified the Equal Rights Amendment (Gangone, 1999).

At the association's 60th anniversary conference, President Barbara Cook, associate dean of women at Purdue University, identified major thrusts for the association. These included "identification, as an Association, with the broad issues which are part of the feminist movement" and "with educational issues which affect particularly girls and women students as well as women educators" (Cook, 1976, p. 202). In her speech, Cook guided the NAWDAC membership as they explored the association's historical foundations. While strongly endorsing feminism and the women's movement, Cook reminded members of the strong and enduring principles that had always been clear in the history of the association: that the woman dean was first of all an educator operating from a centrist point of view; that the association had a consistent concern for the status of women and girls in education and the world beyond; that education occurs over the total life span; and finally, that the association had maintained the determination to keep its uniqueness by remaining a separate association.

Through the efforts of NAWDAC and other women's advocates, barriers to women were falling throughout the administrative and faculty ranks in higher education. Women were moving beyond student affairs and into fund-raising, business, and academic administration. By 1989, the percentage of NAWDAC members employed outside of student affairs had risen to 51%, while those employed in academic affairs had grown to nearly one third of the membership (NAWE, 1998). This shift in membership signaled that by 1989, NAWDAC was no longer a student affairs association, so the culture of the association was beginning to undergo a significant transformation from a single-discipline to a multidisciplinary organization (Gangone, 1999).

NAWDAC 1980–91: Resisting Retrenchment and Redefining Women's Place in the Academy

The headiness of the women's movement gave way, in the 1980s and early 1990s, to retrenchment in higher education and, although the numbers of women undergraduate students were increasing, a continued "chilly climate" for women in the academy existed. In 1984, the U.S. Supreme Court ruled in *Grove City College v. Bell* that Title IX could be limited to only those campus programs that received direct federal funding, rather than the campus as a whole. That court decision sent shock waves through the women's higher education community and was a tangible example of efforts to circumscribe women's equity. NAWDAC joined other women's organizations in grassroots lobbying to limit the effect of Grove (Gangone, 2007). Immediately, legislation was introduced in Congress to restore Title IX's power and the Civil Rights Restoration Act of 1988 reinstated Title IX's broad scope; President Reagan vetoed the new law, but Congress overrode his veto by a wide margin (Chamberlain, 1988). A 1985 *Journal of NAWDAC* article, excerpted from a National Council for Research on Women study, verified the declining federal commitment to research about women (Rubin, 1985). The report examined seven government agencies and showed that while research dollars had risen overall, support for research on women was sharply declining. Decreased funding, conservative legal decisions, and the presence of a "chilly climate" for women in academe were just a few of the indicators that pointed to the backlash against women.

While the debate regarding educational equity was being waged in Congress, NAWDAC joined a coalition of women's education groups in sponsoring a leadership conference for women students, which was the outgrowth of the 1983 demise of the Intercollegiate Association for Women Students (Hanson, 1995b). The coalition included the American Council on Education Office of Women in Higher Education (ACE-OWHE), AAUW, NAWDAC, and other D.C.-based women's organizations. Emily Taylor, former dean of women at the University of Kansas, then director of ACE Office of Women in Higher Education (OWHE), led the effort to create the leadership conference for women students through her Women's Institute. By 1989, NAWDAC had taken on sole responsibility for the conference, which was named the National Conference for College Women Student Leaders (NCCWSL); it was considered part of the association's mission to further the educational opportunities for women students. The NCCWSL and the Women of Distinction Awards program, which linked conference attendees to significant national and international women leaders, provided support and networking for thousands of collegiate women during its tenure; attendance peaked in 1997 with 605 participants (NAWE, 1998).

The association still maintained its conferences (which were annual), its scholarly journal, and now offered NCCWSL to college and university students. Over the years the types of association members had expanded and groups such as the directors of campus-based women's centers found a home in NAWDAC. The ethnic women's caucus and the lesbian caucus allowed women a place to bring their whole selves to the association and work. Discussion around critical personal issues, such as surviving cancer, coexisted with conference sessions that addressed current higher education and women's issues (Gangone, 2007). The continued expansion of the types of women attracted to NAWDAC prompted a fund-raising consulting firm retained by NAWDAC to recommend a name change for NAWDAC; the firm used the concepts of "women in education" and "women's leadership" as their guide and suggested that NAWDAC move in that direction to develop a new organizational identity (NAWE, 1989). In September 1990 the membership of NAWDAC voted to change the association's name to the National Association for Women in Education. The name change was implemented at the Association's 75th anniversary conference in Boston in 1991.

THE NATIONAL ASSOCIATION FOR WOMEN IN EDUCATION (NAWE), 1991–2000

NAWE: "ADVANCING WOMEN IN HIGHER EDUCATION"

In its 75th year, NAWE continued its mission to serve women throughout all facets of education. Its annual conference remained the only national education association meeting fully devoted to issues of women in higher education; its scholarly journal, *Initiatives,* continued to address topics of vital interest to women, from sexual harassment to women's centers and their work. The inclusion of NCCWSL as a service to college women student leaders was a logical extension of the association's commitment to women students. Caucuses for ethnic women, new professionals, lesbians and bisexuals, and women's center directors continued to feed needs expressed by members.

In 1991 Bernice Resnick Sandler, founder of the Project on the Status and Education of Women at the Association of American Colleges and a highly regarded advocate for women's educational equity, best known for her work in the development and implementation of Title IX and for her research on the "chilly classroom climate" (Sandler & Hall, 1982; Sandler, Silverberg, & Hall, 1996), joined NAWE as its senior scholar in residence. With Sandler as primary author, the NAWE publication *About Women on Campus* (AWOC) was introduced in 1991 as part of the Women's Issues Project; AWOC was the second major publication, in addition to the association's journal, *Initiatives,* which focused on women's issues and concerns. Sandler brought with her funds from the Lilly Foundation and the Fund for the Improvement of Post Secondary Education (FIPSE) to develop and publish *The Chilly Classroom Climate* follow-up study, which was completed in 1996 (Gangone, 1999). Like the original landmark study, *The Chilly Classroom Climate* identified areas of the campus that discouraged women students, faculty, and staff and empowered practitioners with suggested remedies for institutional change. *The Chilly Classroom Climate* and AWOC, with their focus on practice, were appropriate complements to *Initiatives* with its research focus, and provided women administrators and faculty with needed resources as campus-based advocates for women.

In April 1996 the Association received notification that it had received $125,000 from Marriott Management Services to assist "the association in the development and implementation of innovative leadership training programs for women within the global world of education" (D. Naughton, personal communication, April 2, 1996). These funds were designated to support the NCCWSL and a new leadership development symposium for entry-to-mid-level women, which ultimately became the Institute for Emerging Women Leaders in Higher Education (IEWL). The IEWL filled an important gap in the professional development of women by targeting the often neglected mid-level professional. The curriculum and the structure of IEWL allowed for women to gain greater exposure to the enterprise of higher education and to consider leadership from whatever position they occupied in their institution (Gangone & Kezar, 2000). In its three years of existence, the IEWL reached nearly 200 entry-to-mid-level professionals, many of whom have gone on to participate in the HERS Bryn Mawr Summer Institute for Women, as well as more discipline-based institutes such as the NASPA Stevens Institute. Through the successful debut of the IEWL, NAWE established itself as a provider of high-quality, professional development programs for women (Gangone, 1999).

At the same time that IEWL was launched, the University of Texas-El Paso sought to transfer the rights of the International Conference on Women in Higher Education (ICWHE) to another 501(c)(3) organization. The NAWE leadership determined that such a conference fit well with the association's work to provide professional development by women for women and in January 1999 offered the first NAWE ICWHE, welcoming 130 women from 13 countries (L.M. Gangone, personal communication to the NAWE Board, February 14, 1999). In January 2000, the ICWHE in New Orleans hosted nearly 200 women from over 20 countries, where issues of global importance to women were discussed and debated.

The NAWE years, though short-lived in comparison to the association's long history, were important in cementing the legacy of the association as one that placed women at the forefront of its work. The association's traditional offerings were supplemented by AWOC, IEWL, and ICHWE, broadening the association's reach and influence among women in higher education. The newer programmatic offerings assisted women with practical strategies for women's advocacy and personal strategies for career advancement. All in all, NAWE met its expressed goal of advancing women in higher education.

CONCLUSION

Despite NAWE's significant contributions to women in education, by the turn of the 21st century increased competition from other professional associations, loss of niche, shrinking professional development dollars, and a societal shift away from single-sex organizations ultimately proved too challenging and the association's members made the painful decision to cease operations in 2000 (Gangone, 1999; NAWE Board, personal communication, June 30, 2000). Nonetheless, the association's vast contributions to the advancement of women students, faculty, and administrators in higher education live on through its historical contributions and in the work of HERS, AAUW, and in the new NASPA Center for Scholarship, Research, and Professional Development for Women. Seventy years after the deans of women introduced their scholarly journal, with Ruth Strang as its editor, the *Journal About Women in Higher Education,* sponsored by NASPA's Center for Scholarship, Research, and Professional Development for Women, and co-edited by Barbara Townsend and Susan B. Twombly, has come into existence. *Initiatives: The Journal of NAWE* now is succeeded by the *Journal About Women in Higher Education*, whose scholarly focus on issues affecting all women in higher education fills a critical void in the academy for researchers and practitioners dedicated to women and their advancement. And so the scholarly work begun by the deans of women continues.

Today, women are the majority of undergraduate students in the United States (Goldin, Katz, & Kuziemko, 2006; King, 2006; Mead, 2006), and many more women are in significant leadership positions in higher education, exemplified by the recent appointment of Drew Gilpin Faust as the Harvard University president (Wilson, 2007). However, the recent ACE report, *The American College President* (2007), shows that men still constitute 77% of all college and university presidents; when minority-serving institutions are excluded, only 10% of presidents are from racial/ethnic minority groups; and while the percentage of women presidents has gone from 10% in 1986 to 23% in 2006, "women's progress has slowed in recent years" (p. viii). No doubt the deans of women would remind us not to be deterred—there is still work to be done, for the issue of women's educational equity and advancement, which they so boldly embraced at the turn of the 20th century, has yet to be achieved in the 21st.

REFERENCES

American Council on Education. (2007, February). *The American college presidency.* Washington, DC: Author.

Bashaw, C. T. (2001). To serve the needs of women: The AAUW, NAWDC, and persistence of academic women's support networks. In J. Nidiffer

& C. T. Bashaw (Eds.), *Women administrators in higher education.* Albany, NY: State University of New York Press.

Brett, R., Calhoun, E. M., Piggott, L. J., Davis, H. A., & Scott, P. B. (1979). Our living history: Reminiscences of Black participation in NAWDAC. *Journal of the National Association for Women Deans, Administrators, & Counselors, 43*(2), 3–13.

Brown, N. B. (1963). *The National Association of Women Deans and Counselors.* Unpublished doctoral dissertation, University of Denver.

Catton, B. (1956). Our association in review. *Journal of the National Association of Deans of Women, 10,* 3–9.

Chamberlain, M. K. (Ed.). (1988). *Women in academe: Progress and prospects.* New York: Russell Sage Foundation.

Cook, B. I. (1976). Sixty years and beyond. *Journal of the National Association for Women Deans, Administrators, and Counselors, 39*(4), 196–204.

Hartmann, S. (1998). *The other feminists: Activists in the liberal establishment.* New Haven: Yale University Press.

Eisenmann, L. (Ed.). (1998). *Historical dictionary of women's education in the United States.* Westport, CT: Greenwood Press.

Eisenmann, L. (2005). *Higher education for women in postwar America, 1945–1965.* Baltimore: The Johns Hopkins University Press.

Fley, J. A. (1978, March). A celebration and recognition of the thirty-four past presidents of the National Association for Women Deans, Administrators, and Counselors. Paper presented at the meeting of the NAWDC, Detroit, MI.

Gangone, L. M. (1999). *Navigating turbulence: A case study of a voluntary higher education association.* Unpublished doctoral dissertation, Teachers College, Columbia University.

Gangone, L. M., & Kezar, A. (2000). Meeting the leadership challenges of the 21st century: An evaluation of a national leadership institute [Electronic Version]. *Initiatives: The Journal of NAWE, 59*(4).

Gangone, L. M. (2007). *Shaping the conversation: The National Association of Women Deans, Administrators, and Counselors 1970–1980.* Unpublished manuscript.

Gilroy, M. (1987). *The contributions of selected Teachers College women to the field of student personnel.* Unpublished doctoral dissertation, Teachers College, Columbia University.

Goldin, C., Katz, L., Kuziemko, I. (2006). The homecoming of American college women: The reversal of the college gender gap. Working Paper

12139. Cambridge, MA: National Bureau of Economic Research. Retrieved March 15, 2006, from http://www.nber.org/papers/w12139

Hall, R. M., & Sandler, B. R. (1982). *The classroom climate: A chilly one for women?* Washington, DC: Association of American Colleges.

Hanson, G. S. (1995a). The organizational evolution of NAWE. *Initiatives: The Journal of NAWE, 56,* 29–36.

Hanson, G. S. (1995b). *Organizational transformation: A case study of the Intercollegiate Association for Women Students.* Unpublished doctoral dissertation, The George Washington University.

Holmes, L. A. (1939). *A history of the position of dean of women in a selected group of coeducational colleges and universities in the United States* (vol. 767). New York: Teachers College, Columbia University.

King. J. (2006). *Gender equity in higher education: 2006.* Washington, DC: The American Council on Education.

Mead, S. (2006). *The truth about boys and girls.* Washington, DC: The Education Sector.

McCall, J. M. (1973). The Women's Movement and NAWDC. *Journal of the National Association of Women Deans and Counselors, 36*(2), 82–83.

NASPA: Student Affairs Administrators in Higher Education. NASPA history. Retrieved January 15, 2007, from http://www.naspa.org/about/index.cfm?show=5

National Association for Women in Education. (1998). *Manual of operations.* Washington, DC: Author.

Nidiffer, J. (2000). *Pioneering deans of women: More than wise and pious matrons.* New York: Teachers College Press.

Phillips, K. S., Kerr, M., & Wells, A. (1926). History of the National Association of Deans of Women. Washington, DC: National Association of Deans of Women.

Potter, M. R. (1926). *Report of committee on history of the National Association of Deans of Women.* Washington, DC: National Association of Deans of Women.

Purdue University, Office of the Dean of Students. Helen Blanche Schleman. Retrieved January 15, 2007, from http://www.purdue.edu/ODOS/counsel/hbschleman.htm

Rubin, M. (1985). A declining federal commitment to research about women, 1980–1984. *Journal of the National Association for Women Deans, Administrators, and Counselors, 48,* 3–7.

Sandler, B. R., Silverberg, L. A., & Hall, R. M. (1996). *The chilly classroom climate: A guide to improve the education of women.* Washington, DC: National Association for Women in Education.

Sayre, M. B. (1950). *"Half a century:" An historical analysis of the National Association of Deans of Women, 1900–1950.* Unpublished doctoral dissertation, Teachers College, Columbia University.

Schetlin, E. M. (1966). Fifty years of association—ninety years of dreams. *Journal of the National Association of Women Deans and Counselors, 29*(2), 111–115.

Schwartz, R. A. (1997). Reconceptualizing the leadership roles of women in higher education: A brief history on the importance of deans of women. *The Journal of Higher Education, 68,* 502–522.

Schwartz, R. A. (1998). Lessons from the past: Women in higher education leadership in the Depression years. *Initiatives: The Journal of the National Association for Women in Education, 58,* 1–21.

Schwartz, R. A. (2002). The rise and demise of deans of men. T*he Review of Higher Education, 26*(2), 217–239.

Solomon, B. M. (1985). *In the company of educated women: A history of women and higher education in America.* New Haven, CT: Yale University Press.

Strang, R. (1966). NAWDC, perspective and prospectus: A symposium. *Journal of the National Association of Women Deans and Counselors, 29*(2), 99–105.

The National Women's History Project. Living the legacy: The women's rights movement 1848–1998. Retrieved February 14, 2007, from http://www.legacy98.org/timeline.html

Thelin, J. R. (2004). *A history of American higher education.* Baltimore: Johns Hopkins University Press.

Thrash, P. A. (1973). *President's report to the membership of NAWE.* Washington, DC: National Association of Women Deans and Counselors.

Truex, D. (1971). Education of women, the student personnel profession, and the new feminism. *Journal of the National Association of Women Deans and Counselors, 35*(1), 13–20.

Tuttle, K. N. (1996). *What became of the dean of women? Changing roles for women administrators in American higher education, 1940–1980.* Unpublished doctoral dissertation, University of Kansas.

Wilson, R. (2007). Harvard's historic choice. *The Chronicle of Higher Education, 53,* A-1.

Gender Differences Over the Span of College: Challenges to Achieving Equity

Linda J. Sax
Associate Professor
Graduate School of Education & Information Studies
University of California, Los Angeles

Emily Arms
Adjunct Assistant Professor
Rossier School of Education
University of Southern California

Although educational and occupational gains made by women in recent decades have given rise to a popular notion that gender equity has been achieved, significant gender differences in the college student population exist across a variety of domains. Focusing on three major areas—(1) Financial Background; (2) Academic Self-Confidence and Engagement; and (3) Degree, Major, and Career Aspirations—this study examines historical trends in gender differences observed among entering college students over the past 4 decades and assesses changes in the gender gap occurring over 4 years of college. Results reveal significant sex differentials across all categories and show that gender differences observed at the point of college entry tend to remain steady over 4 years of college, though some narrowing and/or magnification of gender differences is observed. The implications for improving campus gender equity are discussed.

INTRODUCTION

Educational and occupational gains made by women in recent decades have given rise to a popular notion that gender equity has been achieved

(Conlin, 2003). The fact that women now have higher rates of college attendance—up to 58% of college enrollments nationwide (King, 2006)—is cited as one indicator of not only gender parity but also of women having surpassed men academically. Studies also show that women earn better grades and have higher college persistence rates than men (Astin, 1993; Guido-DiBrito, 2002; Hagedorn, Womack, Vogt, Wetebbe, & Kealing, 2002; Lindholm, Astin, Choi, & Gutierrez-Zamano, 2002). Other research has suggested that the size of the gender gap among students has generally decreased over time, particularly in the areas of degree attainment and career aspirations (Chamberlain, 1988; Astin, Oseguera, Sax, & Korn, 2002). Furthermore, the implementation of Title IX policies has also provided women with unprecedented opportunities in many areas of campus life, most notably in athletics. These gains for women have led some to conclude that what we now have is a national "crisis" for men, as women's achievements are oftentimes perceived to come at a loss for men in a zero sum game (Martino & Meyenn 2001; Hoff Sommers, 2000; Pollack, 1999).

While there is growing evidence that male undergraduates are at risk in certain areas, the recent focus on boys and men often neglects to acknowledge that gender inequity persists. In particular, gender gaps continue in undergraduates' choice of major, their career aspirations, certain areas of graduate degree attainment, and their postcollegiate salaries (Astin, 1993; Christian, 2002; Eccles, 1994; Flowers, Osterlind, Pascarella, & Pierson, 2001; Jacobs, 1996). For example, research continues to document how college men are more likely than women to select majors in lucrative fields such as engineering and computer science, while women still tend to choose majors in the lower-paying fields of education, health, and psychology (U.S. Department of Education, 2004; Margolis & Fisher, 2003).

Studies also show gender differences to persist in the affective domain, with college women reporting less confidence in their self-assessments (Clark & Zehr, 1993; Smith, Morrison, & Wolf, 1994), struggling more with developing autonomy and separating from their parents (Josselson, 1987), and reporting more emotional distress (Sax, Bryant, & Gilmartin, 2004; Sax, Lindholm, Astin, Korn, & Mahoney, 2001) than college men.

Though there is evidence of longstanding differences between college women and men, research on this topic typically takes a "snapshot" approach by reporting on gender gaps among individuals at a given point in time. This study, however, uses nationwide data on students attending

4-year colleges and universities to address the *stability* of the gender gap over the past 4 decades as well as the extent to which the magnitude of the gender gap changes during the college years. The latter question is of particular importance to campus practitioners because it addresses the extent to which male-female differentials change during the pivotal college years. While others have reported gender differences in some areas that have either narrowed or widened during college (Astin, 1993; Smith, Morrison, & Wolf, 1994), such research has not reported on whether the convergence or divergence of the gender gap is statistically significant. It is important to distinguish between gender differences that truly narrow (or widen) from those where changes in the gender gap may be marginal.

Drawing on data from two different surveys on a wide range of topics, this study examines men's and women's responses across three main themes: (1) Financial Background; (2) Academic Self-Confidence and Engagement; and (3) Degree, Major, and Career Aspirations. These particular areas were selected because collectively they tell a story of the progress toward gender equity as well as the persistence and lasting influence of sex differentials among college students. In addition, the gender differences observed in these areas have important implications for campus programming and services, as discussed in this article. Other aspects of students' experience measured on the surveys—such as physical and psychological health, political and social values, and community engagement—are examined in other publications emanating from these data (Sax, forthcoming), but are beyond the scope of this article.

METHODS

Data

This study relies on two databases maintained by the Higher Education Research Institute at UCLA: (1) long-term trend data on successive cohorts of college freshmen collected between 1966 and 2006; and (2) a 4-year longitudinal study of students who were surveyed when they entered college in 1994 and again in 1998.

The database used in trend analysis includes more than 8 million students who participated in the Cooperative Institutional Research Program (CIRP) Freshman Survey between 1966 and 2006. The Freshman Survey, typically administered during orientation or during the first week of classes, asks students about their background characteristics, attitudes, values, educational achievements, and future goals. The data from 1966 to 2006 represent the responses of students attending more than one thousand 4-year colleges and universities nationwide. The institutional sample reflects the diversity of baccalaureate institutions nationwide in terms of size, type (4-year colleges vs. universities), control (public vs. private), and selectivity. Within each year, students' responses are weighted so as to reflect the responses we would expect if students at all 4-year colleges and universities responded to the survey. See Astin et al. (2002) for details on sampling and weighting procedures.

For the longitudinal database, all subjects completed the fall 1994 Freshman Survey and a spring 1998 follow-up survey known as the College Student Survey (CSS). The CSS is similar in format to the Freshman Survey, and it includes information on students' college experiences and their perceptions of college, as well as posttests of items that appear on the Freshman Survey. The longitudinal sample includes a total of 17,637 students (10,901 women and 6,736 men) who completed both instruments at 204 4-year colleges and universities across the United States. Data included in this longitudinal file are weighted to correct for over- or underrepresentation of certain institutional types as well as for the overrepresentation of high-achieving women among follow-up respondents.

Analytical Methods

Within each of the three broad categories (Financial Background; Academic Self-Confidence and Engagement; Degree, Major, and Career Aspirations), we examined long-term trends for women and men dating back to 1966. Most of the trends are current through the 2006 Freshman Survey, though occasionally it was necessary to use other years as the most recent source of data, as noted in the text and figures. Though not all trends could be included in this article, there is discussion of selected trends that reflect: (a) convergence of the gender gap, (b) widening of the gender gap, (c) reversal of the gender gap, or (d) persistent gender gaps over the past 4 decades. Understanding relative changes in the characteristics and experiences of college women and men is critical for campus practitioners, as their ability to enact policies and make decisions depends on knowledge about the unique qualities of any campus subgroup, whether defined by gender, race, family background, or other factors.

Using the longitudinal sample (1994 to 1998), this study reports on gender differences observed for women and men as they entered college and the extent to which those differences became larger or smaller over 4 years. Specifically, cross tabulations were conducted by gender and year to address whether significant differences existed: (a) between women and men at college entry (1994); (b) between women and men as college seniors (1998); and (c) between the gender gap in 1994 and the gender gap in 1998. Tests of significance were employed depending on the type of comparison being made. To test gender differences in 1994 or 1998, we performed independent sample z-tests of the standard error of the gender gap. To test whether there is a significant change in the gender gap over 4 years, we conducted the McNamara test for dependent proportions (Agresti & Finlay, 1997). A p level of .001 was used to assign significance (whether between men and women at a single point in time or between the gender gap in 1994 and the gender gap in 1998).

LIMITATIONS

The primary limitation of this study is that it is entirely descriptive in nature. It examines the sheer magnitude of the gender difference on selected survey items without testing for other factors that may be related to this difference, either as a cause or consequence. The focus on the descriptive differences is intentional, as it provides a "big picture" snapshot of the status of the gender gap across the domains examined in this study. However, a related article (Sax & Harper, 2007) uses the same database to examine, from a multivariate perspective, the extent to which gender differences observed during college are attributable to aspects of the college experience or whether they are due to precollege gender differences. That study finds that gender differences at the end of college are largely unrelated to the college experience and are attributable to gendered patterns of education and socialization prior to college.

A second limitation to the present study is that change during college is examined for students who attended college a decade ago. Reliance on data from the 1990s was necessary as the dataset represents the most recent longitudinal follow-up of freshman survey respondents from a comprehensive set of 4-year colleges and universities. Institutions in this study represent the population of 4-year colleges and universities in terms of size, type, and selectivity; more recent follow-up surveys have not achieved the same institutional representation, though current efforts aim to generate such data for students attending college in the 2000s. Although the longitudinal data may be slightly outdated, the trends do include freshman responses up through 2006.

A related limitation is that 2-year colleges are not included in the present study. Unfortunately, participation in the freshman survey among 2-year colleges is fairly low and the small number of institutions that do participate cannot be used to generalize to the experiences of all 2-year college students. Future research on gender differences should make efforts to include students from 2-year colleges, especially since the population of students at these institutions is often quite different from 4-year institutions. In particular, women comprise an even greater share of students at 2-year colleges, especially among nontraditional-age college students, and they are more likely than women at 4-year colleges to be working full-time and raising children. These factors may account for different results from those observed in this study.

RESULTS

Findings are organized into the three broad categories introduced earlier: Financial Background; Academic Self-Confidence and Engagement; and Degree, Major, and Career Aspirations. Long-term trends analyses are examined first, followed by 4-year longitudinal changes.

Long-Term Trends: 1966–2006

Financial Background

Discussion on the changing demographics of the college student population often centers on gender or race, but less so on socioeconomic status. Yet one of the most important student trends is the emergence of an economic gender gap. Over 40 years ago—when the CIRP Freshman Survey was initiated—college-going men and women reported similar financial backgrounds. Since 1966, however, median family incomes for male students have increased by approximately 40%, relative to a 17% increase among the women (see Figure 1). By 2004, family income for male students was approximately $10,000 higher than for female students. These results extend and highlight findings reported by Lindholm et al. (2002), who found that "the greatest growth in enrollments for women has occurred among low-income women" (p. 34). Their study documented that women are overrepresented among low- and middle-income college students, and underrepresented among students from high-income families.

Figure 1. Median family income of entering freshmen (1966–2004) (in constant 2004 dollars).

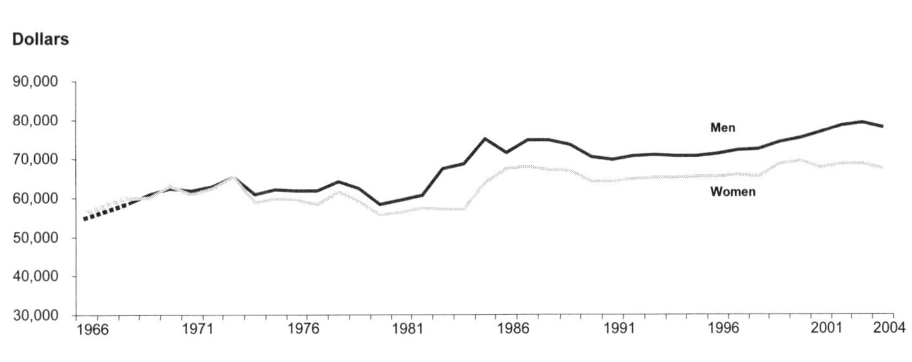

Data unavailable for the year 1967

Women's socioeconomic status relative to men's also can be seen by examining trends in parental education. Although women attending college in the 1960s were more likely than men to have college-educated mothers and fathers, this trend reversed in the in the late 1970s and the gap continues to widen. Among students who entered college in 2006, 56.4% of men and 50.1% of women have fathers who had graduated from college, and 55.5% of men and 50.5% of women have mothers who had graduated from college. In other words, just as we have witnessed a growing gender gap in family income that now favors men, we have also seen emerging disparities in levels of parental education, with men more likely than women to report that their parents graduated from college.

Given their lower family incomes, it is not surprising that the women express greater concern than men about their ability to finance their college education. A full 69.5% of women have "some" or "major" concerns about their ability to pay for college (versus 57.55% among men). Gender differences on this item have widened over the years, as trends since 1966 reveal net increases in financial concern among women and net decreases among men. Further, women are slightly more likely than men to consider the following factors as "very important" in selecting a college: low tuition (22.2 versus 18.5%), offers of financial assistance (37.2 versus 30.7%), or because graduates of that college "get good jobs" (51.8 versus 46.1%).

Also consistent with their greater financial concerns and their family's socioeconomic status relative to men, women are more likely than men to anticipate employment during college. The expectation to seek employment during college has produced one of the more interesting trends in the history of the Freshman Survey. When first asked on the 1976 survey, women and men were equally likely to anticipate employment during college. Since that time, while the expectation to work has fluctuated for both women and men, the overall increase in anticipated employment has been substantially higher for women, resulting in a widening of the gender gap since the mid-1970s. Presently, 50.2% of women and 36.5% of men believe there is a very good chance that they will seek employment while in college. Although one might easily attribute this to women's lower family income, gender differences are readily apparent across *all* income levels, such that regardless of family income, women are notably more inclined than men to report a "very good chance" that they will work to help offset college costs.

Despite women's lower incomes and greater financial concerns relative to men, historically they have expressed less interest than men in the long-term accumulation of wealth. However, this gender gap has converged significantly over time, with 72.4% of women and 74.6% of men reporting that "being very well off financially" is a "very important" or "essential" goal for them (see Figure 2). When it comes to entrepreneurial aspirations, a sizeable gender gap remains, with only 37.9% of women entering college with a commitment to "becoming successful in a business of my own," compared to 46.7% among men.

Figure 2. Freshman goal: being well-off financially (1966–2006) (% of reporting "very important" or "essential").

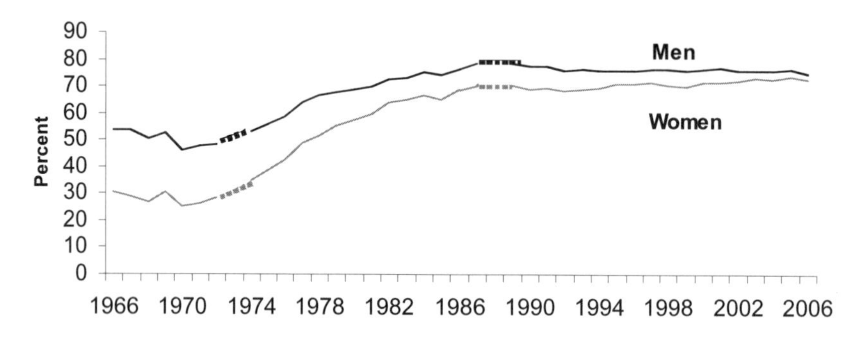

Data unavailable for the years 1973, 1988

Academic Self-Confidence and Engagement

As women have come to dominate enrollments on campuses nationwide, they are often portrayed as an academic success story. Indeed, numerous survey items point to a stronger academic orientation among the women. When it comes to motives for attending college, women are more likely than men to rate the following as "very important" reasons for attending college: to gain a general education and appreciation of ideas (69.9 among women versus 57.5% among men), to learn more about things that interest them (80.6 among women versus 72.1% among men), and to improve their study skills[1] (43.7 among women versus 36.8% among men). Further, women place more importance on a college's academic reputation than do the men, with 61.4% rating this as a "very important" reason for selecting a particular college, versus 52.4% among men.

In addition, women's precollege levels of academic engagement are considerably higher than men's, as women report spending significantly more time studying or doing homework in the last year of high school than do the men (37.6% of women studied 6 or more hours per week, compared to 26.9% among the men). It is worth noting, however, that study time for both genders has decreased significantly over time. Women are also more likely than men to talk with their high school teachers outside of class (51.1% among women versus 43.8% among men) and to participate in student clubs and groups at least 3 hours per week (37.0% among women versus 25.8% among men).

Women's higher levels of time-on-task appear to pay off in terms of their high school grades, with significantly greater proportions of women entering college with "A-" or higher high school grades (50.9% among women versus 40.0% among men) (see Figure 3). The gender gap in high school GPAs has a long history on the survey, even as grades have risen dramatically for all students. Clearly, men and women are equal beneficiaries of "grade inflation," a phenomenon witnessed at both the high school and college levels (Rosovsky & Hartley, 2002; Sax, 2003).

Despite women's stronger academic orientation relative to the men, they report a comparatively low academic self-concept. For example, women rate themselves significantly lower than men on nearly all self-ratings related to academic or intellectual confidence. For example, just over half of the women (52.2%) consider themselves to be "above average"

1. Percentages for "study skills" come from 2003, the last time this item was included on the survey.

Figure 3. High school grade inflation for women and men (1966–2000).

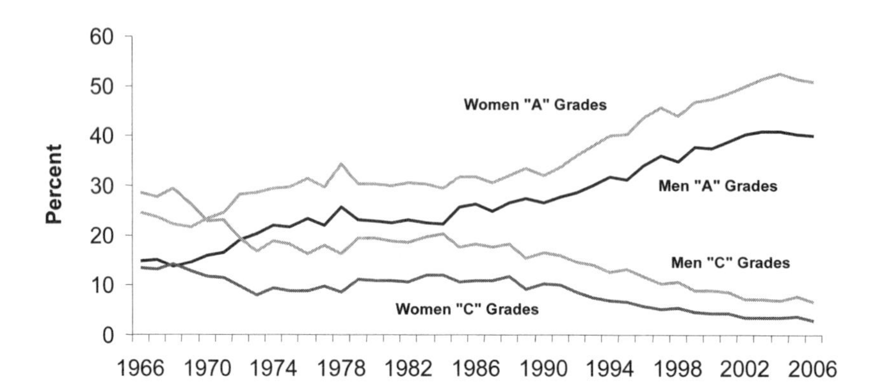

or "highest 10%" in intellectual self-confidence, compared with more than two thirds (68.8%) of the men. Women also are less likely than men to consider themselves to be at least above average mathematical ability (35.9 among women versus 53.1% among men) and academic ability (65.9 among women versus 71.9% among men). Only in the area of writing ability do women report higher levels of confidence than do men (49.3 among women versus 45.7% among men).

These results are consistent with decades of research on gender and self-confidence. While it is clear that women tend to underestimate their skills and abilities, it is less clear *why* this is the case. Do women actually view themselves as less academically capable than the men, or are they simply more modest in their self-assessments? Prior research, for example, has shown women to indicate lower levels of mathematical confidence, even when their *demonstrated* math abilities are equal to or greater than men's (Marsh, Smith, & Barnes, 1985; Sax, 1994a; Sherman, 1983). Sadker and Sadker (1994) also discuss a phenomenon by which "girls, especially smart girls, learn to underestimate their ability" (p. 95) and more often attribute their intelligence to hard work than innate ability. Conversely, adolescent boys have been shown to exhibit a sometimes outsized sense of self not always commensurate with their academic achievement (Sadker & Sadker, 1994).

Perhaps women's lower self-ratings stem from the way these questions are posed on the survey, where students are asked to rate their abilities as "compared to the average person your age." Women may be more reluctant to report their skills as "higher" than others, as that denotes a competitive orientation that may be unappealing to many women. In fact, women do not view themselves as "competitive" as men, as indicated by the fact that 45.2% of women and 69.1% of men view themselves as "above average" or "highest 10%" on this trait.[2] Thus, while we are not sure of the reason, the fact is that women enter college reporting lower confidence in their academic skills than do men. This alone is important for faculty and practitioners to be aware of, as they will encounter students whose outward image may not be the best reflection of their actual talents.

Degree, Major, and Career Aspirations

Despite their reported lack of self-confidence and reluctance to admit high academic ability, college women have become just as likely as men to aspire to graduate degrees. Furthermore, they increasingly aspire to nontraditional majors and careers. Historically, college students' major choices and degree aspirations have been closely related to the career opportunities available to them. Gendered patterns in career choice were accentuated during the 1950s and 1960s, but the wide disparities in choice of major, degree attainment, and career aspirations began to narrow dramatically during the 1970s and 1980s. This was due in no small part to federal legislation regarding equal pay as well as Title IX and affirmative action. Today, with more women pursuing graduate and professional degrees and nontraditional occupations, the public perception seems to be that the gender gap between college men and women has all but disappeared. But the data tell a more complex story. While there has been a significant convergence of the gender gap when it comes to level of degree aspiration, notable gender gaps persist in specific academic and career fields that students plan to pursue.

Degree Aspirations

Marking a significant shift over the past few decades, women are now more likely than men to plan to attend graduate or professional school. The most notable gender difference is in aspiration for doctoral degrees, with 32.3% of women and 29.0% of men planning to earn a Ph.D., an M.D., or a J.D. Aspiration for master's degrees is fairly similar between

2. Percentages for "competitiveness" come from 2001, the last time this item was included on the survey.

the two genders, with 42.3% of women and 41.7% of men aspiring to the master's as their highest degree. Given women's greater interest in attending graduate school, it is not surprising that women are more likely than men to indicate that they were attending college in order to prepare for graduate or professional school (63.1% of women consider this a "very important" reason for college attendance, versus 51.0% of men). Similarly, greater proportions of women than men say that they selected their college because the school's graduates are admitted into top-ranked graduate and professional schools (33.3% among women versus. 26.3% among men).

Intended Major

The Freshman Survey includes a list of 82 academic majors, which have been grouped into 18 different categories for the purpose of analysis. At the point of college entry, women are significantly more likely than men to plan to major in education (12.5% among women versus 5.7% among men), psychology (6.6% among women versus 2.6% among men), and fields in the health professions (11.8% among women versus 3.8% among men). However, women are less likely than men to major in engineering (2.4% among women versus 14.6% among men), business (13.5% among women versus 23.5% among men), and history/political science (4.5% among women versus 5.7% among men). In particular, education and engineering stand out as two major areas from our study that have had an enduring gender gap over the years. For the most part, these results reflect longstanding sex differences in major selection that are well documented in other studies (Astin et al., 2002; Gati, Osipow, & Givon, 1995; Jacobs, 1986, 1996; Little, 2002; Morgan, Isaac, & Sansone, 2001; Sax, 1996; Stickel & Bonett, 1991). And, given women's reported low confidence in their mathematical abilities, it comes as no surprise that women tend to choose less math-intensive fields.

However, in some cases, choice of major signals a reversal of historical patterns. For example, in the 1960s and 1970s, the biological sciences were dominated by male students. Interest in biology converged among the sexes in the 1980s, and during the 1990s a new pattern of female predominance in the biological sciences emerged (see Figure 4). Indeed, by 2000 U.S. women earned over 80% of master's degrees in the health professions and related sciences, and over 40% of degrees in medicine (U.S. Department of Education, 2004).

Figure 4. Entering freshmen who intend to major in biological science (1966–2006).

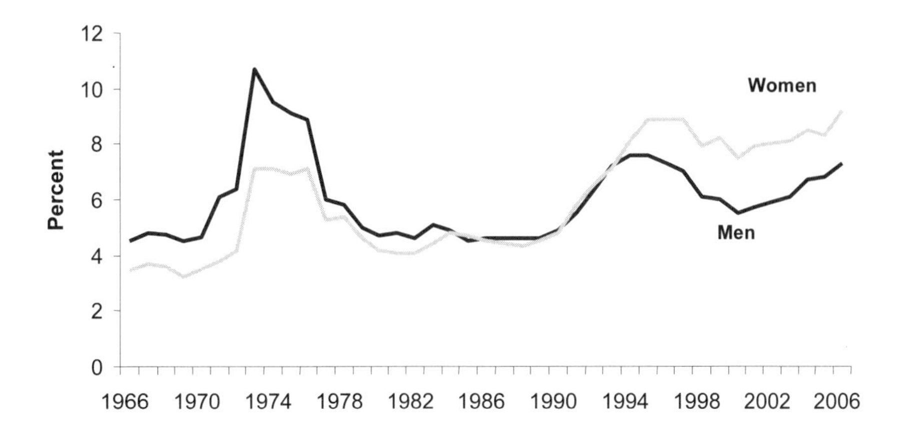

Career Aspirations

Gender differences in career choice mirror those found for major preferences. Upon entering college, women are more likely than men to plan to become elementary school teachers (7.9% versus 1.0%), health professionals (7.2% versus 4.0%) and nurses (6.8% versus 0.8%). Men are more likely than women to aspire toward careers in engineering (11.7% versus 2.0%), business (18.3% versus 10.0%), and computer programming (3.4% versus 0.3%). These differences generally reflect historical trends in men and women's relative career aspirations.

However, it is important to point out areas in which sex differences in career choice have been eliminated or have reversed direction. For example, interest in the historically male-dominated careers of law and medicine converged in the 1980s and 1990s respectively (see Figures 5 and 6). These trends reflect the dramatic narrowing of the gender gap in law and medical degrees conferred in the United States over the past several decades (U.S. Department of Education, 2003).

In one instance, the genders have converged on a career choice that was once dominated by women: secondary education. When the survey began in 1966 women were approximately twice as likely as men to express interest in secondary education, a gap that has since converged completely, with 4.9% of women and 4.6% of men planning to become secondary school teachers. Incidentally, gender differences in interest in elementary education have also narrowed over the history of the survey, but women remain far more likely to aspire toward this career than men (7.9% versus

Figure 5. Entering freshmen who aspire to become lawyers (1966–2006).

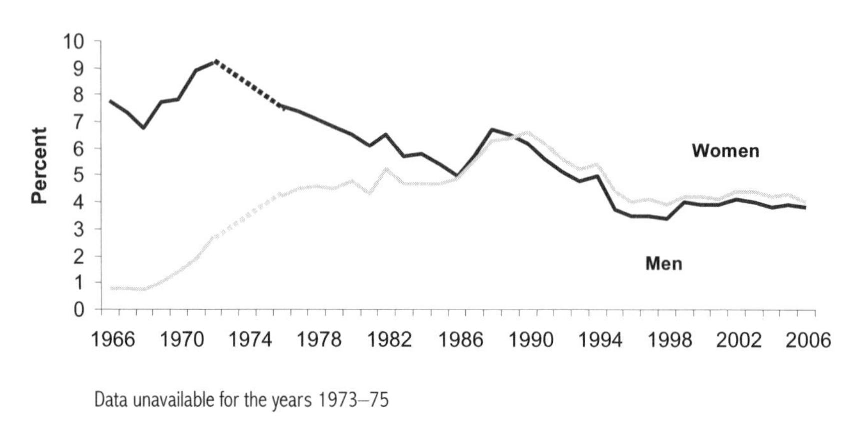

Figure 6. Entering freshmen who aspire to become medical doctors (1966–2006).

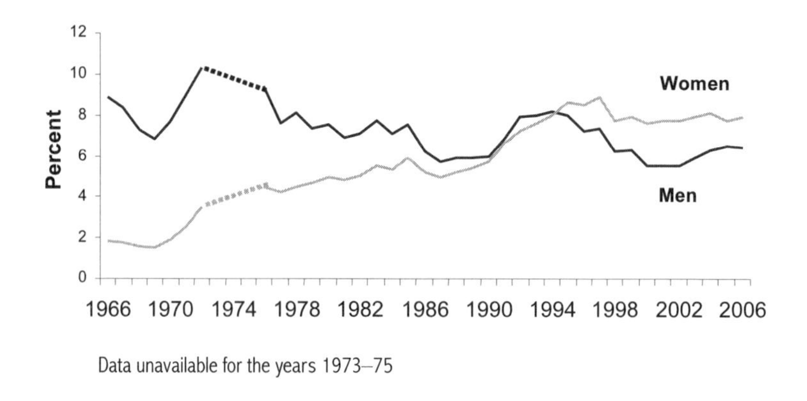

1.0%). The narrowing of the gender gap in teaching aspirations is almost entirely due to the significant decline in women's interest in this field, as evidenced by the shift of women into law, medicine, and business.

Change During College: 1994–98

The long-term trends described in the prior section provide clear evidence that numerous longstanding gender gaps continue to be evident among students entering college, though some differences between women and men have disappeared over time. What the trends do not reveal is how the gender gap changes over the span of students' college years. Thus, this section describes changes in the gender gap occurring over 4 years of college. As noted earlier, this section relies on longitudinal data on students attending college in the 1990s; thus, freshman year percentages will differ from the more current percentages reported in the prior section. Future studies will need to address whether changes in the gender gap observed for these students in the 1990s are observed for more recent cohorts.

Financial Background

The long-term trends described above reveal a growing economic gender gap among entering college freshmen, with women coming from lower-income families and experiencing greater financial concerns relative to the men. Though the follow-up survey does not reassess students' financial standing after 4 years, it does indicate which students actually sought employment to pay for college expenses. Specifically, after 4 years of college, women in the longitudinal sample are only slightly more likely than the men to hold part-time jobs (58.1 versus 53.8%). Further, men are slightly more likely than women to work full-time while attending college (11.4 versus 9.0%). Thus, the gender gap in actual employment is much smaller than the gender gap in anticipated employment. Perhaps this reflects the fact that although women report greater financial worries, the costs of college are just as high for the men as the women. Future research should investigate why women's employment rates during college are similar to men's, especially at a time when women tend to come from lower-income families.

Academic Self-Confidence and Engagement

As indicated by trends over the past 40 years, women enter college with significantly higher levels of academic engagement, but consistently lower levels of academic self-confidence. What happens to women and men's intellectual self-confidence over the span of college? The results are not favorable to women, as the differential between women and men either remains stable or becomes more pronounced over time (see Table 1). For example, while both women and men experience gains in intellectual self-confidence during college, these gains are larger for men, resulting in a significant widening of the gender gap. Similarly, in the realm of mathematical abilities, both groups become less confident during college, with the decline greater among women, again resulting in a significantly larger gender difference 4 years after college entry. This latter result is consistent with findings reported on students attending college in the 1980s (Sax, 1994a, 1994b), in which the decline in math confidence that is observed among all students is generally not witnessed among students

Table 1. Gender differences in academic self-confidence and engagement.

	1994			1998			Significant Change[a] in Gender Difference?
	Women	Men	Diff.	Women	Men	Diff.	
	(%)	(%)	(W-M)	(%)	(%)	(W-M)	
Self-Ratings (above average or highest 10%):							
Intellectual self-confidence	48.8	63.1*	-14.3	59.4	78.1*	-18.7	Widens
Math ability	43.6	54.6*	-11.0	37.3	51.4*	-14.1	Widens
Academic ability	68.2	73.9*	-5.7	70.5	75.9*	-5.4	
Writing ability	47.1*	40.5	+6.6	58.2	56.8	+1.4	Widens
Competitiveness	44.4	69.8*	-25.4	48.7	71.8*	-23.1	
Studying or homework 6+ HPW	50.1*	38.6	+11.5	76.5*	66.6	+9.9	
Student clubs/groups 3+ HPW	45.4*	30.4	+15.0	34.8*	32.4	+2.4	Narrows
Talking with instructors 1+HPW	49.6*	45.5	+4.1	56.3*	53.3	+3.0	
Activities (frequently or occasionally):							
Didn't complete homework on time	59.5	69.7*	-10.2	52.1	64.4*	-12.3	
Overslept/missed class or appointment	24.7	27.1*	-2.4	49.9	60.9*	-11.0	Widens
Grades							
A or A+	22.1*	16.7	+5.4	11.4*	9.1	+2.3	Narrows
B+ or A-	42.1*	37.9	+4.2	37.4*	30.0	+7.4	Widens
B	26.4	30.5*	-4.1	34.9	37.0	-2.1	Narrows
B- or C	8.7	13.2*	-4.5	13.3	18.4*	-5.1	Widens
C or less	0.6	1.6	-1.0	2.3	4.4*	-2.1	Widens

*Percentage is significantly larger ($p<.001$) for that group.
[a]Only changes significant at $p<.001$ are designated as widening or narrowing.

majoring in math-intensive fields (e.g., engineering, physical science, mathematics, statistics, and computer science). In fact, persisting in a math-intensive curriculum—in fields typically dominated by men—promotes women's confidence in their abilities as well as their willingness to admit that confidence. For women in other fields, who are likely to have minimal exposure to mathematics during college, their sense of math confidence falls even further behind men's during college.

In college, although grades decline relative to those earned in high school, women continue to earn higher grades than men, as shown in Table 1. Further, women continue to spend more time than men studying and doing homework in college. The small gender gap in time spent talking with instructors also persists from high school to college, with women spending more time interacting with their professors than did the men. Further, as another sign of greater academic disengagement, men become significantly more likely than the women to oversleep and miss class or an appointment. In fact, a full 60.9% of men and 49.9% of women report oversleeping in college. Finally, one area of initial gender differences in academic engagement narrows significantly during college: student clubs and groups. Although women spend more time than men on these extracurricular activities in high school, gender differences are nearly nonexistent during college (due primarily to a decline in involvement in clubs and groups among the women). Quite possibly, women elect to tone down their extracurricular activities in order to adjust to the greater studying demands in college.

Degree, Major, and Career Aspirations

Over 4 years of college, gender differences in degree aspirations shift only slightly. Aspirations for terminal bachelor's degrees increase among men, while plans to earn master's degrees grow more common among women. Thus, gender gaps in aspiration for these degrees grow wider over time. However, gender differences in students' aspirations for doctoral degrees (Ph.D., M.D., J.D.) remain significant over 4 years.

What happens to men's and women's major choice and career aspirations during college? As seen in Table 2, in some majors gender differences observed at the point of college entry are observed again 4 years later (business, psychology, and education), although for both sexes, interest in psychology grows while interest in education declines. Initial gender differences that are observed in engineering and the health professions majors narrow significantly during college as men's interest in engineering declines more so than women's, and as women's interest in the health professions declines more so than men's.

Among intended careers, initial gender differences observed in the fields of business and nursing are maintained over 4 years (see Table 3). For one career choice—social work—gender differences that are seemingly nonexistent in the freshman year emerge 4 years later as significantly more women than men aspire to careers in social work. Just as was observed with choice of major field, gender differences narrow (but remain significant)

Table 2. Gender differences in major field.

	1994			1998			Significant Change[a] in Gender Difference?
	Women (%)	Men (%)	Diff. (W-M)	Women (%)	Men (%)	Diff (W-M)	
Engineering	3.3	12.5*	-9.2	2.6	9.3*	-6.7	Narrows
Business	12.5	18.8*	-6.3	12.4	17.7*	-5.3	
History or Political Science	3.4	5.5*	-2.1	3.2	6.2*	-3.0	
Computer Science	1.0	2.2*	-1.2	1.0	2.6*	-1.6	
Agriculture or Forestry	1.2	2.0*	-0.8	1.6	2.5*	-0.9	
Architecture/Urban Planning	0.9	1.7*	-0.8	0.5	0.9*	-0.4	
Mathematics or Statistics	0.9	1.6*	-0.7	1.2	1.1	+0.1	Reverses
Technical/Applied Majors	1.2	1.0	0.2	1.1	1.0	+0.1	
Physical Sciences	1.9	2.4	-0.5	1.3	3.4*	-2.1	Widens
Fine Arts	2.6	3.1	-0.5	2.8	2.6	+0.2	
Undecided	9.0	8.8	+0.2	0.4*	0.0	+0.4	
Humanities/English	3.5	3.1	+0.4	6.5*	4.3	+2.2	Widens
Journalism/Communications	3.5*	2.4	+1.1	3.6	3.8	-0.2	Reverses
Social Sciences	3.1*	1.9	+1.2	7.3*	5.0	+2.3	
Biological Sciences	8.6*	7.2	+1.4	8.2	8.2	0.0	Narrows
Psychology	5.5*	2.1	+3.4	6.5*	3.5	+3.0	
Health Professional	15.6*	7.4	+8.2	5.5*	1.5	+4.0	Narrows
Education	15.1*	6.8	+8.3	13.4*	5.0	+8.4	

*Percentage is significantly larger ($p<.001$) for that group.
[a]Only changes significant at $p<.001$ are designated as widening or narrowing.

in the career categories of engineering and the health professions. Finally, the gender gap becomes notably wider over 4 years in one field—computer programming—as the influx of men into that field is nearly four times that of women. This reflects a national trend of male dominance in computing that is well documented by Margolis and Fisher (2003).

SUMMARY AND CONCLUSION

The data presented in this study paint a picture of both dynamic changes and perplexing stasis among U.S. college students. Today's college student population is much different than it was 40 years ago, with women

Table 3. Gender differences in career aspirations.

	1994			1998			Significant Change[a] in Gender Difference?
	Women	Men	Diff.	Women	Men	Diff.	
	(%)	(%)	(W-M)	(%)	(%)	(W-M)	
Engineer	3.3	11.8*	-8.5	2.2	8.0*	-5.8	Narrows
Business	11.6	16.5*	-4.9	16.0	21.1*	-5.1	
Computer Programmer	0.9	3.4*	-2.5	1.9	7.3*	-5.4	Widens
Law Enforcement	0.4	2.2*	-1.8	0.7	2.6*	-1.9	
Doctor/Dentist/Physician	6.8	7.9	-1.1	2.7	4.1*	-1.4	
Farmer/Forester	0.8	1.9*	-1.1	0.6	1.0	-0.4	Narrows
Lawyer	3.5	4.4	-0.9	2.7	3.5	-0.8	
Clergy	0.2	1.0*	-0.8	0.3	1.2*	-0.9	
Military	0.3	1.0*	-0.7	0.5	1.6*	-1.1	
Education (Secondary)	4.8	5.5	-0.7	4.8	4.7	+0.1	
Artist	4.9	5.6	-0.7	5.3*	4.2	+1.1	Reverses
Architect	1.0	1.6*	-0.6	0.9	1.1	-0.2	
Research Scientist	2.0	2.5	-0.5	3.2	3.0	+0.2	
College Teacher	0.4	0.6	-0.2	1.2	1.8*	-0.6	
Homemaker	0.2*	0.0	+0.2	0.3*	0.0	+0.3	
Business Clerk	1.2*	0.4	+0.8	0.5	0.3	+0.2	Narrows
Social Worker	1.7*	0.7	+1.0	6.5*	1.0	+5.5	Widens
Undecided	13.7	12.6	+1.1	3.9	3.5	+0.4	
Psychologist	2.2*	0.7	+1.5	1.7*	0.5	+1.2	
Nurse	3.2*	0.4	+2.8	3.2*	0.3	+2.9	
Health Professional	11.7*	4.7	+7.0	5.9*	2.2	+3.7	Narrows
Education (Primary)	10.7*	2.8	+7.9	11.9*	2.8	+9.1	Widens

*Percentage is significantly larger ($p<.001$) for that group.
[a]Only changes significant at $p<.001$ are designated as widening or narrowing.

now comprising nearly 60% of all undergraduate college students. And their strength is not only in their numbers. College women today earn higher grades and, overall, are more academically engaged when compared to male college students. Women also increasingly aspire to traditionally "male" majors and careers such as medicine and law. But despite these gains in access and opportunity for women, there continue to be fundamental differences in values, beliefs, attitudes and, most importantly, outcomes between men and women. Simply put, there remains a significant gender gap on U.S. college campuses.

Focusing on three major domains—Financial Background; Academic Self-Confidence and Engagement; and Degree, Major, and Career Aspirations—this article reports on gender differences observed for women and men as they enter college and the extent to which those differences become larger or smaller over 4 years. At the point of college entry, significant gender differences are observed across all categories. Some of the most significant gaps are found in the area of self-confidence, with women rating their intellectualism, mathematical ability, and competitiveness all at much lower levels than do the men. Women entering college also come from families with lower socioeconomic status and parental education levels than those of college men, and they are more concerned than men about how they will pay tuition; thus, women anticipate spending more time than men working in college (though actual employment rates during college are more equivalent).

Gender differences observed at the point of college entry tend to remain steady over 4 years of college. In other words, if women and men differ in certain ways when they begin college, it is likely that they differ in those same ways at the end of college. However, there are a number of items in which gender differences grow larger, and an equivalent number of items in which differences narrow. For example, women and men move closer together in several ways that differentiate them as freshmen: interest in engineering, mathematics/statistics, and the health professions. But the sexes grow farther apart in key aspects of self-confidence—intellectual, mathematical, and academic—and in their orientation toward certain gender-imbalanced careers, such as elementary education, social work, and computer programming.

What implications do these gender differences have for campus personnel? After all, many of these differences exist well before students set foot on campus and are simply maintained as students move through their undergraduate years. One may argue that institutions are not in a position to eradicate gender differences that exist prior to college matriculation, as these differentials result from years of gender-based socialization occurring in homes, schools, peers, the media, and other major sources of influence (Anderson, 2000; Barnett & Rivers, 2004; Sax & Harper, 2007).

However, college and university practitioners can utilize the information presented here to better understand their students and to create opportunities to maximize the success of all students. For example, this study documents socioeconomic shifts over the last 40 years that have resulted in a generation of college women who have significantly more financial concerns than their predecessors, and more than their male counterparts. Importantly, this growing population of women "at risk" may not be readily apparent to campus practitioners, especially since women's achievement levels are higher than men's. Through vehicles such as financial aid, work-study, and other assistance, campuses can help to minimize the financial burden carried by many women. Further, campuses should expand opportunities for on-campus employment for women (and for men as well) given research documenting the benefits that students accrue—both academically and socially—when they are afforded part-time employment on campus. In fact, Astin's (1993) research has shown that working on campus yields more benefits to students than not working at all.

In addition, campuses must address the gender disparities in the academic realm. Though college women spend more time than men studying, completing assignments, attending class, and meeting with faculty, they suffer from comparatively low academic and intellectual self-confidence—differences that grow larger during college. Clearly, campus practitioners must be attuned to the differential needs and experiences of both genders. For women, there is a need to encourage a stronger sense of self-confidence. Getting good grades does not guarantee that women will make favorable academic or intellectual self-assessments. In other words, competence does not always translate into confidence. Thus, faculty and practitioners should not discount the concerns of female students who, despite a string of academic successes, doubt their ability to do well in their classes, thrive in their major, or pursue graduate school. Of particular concern is women's low confidence in their mathematical abilities and their reluctance to pursue math-intensive majors and careers. Both of these factors have severe economic consequences for women who still face a lifetime of lower wages than men.

Awareness of shifting career interests of women and men is vital for campus personnel, most notably academic advisors, career counselors, and faculty. Students should be advised that no career is inappropriate for their gender, but that they ought to be prepared for the realities that they may face in their chosen field. In computer science and engineering, for example, though women increasingly possess the interest and academic preparation to succeed, they often are not prepared for the unwelcome or "chilly" climate that often exists in these fields (Margolis & Fisher, 2002; Seymour & Hewitt, 1997). By the same token, men should be encouraged to keep an open mind regarding careers traditionally dominated by women, such as education—a field that faces a teacher shortage and stands to benefit from increased interest among both genders.

Furthermore, campuses should regularly evaluate their policies and programs with an eye toward differential outcomes experienced by women and men. Presently, there is little evidence on whether student experiences and collegiate environments yield differential effects for the two genders. The vast majority of research on college impact examines men and women in the aggregate, typically using gender as an independent variable to address whether being female (versus male) makes a difference in predicting a particular college outcome. However, as suggested by numerous scholars, the next generation of research on college impact must be attuned to "conditional" effects of college; that is, the ways in which certain college environments and experiences (e.g., classroom climate, peer culture, extracurricular activities, and so on) differentially affect students on the basis on gender, race, ethnicity, or other characteristics (Pascarella & Terenzini, 2005). While some studies have addressed gender differences in the impact of college on certain outcomes, the field of higher education has not yet developed an understanding of whether there exist gender-based patterns in the influence of college. Such an examination is presently underway by examining, separately for women and men, the impact of a wide range of college environments and student experiences on more than two dozen college outcomes (Sax, forthcoming). That study aims to put this paper's findings in context by addressing whether the differential changes experienced by women and men during college are actually the result of exposure to differential college environments, differential reactions to similar college environments, or to differential patterns of human development that may not be dependent on college attendance at all.

REFERENCES

Agresti, A., & Finlay, B. (1997). *Statistical methods for the social sciences* (3rd ed.). New Jersey: Prentice Hall.

Anderson, M. L. (2000). *Thinking about women: Sociological perspectives on sex and gender* (5th ed.). Boston: Allyn and Bacon.

Astin, A. W. (1993). *What matters in college? Four critical years revisited.* San Francisco: Jossey-Bass.
Astin, A. W., Oseguera, L., Sax, L. J., & Korn, W. S. (2002). *The American freshman: Thirty-five year trends, 1966–2001.* Los Angeles: Higher Education Research Institute, UCLA.
Barnett, R., & Rivers, C. (2004). *Same difference: How gender myths are hurting our relationships, our children, and our jobs.* New York: Basic Books.
Baxter Magolda, M. B. (1992). *Knowing and reasoning in college: Gender-related patterns in students' intellectual development.* San Francisco: Jossey Bass.
Chamberlain, M. K. (1988). *Historical background and overview.* In M. K. Chamberlain (Ed.), *Women in academe* (pp. 3–12). New York: Russell Sage Foundation.
Christian, P. M. (2002). Graduate students. In A. M. Martínez Alemán & K. A. Renn (Eds.), *Women in higher education: An encyclopedia* (pp. 309–312). Santa Barbara, CA: ABC-CLIO.
Chodorow, N. (1978). *The reproduction of mothering.* Berkeley, CA: University of California Press.
Clark, J., & Zehr, D. (1993). Other women can: Discrepant performance predictions for self and same-sex other. *Journal of College Student Development, 34,* 31–35.
Conlin, M. (2003). The new gender gap. *Business Week,* May 26, 2003.
Eccles, J. S. (1994). Understanding women's educational and occupational choices: Applying the Eccles et al. model of achievement-related choices. *Psychology of Women Quarterly, 18,* 585–609.
Erikson, E. H. (1968). *Identity: Youth and crisis.* New York: W. W. Norton.
Flowers, L., Osterlind, S. J., Pascarella, E. T., & Pierson, C. T. (2001). How much do students learn in college? Cross-sectional estimates using the College BASE. *Journal of Higher Education, 72,* 565–583.
Gati, I., Osipow, S. H., & Givon, M. (1995). Gender differences in career decision making: The content and structure of preferences. *Journal of Counseling Psychology, 42,* 204–216.
Gilligan, C. (1982). *In a different voice: Psychological theory and women's development.* Cambridge, MA: Harvard University Press.
Guido-DiBrito, F. (2002). Women students: Overview. In A. M. Martínez Alemán & K. A. Renn (Eds.), *Women in higher education: An encyclopedia* (pp. 249–260). Santa Barbara, CA: ABC-CLIO.

Hagedorn, L. S., Womack, F. I., Vogt, C., Westebbe, S., & Kealing, J. (2002). Persistence. In A. M. Martínez Alemán & K. A. Renn (Eds.), *Women in higher education: An encyclopedia* (pp. 339–343). Santa Barbara, CA: ABC-CLIO.

Hoff Sommers, C. (2000). *The war against boys: How misguided feminism is harming our young men.* New York: Simon and Schuster.

Jacobs, J. A. (1986). The sex-segregation of fields of study: Trends during the college years. *Journal of Higher Education, 57,* 134–154.

Jacobs, J. A. (1996). Gender inequality and higher education. *Annual Review of Sociology, 22,* 153–185.

Josselson, R. (1987). *Finding herself: Pathways to identity development in women.* San Francisco: Jossey-Bass.

King, J. (2006). *Gender equity in higher education.* Washington, DC: American Council on Education.

Kohlberg, L. (1975). The cognitive-developmental approach to moral education. *Phi Delta Kappan, 56,* 670–677.

Lindholm, J. A., Astin, H. S., Choi, J. Y., & Gutierrez-Zamano, E. (2002). *The educational paths of recent high school graduates: College, work, and future plans.* Los Angeles: Higher Education Research Institute, UCLA.

Little, C. A. (2002). Curricular and professional choices. In A. M. Martínez Alemán & K. A. Renn (Eds.), *Women in higher education: An encyclopedia* (pp. 292–294). Santa Barbara, CA: ABC-CLIO.

Margolis, J., & Fisher, A. (2002). *Unlocking the clubhouse: Women in computing.* Massachusetts: MIT.

Margolis, J., & Fisher, A. (2003). Geek mythology. *Bulletin of Science, Technology & Society, 23*(1), 17–20.

Marsh, H. W., Smith, I. D., & Barnes, J. (1985). Multidimensional self-concepts: Relations with sex and academic achievement. *Journal of Educational Psychology, 77*(5), 581–596.

Martino, W., & Meyenn, B. (Eds.). (2001). *What about the boys?* Buckingham, England: Open University Press.

Morgan, C., Isaac, J. D., & Sansone, C. (2001). The role of interest in understanding the career choices of female and male college students. *Sex Roles, 44,* 295–320.

Mortenson, T. (2005). College continuation rates for recent high school graduates: 1959–2004. *Postsecondary Education Opportunity,* 154.

Pascarella, E. T., & Terenzini, P. T. (2005). *How college affects students: A third decade of research.* San Francisco: Jossey-Bass.

Perry, W. G. (1970). *Forms of intellectual and ethical development in the college years: A scheme.* Troy, MO: Holt, Rinehart, & Winston.

Pollack, W. (1999). *Real boys: Rescuing our sons from the myths of boyhood.* New York: Henry Holt.

Rosovsky, H., & Hartley, M. (2002). *Evaluation and the academy: Are we doing the right thing?* Cambridge, MA: American Academy of Arts and Sciences.

Sadker, M., & Sadker, D. (1994). *Failing at fairness: How America's schools cheat girls.* New York: Charles Scribner's Sons.

Sax, L. J. (1994a). Predicting gender and major-field differences in mathematical self-concept during college. *Journal of Women and Minorities in Science and Engineering, 1,* 291–307.

Sax, L. J. (1994b). Mathematical self-concept: How college reinforces the gender gap. *Research in Higher Education, 35,* 141–166.

Sax, L. J. (1996). The dynamics of "tokenism": How college students are affected by the proportion of women in their major. *Research in Higher Education, 37,* 389–425.

Sax, L. J. (2003). Our incoming students: What are they like? *About Campus, 8*(3), 15–20.

Sax, L. J. (in press). *The gender gap in college.* San Francisco: Jossey-Bass.

Sax, L. J., Bryant, A. N., & Gilmartin, S. K. (2004). A longitudinal investigation of emotional health among male and female first-year college students. *Journal of the First Year Experience and Students in Transition, 16*(2), 39–65.

Sax, L. J., & Harper, C. (2007). Origins of the gender gap: Pre-college and college influences on the differences between men and women. *Research in Higher Education, 48*(6), 669–694.

Sax, L. J., Lindholm, J. A., Astin, A. W., Korn, W. S., & Mahoney, K. (2001). *The American freshman: National norms for fall 2001.* Los Angeles: Higher Education Research Institute, UCLA.

Sherman, J. (1983). Factors predicting girls' and boys' enrollment in college preparatory mathematics. *Psychology of Women Quarterly, 7*(3), 272–281.

Smith, D. G., Morrison, D. E., Wolf, L. E. (1994). College as a gendered experience: An empirical analysis using multiple lenses. *Journal of Higher Education, 65,* 696–725.

Stickel, S. A., & Bonett, R. M. (1991). Gender differences in career self-efficacy: Combining a career with home and family. *Journal of College Student Development, 32,* 297–301.

U.S. Department of Education (2003). *Degrees and other formal awards conferred.* Washington, DC: National Center for Education Statistics.

U.S. Department of Education, (2004). *Trends in educational equity of girls & women.* Washington, DC: National Center for Education Statistics.

Leadership in a World of Divided Feminism

Adrianna Kezar
Associate Professor
University of Southern California, Los Angeles

Jaime Lester
Assistant Professor
George Mason University
Fairfax, Virginia

On college campuses today, women from a variety of generations—baby boomers, generation Xers, and nexters—come together to work, learn, and lead. Women of different generations were born and raised under different social, economic, and political conditions; approach feminism in a different ways; and have experienced more or less overt forms of discrimination. Not only is there minimal research that provides a description of the impact of generational differences on organizational functioning, little information exists to help women faculty and staff as leaders to more deeply understand and navigate these important differences. The purpose of this article is to illuminate generational differences and similarities between women leaders on college campuses and illustrate the potential impact of these generational differences on leadership practices. This article concludes with specific strategies of how postsecondary institutions can create more cross generational dialogues, which may help improve campus leadership and functioning.

"I am not sure I am interested in advancing up the administrative chain, it seems like too much of a sacrifice in terms of family, maybe later in life."

"I am worried I will not fit in with other women at the top, I do not want to 'act like a man' and that is what I tend to see happening."

"I am concerned there is not another generation of woman leaders coming up through the ranks—they are not willing to work the hours, put in the extra effort of going to events and meeting the right people."

INTRODUCTION

On college campuses today, individuals from a variety of generations—baby boomers, generation Xers, and nexters—come together to work, learn, and lead. These generations came of age in markedly different sociopolitical conditions that create and inflate generational differences. Baby boomers, for example, take a collegial approach to leadership with a focus on group building and consensus. These leadership characteristics were developed and impacted by World War II, the civil rights movement, and other social movements inspired by strong leaders like Martin Luther King, Jr. (Zemke, Raines, & Filipczak, 2000). In contrast, generation Xers approach leadership as an opportunity to create change and adopt creative and new organization styles, cultures, and structures inspired by the rise of the Internet, the Challenger accident, and Desert Storm (Howe & Strauss, 1991; Tapscott, 1998; Zemke, Raines, & Filipczak, 2000).

Recently a few researchers have explored the ways that generational differences[1] shape perspectives about leadership and how a lack of awareness about these differences can be problematic (Arsenault, 2003; Bennis & Thomas, 2002; Lancaster & Stillman, 2002; Smola & Sutton, 2002). For example, Arsenault (1993) found that different generations create their own traditions and culture related to leadership and have different attitudes, preferences, and dispositions. The breakdown of bureaucratic

1. The generational differences noted in the studies were all conducted on groups of people in the United States.

organizations in favor of horizontal structures has led to greater interaction across generations (Arsenault, 2003; Kinball, 2005; Lancaster & Stillman, 2002). If not managed properly, generational differences can result in conflict, misunderstanding, low morale, and organizational inefficiency and ineffectiveness (Lancaster & Stillman, 2002). Conversely, generational differences that are facilitated in healthy ways can lead to more creativity and innovation within organizations including colleges and universities.

One of the more intense generational differences on college campuses is between women of different generations who were born and raised under different social, economic, and political conditions; who approach feminism in a different ways; and who have experienced more or less overt forms of discrimination. As the women's movement emerged in the 1970s and early 1980s, a solidarity of purpose and a singular vision developed that had not existed to the same degree in previous movements. Throughout the 1980s, feminism expanded to encompass new views from women of color and women from countries around the world. A variety of articles and books, usually from women's or feminist studies, have been written about the generational divides among women and their effect on varying issues from the production of art and literature to the well-being of religious institutions to the way organizations operate; but the issue remains mostly unspoken among college and university staff, administrators, and faculty (Craigo-Snell, 2005; Edut, Logwood, & Edut, 1997; Henry, 2004; Heywood & Drake, 1997; Kinball, 2005; Sidler, 1997; Whittier, 1995).

A few studies in higher education have hinted at the significance of generational divides in leadership and gender such as Lynn Safarik's (2003) examination of how a woman's studies department helped propel organizational change on a college campus. In a similar study, Astin and Leland (1991) documented three different generations of woman—predecessors, inheritors, and instigators—who contributed to the woman's movement on campuses and explored the unique ways they approached the task of transforming campuses. Although these two studies suggest some differences in leadership style, aims, and outcomes, the studies do not explore these differences and do not examine the implications of different generations for organizational functioning. While a few recent pieces have touched on the way that generational differences in feminism impact campus progress in addressing the needs of women, there is very little information that exists to help women faculty and staff as leaders to more deeply understand and navigate these important differences.[2] We draw from leadership studies outside higher education to synthesize and inform the field.

As a result of this significant gap in knowledge, this article has three main goals: (1) illuminate generational differences between women leaders on college campuses based on a review of literature on generational differences (part 1 of the article); (2) illustrate the impact of these generational differences on leadership practices (parts 1 and 2 of the article), also based on a review of the literature; and (3) describe one process for negotiating the generational differences and their resultant impact on leadership—intergenerational dialogues (part 3). Although we acknowledge that there is a great deal of diversity within generations and feminist waves, an understanding of generational differences and their effect on leadership practices helps set the context for why dialogue is necessary. The various differences also help to provide a framework for discussion and areas to explore in intergenerational dialogues. We hope that this knowledge of differences and the creation of dialogues will help women on college campuses across generational lines to better communicate and understand each other and to work together toward common goals—equity for women.

PART 1: GENERATIONAL DIFFERENCES AND LEADERSHIP

Most authors agree that generation refers to a group of people who develop a shared or collective culture that reflects specific attitudes, preferences, and dispositions, which in turn alters their activities and practices. A generation is influenced by a collective culture based on certain key experiences that occurred during its lifetime and eventually shape collective memory (Arsenault, 2003; Schewe & Evans, 2000). A generation is also viewed as a cohort of individuals that develops around sociohistorical events, termed watershed moments (Ryder, 1965). In this

---

2. It should be noted that there are several articles on generational differences related to college students, but almost all of these refer to generic generational differences and do not examine specific groups such as feminists. In addition, most of these articles that examine generational differences relate to student behavior and preferences; instead, this article is focused on the way that generational differences affect leadership among faculty and staff.

life course model, cohorts (generations) share similar collective memories that are formed by significant watershed events, such as the second world war, civil rights and feminist movements, the Challenger accident, AIDS, and the recent events of September 11, 2001 (Arsenault, 2003).

In the workforce, there are currently four generations that have been formed by year of birth and the collective memory of watershed events: veterans born between 1922 and 1943, baby boomers born between 1944 and 1960, generation Xers[3] born between 1961 and 1980, and generation nexters born between 1981 and 2000. Each of these generations are shaped by significant watershed events—veterans experienced the Great Depression and World War II, baby boomers witnessed and participated in the civil rights and women's movement, generation Xers were affected by AIDS and the Challenger accident, and generation nexters were the first generation to grow up experiencing terrorism and extensive use of personal computers (Zemke, Raines, & Filipczak, 2000). Due to the experiences of these different generations and the impact of watershed moments, leadership styles differ. Conger (2001) discovered that the veteran generation preferred directive leadership, well-defined hierarchy, and respected loyalty to the organization. The veteran generation views of leadership were formed by a variety of military leaders of World War II, Harry Truman, and Winston Churchill. Each of these leaders expressed loyalty and led in an authoritative style.

In contrast, the baby boomer generation prefers a collegial and consensual approach to leadership; they are highly engaged in their organizations and believe in shared responsibility and dislike traditional hierarchy. Baby boomers are concerned about the culture of the workplace and are passionate about equal participation (Zemke, Raines, & Filipczak, 2000). Significant leaders of this generation included John F. Kennedy, Martin Luther King, and Mother Teresa, who exhibited a collective approach to leadership. Generation X, however, does not respect authority and prefers an egalitarian leadership style. They like to be challenged and thrive on change and prefer leaders who communicate regularly and honestly (Kunreuther, 2002; Zemke, Raines, & Filipczak, 2000). Generation Xers prefer organizational models that rely on flat structures rather than

---

3. Several researchers have argued that generation X is most appropriately applied to White, middle- to upper-class individuals with an interest in technology (Kaminow, 1999; Strauss & Howe, 1991). We adopt a more inclusive definition of generations Xers while acknowledging the intragenerational differences among race, gender, and class.

hierarchies and have a significant focus on the workplace quality. Admired leaders exemplify a creative and competent approach, such as Bill Gates who created a Microsoft campus that has a variety of amenities, including a recreation center to cater to a flexible and creative work environment. Nexters prefer a polite relationship with authority and like leaders who pull people together. They believe in collective action in opposition to the autonomy that characterizes baby boomers and generation Xers. A collective leadership style is exemplified by Michael Jordan, Bill Clinton, and Tiger Woods.

Although generational differences are consistently noted in the leadership literature, similarities also emerge among the generations. Generation Xers and nexters consistently describe competence and change agents as preferred leadership qualities (Arsenault, 2005). Change agents, however, are defined, not as individuals who inspire social movements, but leaders who are able to create change in technology and those who exemplify extreme competence and talent. For example, Bill Gates created change via personal computing operating systems, while Michael Jordan expressed talent and leadership on a basketball team. Several studies note that all generations agree that trust, honesty, and loyalty are admirable qualities of leaders (Arsenault, 2005; Kouzes & Posner, 2002).

In addition to the shared leadership styles of these generations, intragenerational variability is also found that is often mediated by gender, race, socioeconomic class, and life stage (Elder, 1991, 1998; Estes, 1991).[4] Black women educational administrators, for example, are found to have a notably different leadership style if they were born before or after the civil rights movement. Their leadership styles and values also vary dramatically from their White female counterparts. Women who were born prior to the Civil Rights Movement prioritized family over work, felt considerable barriers based on race and gender, and had significantly more household responsibilities then the "younger" postcivil rights generation (Loder, 2005). Differences also emerged between White and Black women within each generation. White women were less likely to rely on kinship networks to assist with family responsibilities and were more likely to prioritize career aspirations over family. Despite the continued conflicts with balancing work and family and maintaining traditional gender roles that younger

4. It should also be noted that research has identified life, developmental stage, and lineage position as significant in understanding generational differences (see Clark & Gunn Jr., 1985).

White women experience, they believe that many gender-based issues were solved by the older generations (Loder, 2005).

Generational Differences and Feminism

One of the more significant watershed moments that distinguishes generations of women is the different waves of feminism; the first wave was from 1848 to 1925, the second wave was from the 1960s to 1980s, and the third wave began in the 1990s. Most of the senior administrators and faculty on campus belong to the baby boomer generation, which coincides with the second wave feminist movement. They tend to be in their 50s and 60s—often at the peak of their careers—and fought for equal rights for women alongside civil rights activists in the 1960s, who crafted and supported the Equal Rights Amendment and created modern feminist organizations such as the National Organization of Women (NOW) (Whittier, 1995). These women were born in the 1940s and 1950s and grew up during the Civil Rights Movement, the Vietnam War, and the Kennedy era. This generation was shaped by a profound connection to politics and witnessed great changes in the world. They are committed to the Equal Rights Amendment, the Equal Credit Opportunity Act, and Title IX; they developed an awareness of sexism throughout organizations and society that helped to create many fundamental policy changes (Astin & Leland, 1991). This generation worked in a broad-based network through local consciousness-raising organizations; but it was also centered around large organizations, such as NOW, and developed a series of leaders including Gloria Steinem, Betty Friedan, Brenda Feigan, and Bella Abzug. On college campuses, this generation is associated with the rise of women's studies, feminist research, and women's centers on campuses (Astin & Leland, 1991).

A variety of authors have termed the most recent approach to feminism the third wave, which coincides with generation X (Baumgardner & Richards, 2000; Craigo-Snell, 2005; Edult, Logwood, & Edut, 1997). It emerged in the early 1990s and continues today. Most of the individuals within third wave feminism were born in the 1960s or 1970s and were shaped by events in the 1980s and 1990s and the changes in the world including the Internet, globalization, the rise of consumerism, and the evolution of hip-hop and rap. The critical incidences and experiences that shape this generation are powerful women such as Madonna, the Reagan backlash against feminism, the proliferation of women's studies departments, rise of queer theory, AIDS, and the rise of alternative forms of media that allowed women more ways to communicate through alternative structures. The third wavers are also the first generation to grow up in destabilized family homes with over a 50% divorce rate and were raised in families with both parents working (Baumgardner & Richards, 2000). Generation Xers had more female role models who worked outside the private sphere and who often held positions of power (e.g., Hillary Clinton).

Generation Xers were also one of the first generations to benefit from the dramatic gender role transformation that began with women entering the workforce and higher education institutions in large numbers. Unlike their mothers in the second wave, baby boomer generation, generation Xers were not susceptible to strict gender roles that placed women in the private sphere; rather, third generation feminists have had an opportunity to negotiate the contradictions of gender roles and to carve out a space for women that incorporates a variety of roles (Reed, 1997). For example, women are able to be aggressive, successful, intelligent, perky, and hyper-feminine. (See the representation of women in movies such as *Legally Blonde*).

Among third wave feminists, politics were much less influential. Third wave feminists include individuals such as Naomi Wolf, Rebecca Walker, Astrid Henry, and Susan Faludi. They see themselves as reinventing the image of feminism and bringing new life to the movement by embracing the feminine, by destroying stereotypes that feminists are not sexual and do not want family, and by embracing alternative cultural trends such as hip-hop. This generation used alternative forms of protest including punk rock, alternative arts and film, Lilith fair, *Bust,* zines, Queen Latifah, and the Internet to create a new feminism that incorporates the voices of women of color, other social classes, and women from around the globe (Baumgardner & Richards, 2000). The third wavers have also come of age in a time of economic changes. Job insecurity, lower wages, and a high cost of living have created an economic situation where women do not have a choice to enter the job market (Sidler, 1997).

PART 2: GENERATIONAL CONFLICTS RESULTING IN FAULT LINES[5]

Zemke et al. (2000) states that the attitudes and beliefs of a generation affects how each generation views leadership. To examine how the different perspectives of feminism and the significant generational differences create tensions and conflicts among women leaders in colleges and universities, we review some of the differences and misunderstandings that create *fault lines* that can pull women apart and create deep generational divides.

We focus on the relationship between these two generations of women (second and third wave), as they are the two major groups within leadership roles on campuses. Of the many generational conflicts between second and third wave feminists, the existence of different types of feminists (e.g., liberal, radical, postmodern) that hold conflicting values and beliefs about feminism has exacerbated significant generational fault lines. Older feminists tend to believe that younger feminists do not have a political commitment and are not invested in creating a better world for women (Baumgardner & Richards, 2000; Craigo-Snell, 2005). Although younger feminists feel that they are misunderstood by baby boomers, baby boomers feel that younger feminists have betrayed the movement.

Another major generational conflict that leads to fault lines lies is the tenuous relationship that arises when one generation attempts to simultaneously respond and differentiate itself from the previous generation. A significant critique of second wave feminism is that it was for White, heterosexual women from the middle to upper class (see Collins, 1993 and Mohanty, 2003). As mentioned previously, third wave feminists have attempted to create a more inclusive feminism that includes women from social identities and social classes to respond to the criticism of the second wave. However, third wave feminism is also attempting to redefine feminism. Henry (2004) describes the relationship between second and third wave feminism as a mother-daughter relationship where the daughter, the third wave, is attempting to resist the teaching of the mother and create a new identity. To do so, third wavers have formulated a new identity

5. The fault lines presented in this section are not intended to suggest that all women in particular generations and waves of feminism think and feel uniformly. We acknowledge that there is vast diversity within generations and waves of feminism.

focused on individualism while paradoxically trying to create an inclusive feminist ideology (Henry, 2004).

The specific fault lines that impact women faculty and staff at postsecondary institutions that we highlight include being unwilling to sacrifice family versus making sacrifices for career advancement; changing day-to-day practice versus focusing on revolutionary change; focusing on culture and a "girlie culture" versus an emphasis on politics; emphasizing individuality and a rejection of a feminist label versus embracing feminist ideals and collective action; and the importance of leadership as nonpositional versus focusing on placing women in traditional leadership roles.

While these are not all the differences, they highlight key areas that can result in miscommunication and difficulty in working and understanding each other. While generalizations can be problematic, as there are always individuals who act uniquely and issues are multifaceted and complex, these general differences have been identified in studies/literature and do help to understand global patterns that women may need to address. The goal of the article is not to understand each of these differences in depth, but to understand the range of topics women might need to discuss in intergenerational dialogues. In their real life discussions, the nuances and complexity will emerge. But, these issues provide a roadmap or framework of areas for people to examine what they see as intergenerational tensions of their campuses and potential ways to understand and interpret these tensions.

Willingness to Sacrifice Family

One of the many differences between women in the baby boomer and generation X cohorts is the value placed on family versus career advancement (Baumgardner & Richards, 2000; Craigo-Snell, 2005; Edult, Logwood, & Edut, 1997). While many women of the baby boomer generation within higher education were willing to forgo having children or marriage for career advancement, women of the third wave and of generation X are unwilling to forgo childbearing or developing a meaningful relationship with a partner. Women who grew up as part of generation X watched their parents divorce and grew up in unstable family environments (Baumgardner & Richards, 2000). As a consequence, many have a strong desire to create a meaningful and stable family environment. Generation X has a strong resolve to find and commit time to a partnership and family.

We suggest that the specific conflicts that arise in an organizational setting relate to the level of support that baby boomers might provide to those generation Xers with families, the understanding of the importance of work–family balance, and the creation of family-friendly policies by those baby boomers who are often in higher level leadership positions. Without support and policies, generation X is often searching for a balance between work and personal life that they believe was lacking in their parents' lives (Kunreuther, 2002). There is no other time in higher education where work and family balance has received more attention. Foundations, organizations, and individual institutions have begun to create new policies that address work and family balance. Women leaders from the baby boomer generation are poised to address and lead the efforts for greater career flexibility. These generational fault lines have not only made evident the tensions between groups, but also they have created the need for additional policies and new practices that require a discussion and understanding of generational differences.

Short-Term Sacrifices for Long-Term Gain

Third wave feminists and generation X faculty and staff tend to desire job satisfaction in the short term and are not willing to sacrifice happiness and meaning for long-term career advancement (Baumgardner & Richards, 2000; Craigo-Snell, 2005; Edult, Logwood, & Edut, 1997; Kunreuther, 2002). Whereas second wave feminists often took positions that they might not have enjoyed in order to foster their long-term career advancement, third wavers are unwilling to take positions that they do not find meaningful. An important misunderstanding between the two generations arises when third wavers reject undesirable lateral career moves with the long-term potential to move up at a later date (Baumgardner & Richards, 2000). Many second wave feminists feel unappreciated for the sacrifices that they made in order to provide third wave feminists with opportunities to have a more meaningful career.

This does not suggest that third wavers do not value the progress and advancement of women in leadership positions. Rather, we argue that the women of generation X believe in the importance of asserting their own empowerment and career mobility as a form of progress in the movement. They also try to work with individuals in their immediate sphere to help them propel their careers. They are less likely to work in a political fashion, mobilizing women collectively across campus to empower a group of women and create a network. Furthermore, women in generation X who watch baby boomers in higher level leadership positions work long hours, make sacrifices, and participate in power struggles to create change may not perceive of progress up the hierarchy as a way to increase job satisfaction (Kunreuther, 2002). The benefits that baby boomers once saw in moving up the hierarchy may not be apparent to women of generation X.

Changing Day-to-Day Practice Versus Focusing on the System: Incremental Versus Radical Change

The baby boom generation was part of a series of social movements that were able to create fundamental changes in social, political, and economic structures (Astin & Leland, 1991; Howe & Strauss, 1991; Zemke, Raines, & Filipczak, 2000). As a result of these fundamental experiences, this generation tends to approach change by focusing on the overall system and using the political process to create broad-based change. Generation X grew up in a time where the overall system reasserted itself and criticized the ability of the entire system to change (Kunreuther, 2002; Tapscott, 1998; Zemke, Raines, & Filipczak, 2000). Third wave feminists grew up in the midst of a backlash against feminism and as a result saw many of the changes that occurred be dismantled or ridiculed (Baumgardner & Richards, 2000; Craigo-Snell, 2005). Rather than joining a feminist group on campus and trying to promote schoolwide changes, they are more likely to try to alter practices within their specific units and infuse changes in the ways that they approach their work (Baumgardner & Richards, 2000). They characterize themselves more as "individuals quietly living determined lives rather than radicals on the ramparts" (Baumgardner & Richards, 2000, p. 36). They also fear a backlash that many second wave feminists experienced and prefer to work in more incremental ways in which they are less threatening to the system. Second wave feminists are committed to more revolutionary change and are frustrated by the current slower pace of change (Zemke, Raines, & Filipczak, 2000). While they recognize that the women's movement is a long-term journey, they remain committed to more revolutionary and systemic change.

We argue that the ways in which women in higher education leadership positions approach change has the potential to create substantial fault lines. As many women in high-level leadership positions look to the next generation of third wavers to take over the struggle for equity, second wavers expect women of the third wave to value, recognize, and continue the same strategies. However, third wavers take a markedly different approach that seeks to more subtly and subversively create change within the system. Different approaches lead to conflicts within leadership teams, among groups of activist women, a lack of acknowledgement of activist efforts, and concern that the work of the second wavers will be erased by a lack of direct action by the new third wave leaders.

Embracing and Celebrating "Girlie" Culture

The unifying vision for third wave feminism focuses not only on political changes to help advance women in society, but also on expressing the value and beauty of women and their perspectives (Baumgardner & Richards, 2000; Craigo-Snell, 2005). They are less likely to host a rally with a political theme than to put on a concert such as Lilith Fair. Consciousness-raising takes the form of women sharing and enjoying their contributions and culture and is less directly focused on the inequities that they face, although these inequities are not ignored. This generation of women embraces the contributions and experiences of women more and wants to celebrate women's culture (Baumgardner & Richards, 2000; Craigo-Snell, 2005). Second wave feminists worry that the focus on culture rather than politics diverts feminism from its goals of equity. They also are concerned that third wave feminists are missing a framework or strategy for transforming sexism and confronting the inequities that lie before women (Astin & Leland, 1991). The "girlie culture" of third wave feminists leads to indirect criticism of inequitable policies rather than the direct activist strategies—letter writing and petitions—that are traditionally practices of second wave feminism. In leadership teams and in groups that are attempting to address inequities, these different tactics and strategies create tensions within the group and may prevent action.

Furthermore, baby boomers often downplay differences between men and women, emphasizing that women are equal to and therefore just like men (Loder, 2005). The women of generation X do not want to act like men and want to celebrate what they call "girlie culture" (Baumgardner & Richards, 2000). Rather, generation X women reject the idea that they should dress and act like a man in order to be respected as leaders. They even want to assert their sexuality and femininity and enjoy using their sexual power to create change and navigate difficult situations. Baumgardner and Richards (2000) note that "girlie culture is a rebellion against the false impression that since women don't want to be sexually exploited, they don't want to be sexual; against the necessity of brass button, red-suited seriousness to infiltrate a man's world; against the anachronistic belief that because women could be dehumanized by power they must be; and the idea that girls and power don't mix" (p. 137). The different expressions of gender between the second and third wave feminists lead to contradictory approaches to activism and also misinterpretations of leadership qualities. While women of the second wave are more likely to adopt masculine performances that express traditional management styles (e.g., authoritative, confident, decisive), women of the third wave adopt a more inclusive leadership style. These different styles may lead to criticism and tensions between women who lead in seemingly contradictory ways.

Embracing or Rejecting a Feminist Label

Women of the third wave often reject the label of feminist. During the backlash of the 1980s, feminism became a pejorative term associated with angry, militant lesbians (Baumgardner and Richards, 2000). Baumgardner and Richards (2000) relay this common stereotype: "Some feminists think all sex is rape, all men are evil, you have to be a lesbian to be a feminist, you can't wear girlie clothes or makeup, married women are lame, etc." (p. 62). Unable to see beyond the stereotype or afraid to experience the backlash of using the title, many of the more recent women do not assert their connection to the larger feminist movement. However, their day-to-day actions usually demonstrate that they are feminists working toward helping women to gain greater equality and equity in the world. Third wave feminists believe that their emphasis on a "girlie culture" will help bring more women back to feminism and that the second wave feminists do not understand the potential (Baumgardner & Richards, 2000).

Rejecting the feminist label is also a response to the critique of second wave feminism. Rather then creating an all-inclusive form of feminism, third wavers tend to focus on individuality that prevents the formation of meta-narratives that essentialize groups of women. Third wavers ask, "Which person? and Whose politics?" (Heywood & Drake, 1997, p. 56). We suggest that the implication for leadership is that collective action, focused specifically around gender, seems to be invisible on campus, but it is often happening and women leaders need to search hard to join networks and find like-minded people. The networks are less visible because many of the actions are occurring within the system rather than trying to change the system, are individual and not collective practices, and are less assertive. For these reasons, the efforts of third wavers remain out of the purview of the public and are not visible to the second wavers, who are more apt to identify, direct, and use collective strategies as activist movements. Women leaders on higher education campuses may not be able to identify or see the value in the more subversive and individually based approach if those approaches are difficult to identify and the resulting changes are not made public.

Embracing or Dismantling Mainstream Organizations

Second wave feminists often hope to create new feminist organizations or to alter existing patriarchal organizations and their practices (Astin & Leland, 1991). The second wave feminists worked to fundamentally change the policies and practices of organizations that discriminated against women such as maternity leave, equal pay, and sexual harassment. They believed in the vision of fundamentally different organizations. Third wave feminists are happy to work within mainstream organizations working patiently day-to-day to change the field of practice within mainstream organizations (Baumgardner & Richards, 2000; Craigo-Snell, 2005). They no longer believe in a vision of fundamentally altering patriarchal structures within a single generation, but believe that over time, "girlie culture" will become more respected and women will make small inroads to create more equity. Because second and third wave feminists often have different approaches for achieving equity and defining what equity means, they tend to clash in discussions.

This change from dismantling to embracing mainstream organizations is illustrated in the decline of national higher education organizations dedicated to women. In the early 2000s, the long-standing National Association for Women in Higher Education closed its doors because membership had declined rapidly in the previous decade (Gangone, 1999). Women no longer see themselves as part of a broader movement and tend to work at the local, not national, level. As leaders, third wave feminists work locally, rather than nationally, as part of a systems orientation to change within mainstream structures. Leadership has taken on different attributes, styles, and qualities among third wave feminists. This results in a decline in collective action and a decline of those organizations that rely on direct criticism and activism to achieve the goal of equity. Therefore, we conjecture that women leaders in higher education are more apt to have conflicts regarding the actual issues that require change and strategies to create change.

Consciousness-Raising

Because many of the third wave feminists grew up having many opportunities and experiencing less sexism, they often do not recognize the importance of raising consciousness and making sexism apparent in society and organizations (Baumgardner & Richards, 2000; Craigo-Snell, 2005; Edult, Logwood, & Edut, 1997; Kunreuther, 2002; Tapscott, 1998; Zemke, Raines, & Filipczak, 2000). These women experience great confidence in much of their early education and career and have not experienced the glass ceiling that second wave feminists experienced throughout their education and early careers. Many early and midcareer faculty and staff on campuses have experienced little overt sexism and may be unaware of more subtle sexism they experience because they often lack consciousness. As a result, third wave feminists do not spend much of their time conducting consciousness-raising, which was one of the fundamental tools of the early women's movement. Without consciousness-raising, generation X has difficulty setting an agenda and being cognizant of current societal barriers (Craigo-Snell, 2005; Edult, Logwood, & Edut, 1997). We argue that third wave feminists may not be able to see needed changes on campus and may lack the skills to help others to understand sexist norms and practices that subtly discriminate against women; third wavers are often unaware of how to read and analyze these structures.

The Importance of Visible, Hierarchical Leaders

Second wave feminism emphasizes the importance of women obtaining positions of leadership from which they had been traditionally excluded (Astin & Leland, 1991; Glazer-Raymo, 1999; Wenniger & Conroy, 2001). Programs such as the American Council on Education Fellows Program emerged to help women move up the ladder into senior faculty, dean, provost, vice president, and presidential positions. Ironically, although many second wave feminists were working to dismantle patriarchal organizations and hoped to use unique approaches to leadership, they also recognized the importance of getting into positions of power to be able to create change of a more radical nature in the system. In addition, the women's movement in the 1970s and 1980s had many visible leaders that people identified with and that marked the movement (Astin & Leland, 1991; Wenniger & Conroy, 2001) In contrast, members of generation X and third wave feminists are cynical of individuals and positions of power and do not strive to be in these positions (Baumgardner & Richards, 2000;

Craigo-Snell, 2005; Edult, Logwood, & Edut, 1997; Kunreuther, 2002). Instead, they believe in the importance of people creating change and being activists in whatever position or organization they are located (Baumgardner & Richards, 2000). The implication for leadership is that new staff are not drawn to or striving for positions of hierarchy. We assert that third wavers in higher education have a fundamental belief that leadership can be exercised from all positions within the hierarchy and do not move up the institutional hierarchy before they attempt to create change.

Using the Tools of Patriarchy

Many second wave feminists believe that the women's movement should adopt different approaches to creating change and playing a leadership role (Glazer-Raymo, 1999; Wenniger & Conroy, 2001). While not universally endorsed, many second wave feminists believed in using different leadership tactics and strategies than those typically used by men. Second wavers emphasize networks rather than hierarchy, empowerment rather than manipulation of power, the sharing of information rather than the controlling of it, relationship-building rather than autonomy, and consciousness-raising and education rather than persuasion and influence. In contrast, third wave feminists often use the tools of patriarchy and believe it can be used against the patriarchy to dismantle it. Third wave feminists are not afraid to yield power, control information, and manipulate hierarchy. They see themselves as willing to use the tools of patriarchy from inside patriarchal organizations.

Tools of the patriarchy are particularly relevant for the third wavers who consume pop culture regularly, are computer savvy, and rely on personal anecdotes. For example, when a group of women came together to create *HUES Magazine*—a grassroots magazine created as a forum to promote sisterhood and empowerment—the group purposefully used personal anecdotes to illustrate individualistic definitions of feminism and relied on appealing graphics to attract generation Xers who are used to sensory overload (Edut, Logwood, & Edut, 1997). The HUES founders purposefully used pop culture and the media—commonly considered patriarchal structures—to disseminate a message of empowerment and "girlie culture." Using these tools of patriarchy allowed for mass dissemination and exposure to reach more women. Examples of third wavers using the tools of patriarchy in a higher education context include co-opting campus newspapers with advertisements and editorials about inequities, developing student organizations to raise consciousness, populating hiring committees to hire more women and people of color, and strategically becoming a part of planning committees to subtly push an agenda forward. Women leaders in higher education who identify with the third wave use these strategies to work within the systems to create change that stands in direct contrast to the direct activist strategies of second wave leaders.

PART 3: NEEDED CONVERSATION AND CROSS-GENERATIONAL DIALOGUE

These various differences in approaches to and tactics of leadership might make it difficult for members of these two generations to work together. In our experiences working with leadership development programs across the country and with leaders on various campuses, these differences are mostly not understood among different generations of women on campuses, and they prevent collective action and progress. Baumgardner and Richards (2000) note: "we have seen up close and personal the biggest conflict between the generations is a lack of communication, mutual ignorance of each other's accomplishments, and sometimes suspicion about each other's tactics" (p. 220).

Colleges and universities need to recognize generational differences as a diversity issue. Generations have different perspectives, values, beliefs, and leadership styles that can, by being recognized, create unique leadership and workplace challenges. What is needed both nationally—with an organization such as NASPA—and locally on individual campuses are opportunities for intergenerational dialogues that help to create common ground by blending the individual and different voices into a unified women's movement that has been lost nationally and at the campus level. National associations provide a forum to foster mentoring, networking, and support building activities, which are essential in promoting and developing more women leaders. However, organizational context has a significant effect on the ways in which generational differences emerge (Kunreuther, 2002). Having institutional-specific dialogues is important for challenging cultural and structural barriers and definitions of leadership that emphasize these generational differences. These dialogues need to have three primary elements: (1) a discussion of common ground, (2) an acknowledgment and discussion of the fault lines outlined above respecting both the positions, and (3) a recognition and appreciation of the contributions of both generations.

Common Ground

Intergenerational dialogues need to begin with seeing this common ground—both want equal pay for women on campus and family-friendly policies that allow women to advance and be more satisfied in their careers. Research has noted that pay for women in higher education is consistently lower than that of men, regardless of the level of the position, age, or other generational-specific differences (Perna, 2002). In addition, family-friendly policies encompass child bearing and caring for elderly parents, significant issues for both baby boomers and generation Xers. Both groups want women students to have opportunities and choices in terms of majors or career choices and seek to create a campus environment to help women in advancing. By creating dialogues to come together, groups of women from different generations may understand the needs and similarities of these in broader issues. There are commonalities in the ways different generations think about leadership such as the importance of honesty or integrity that can serve as a common ground (Arsenault, 2005; Kouzes & Posner, 2002). Therefore, starting a dialogue about some important traits and characteristics desirable in leaders, leadership processes, or organizational change that ascertain qualities such as wisdom, caring, or civility, mutual respect can help groups to see some of the core areas where they can come together and emphasize when working together and communicating becomes difficult.

There are several ways to begin dialogues of common ground between generations. First, these discussions may be guided by readings that identify generational differences and address the implications of how generational differences create contradictory perspectives and approaches to change (see Baumgardner & Richards, 2002 and Meyerson, 2003). Second, campus data can identify issues that cross generational lines, particularly data that show inequities over time and among leadership positions. Data on salary inequities and the representation of women in faculty and leadership positions will show sustained inequity. Third, these dialogues need to occur in a variety of settings and may be most effective in existing groups. For example, current leadership development programs should consider adding these dialogues to curricula. Groups may not be moving forward because these underlying tensions exist and individuals are not able to identify the common group.

Discussion of Fault Lines

Intergenerational dialogues cannot stop with acknowledging common ground, as miscommunication will occur if differences and fault lines are not identified and brought to light. This article is meant as a tool to be distributed to groups conducting intergenerational dialogues so that they can reflect on differences within the experiences and background of different generations (described in parts one and two). The historical grounding in part 1 also helps all groups to understand why generations have different perspectives based on their different histories. People are much more likely to understand each other when they can see how people's experiences affect their opinions, beliefs, and preferences (Conger, 2001). The specific differences in beliefs and how they manifest in leadership makes these fault lines more tangible—demonstrating how they affect how individuals may work together within institutions (part 2 of the article). Intergenerational groups can be structured around the following questions:

1. What are the generational groups on our campus? Are there large numbers of one group? Is there a dominant perspective that overshadows others?
2. Do we allow for multiple feminist voices of different generations? In what ways?
3. What are the areas of difference related to leadership and change that have emerged on our campus and that have lead to miscommunication and misunderstanding?
4. How might we think about these differences in a synergistic rather than a competing manner?

In addition to using the fault lines to understand differences that can lead to miscommunication, the fault lines can also be used as ways to brainstorm and create strategies for advancing equity that combine elements of both approaches to leadership and creating change. Using the baby boomer focus on creating social change and the generation Xer focus on daily and small-scale forms of activism can benefit a mutual movement. We can capitalize on the power of both strategies rather than continue to see them as competing strategies and arguing for the benefit of one over the other. Generation Xers and baby boomers need to have opportunities to see the common ground (as suggested in the first phase of the dialogues), while also acknowledging and taking advantage of the ways to approach leadership and change from their distinctive approaches building a more robust women's movement.

Recognition and Appreciation

The last issue of recognition and appreciation of the contributions of both generations is also important for extending and building the common ground. In the past, both generations have acted in ways that broke down dialogue and communication. Younger women have often ignored sacrifices and contributions of older feminists as well as ridiculed their techniques and approaches. As a result, second wave feminists feel misunderstood and belittled by these actions. Older feminists often critique third wave feminists for being apathetic, lacking political skills, being frivolous in their emphasis on girlie culture, and exhibiting a lack of ambition and a lack of desire for positional leadership and making sacrifices. Third wave feminists can learn much from the second wave feminists about the power of agenda-setting, consciousness-raising, and dismantling problematic policies. Conversely, the second wave feminists can learn from third wave feminists about ways to attract more women into the women's movement, about the power of working within traditional organizational systems, or using patriarchal tools against the system.

Questions to help groups in moving toward greater recognition and appreciation include:

1. Describe three of the best qualities of the second wave feminists on your campus. Describe three characteristics, skills, or strategies that second wave feminists can teach third wave feminists.
2. Describe the three best qualities of third wave feminists on your campus. Describe three characteristics, skills, or strategies that third wave feminists can teach second wave feminists.
3. What are the most successful strategies that the two generations can develop together?
4. What is a combined agenda that the two groups might develop using the best characteristics and strategies of each group?

CONCLUSION

Student affairs has long taken a leadership role in issues of diversity. In fact, it is probably not an exaggeration to say that student affairs is a campus's soul or conscience on issues of diversity. However, one important issue of diversity remains mostly unaddressed—generational differences, specifically as they relate to women and efforts to create gender equity (another key area of diversity). Leaders in student affairs can help to make a difference on college campuses if they help to foster a recognition of generational issues among women leaders and create intergenerational dialogues that help to create a more unified movement toward gender equity, capitalizing on the power of all women working together.

This paper also has broader implications as well. These generational differences are not limited to women; they also exist among men and are likely to impact organizational functioning and leadership. General dialogues related to generational differences that exist among campus staff would also be important. The framework presented in part 3 could also be used for such dialogues as well, with the set of questions being altered slightly to provide direction.

Lastly, leadership programs, particularly those that work to develop and promote women into leadership positions, need to adopt new pedagogical tools that appeal to generation Xers—most have been modeled on the baby boomers. For example, successful leaders need to consider the qualities that different generations value. In addition, programmatic materials may also need to incorporate more collective forms of leadership that discuss change agents. Recent books, such as *Tempered Radicals* by Meyerson (2003) and *Grassroots Leadership: A Field Guide for Feminist Activism* (2000) by Baumgardner and Richards, conceptualize leadership as nonpositional and collegial. Using these new resources that represent a new generation's way of conceptualizing leadership can help to make leadership development programs more relevant for a new generation of leaders. While programs should not abandon all the skills and competencies that baby boomers found effective, the individuals who develop leadership programs should be more sensitive to being inclusive as they design the curriculum.

In closing, we challenge student affairs leaders to develop their knowledge of generational differences, to understand how these differences affect leadership and change on campus, and create intergenerational dialogues when necessary to help create more functional environments where all generations can thrive.

REFERENCES

Astin, H., & Leland, C. (1991). *Women of influence, women of vision.* San Francisco: Jossey Bass.

Arsenault, P. (2004). Validating generational differences: A legitimate diversity and leadership issue. *Leadership and Organizational Development Journal, 25*(1/2), 124–141.

Baumgardner, J., & Richards, A. (2000). *Manifesta: Young woman, feminism, and the future.* New York: Farrar, Strauss, & Giroux.

Bennis, W., & Thomas, R. (2002). *Geeks & geezers: How era, values and defining moments shape leaders.* Boston: Harvard Business School Press.

Collins, P. (1993). Learning from the outsider within. The sociological significance of black feminist thought. In J. Glazer, E. Bensimon, & B. Townsend (Eds.), *Women in higher education: A feminist perspective* (pp. 45–65). Needhman Heights, MA: Ginn Press.

Conger, J. (2001). How gen X manage. In J. Osland, D. Kolb, & I. Rubin, (Eds.), *Organizational behavior reader* (pp. 9–19), Upper Saddle River, NJ: Prentice-Hall.

Craigo-Snell, S. (2005). Multiplication and division: Feminist theology from 1980 to 2000. In G. Kimball (Ed.), *Women's culture in a new era* (pp. 215–222). Lanham, MD: The Scarecrow Press.

Edut, T., Logwood, D., & Edut, O. (1997). HUES magazine: The making of a movement. In L. Heywood & J. Drake (Eds.), *Third wave agenda: Being feminist, doing feminism* (pp. 83–98), Minneapolis, MN: University of Minnesota Press.

Elder, G. H. Jr. (1991). Lives and social change. In W. R. Heinz (Ed.), *Theoretical advances in life course research* (pp. 58–86). Weinheim Germany: Deutscher Studien Verlag.

Elder, G. H. Jr. (1998). The life course as development theory. *Child Development, 69,* 1–12.

Estes, C. L. (1991). The new political economy of aging: Introduction & critique. In M. Minkler & C. L. Estes (Eds.), *Critical perspectives on aging* (pp. 19–36). Amityville, NY: Baywood.

Henry, A. (2004). *Not my mother's sister: Generational conflict and third-wave feminism.* Bloomington, IN: Indiana University Press.

Findlen, B. (2001). *Listen up: Voices from the next feminist generation.* New York: Seal.

Gangone, L. (1999). *Navigating turbulence: A case study of a voluntary higher education association.* Columbia Unvieristy, Teachers College, Unpublished dissertation.

Glazer-Raymo, J. (1999). *Shattering the myths: Women in academe.* Baltimore: John Hopkins Press.

Hernandez, D. Rehman, B (2002). *Colonize this!: On feminism today.* Emeryville, CA: Seal.

Heywood, L. & Drake, J. (1997). Introduction. In L. Heywood & J. Drake (Eds.), *Third wave agenda: Being feminist, doing feminism* (pp. 1–20), Minneapolis, MN: University of Minnesota Press.

Heywood, L. & Drake, J. (1997). We learn America like a script: Activism in the third wave; or, enough phantoms of nothing. In L. Heywood & J. Drake (Eds.), *Third wave agenda: Being feminist, doing feminism* (pp. 40-54), Minneapolis, MN: University of Minnesota Press.

Hoagland, S. (1988). *Lesbian ethics homeland toward a new value.* Chicago: Institute of Lesbian Studies.

Howe, N., & Strauss, B. (1991). *Generations.* New York: Quill Publications.

Kinball, G. (Ed.) (2005). *Women's culture in a new era.* Lanham, MD: The Scarecrow Press.

Kouzes, J. M., & Posner, B. Z. (2002). *The leadership challenge.* San Francisco: Jossey-Bass.

Kunreuther, F. (2002). *Generational changes and leadership: Implications for social change organizations.* New York: Building Movement Project.

Lancaster, L. C., & Stillman, D. (2002). *When generations collide: Who they are. Why they clash. How to solve the generational puzzle at work.* New York: HarperCollins.

Loder, T. L. (2005). Women administrators negotiate work-family conflicts in changing times: An intergenerational perspective. *Educational Administration Quarterly, 41*(5), 741–776.

Meyerson, D. E. (2003). *Tempered radicals: How everyday leaders inspire change at work.* Boston: Harvard Business School Press.

Mohanty, C. (2003). *Feminism without borders: Decolonizing theory, practicing solidarity.* Durham, NC: Duke University Press.

Perna, L. W. (2002). Sex differences in the supplemental earning of college and university faculty. *Research in Higher Education, 43*(1), 31–58.

Tapscott, D. (1998). *Growing up digital: The rise of the net generation.* New York: McGraw Hall.

Safarik, L. (2003). Feminist transformation in higher education: Discipline, structure, and institution. *The Review of Higher Education,* 26(4), 419–445.

Ryder, N. B. (1965). The cohort as a concept in the study of social change. *American Sociological Review, 30,* 843–861.

Schewe, C. D., & Evans, S. M. (2000). Market segmentation by cohorts: The value and validity of cohorts in American and abroad. *Journal of Marketing Management, 16,* 129–142.

Shoemaker, L. (1997). Part animal, part machine: Self-definition, Rollins style. In L. Heywood & J. Drake (Eds.), *Third wave agenda: Being feminist, doing feminism* (pp. 103–133), Minneapolis, MN: University of Minnesota Press.

Sidler, M. (1997). Living in Mcjobdom: Third wave feminism and class inequity. In L. Heywood & J. Drake (Eds.), *Third wave agenda: Being feminist, doing feminism* (pp. 25–39), Minneapolis, MN: University of Minnesota Press.

Siegel, D. L. (1997). Reading between the waves: Feminist historiography in a "postfeminist" moment. In L. Heywood & J. Drake (Eds.), *Third wave agenda: Being feminist, doing feminism* (pp. 55–82), Minneapolis, MN: University of Minnesota Press.

Smola, K. W., & Sutton, C. D. (2002). Generational differences: Revisiting generational work values for the new millennium. *Journal of Organizational Behavior, 23*(4), 363–332

Walker, R. (1995). *To be real: Telling the truth and changing the face of feminism.* New York: Anchor Books.

Wenniger, M. D., & Conroy, M. (2001). *Gender equity or bust: On the road with women in higher education.* San Francisco: Jossey-Bass.

Whittier, N. (1995). *Feminist generations: The persistence of the radical movement. P*hiladelphia: Temple University Press.

Zemke, R., Raines, C., & Filipczak, B. (2000). *Generations at work: Managing the clash of veterans, boomers, xers, and nexters in your workplace.* New York: AMACOM.

A Window Into the Culture of Leadership Within Higher Education Through the Leadership Definitions of Women Faculty: A Case Study of ELAM Women Faculty Alumnae

Sharon A. McDade
Associate Professor, Higher Education Administration
The George Washington University
Washington, D.C.

Phillip J. King
Associate University Registrar for Academic Course Planning and Scheduling
Florida International University
Miami, Florida

Yu-Chuan Chuang
Doctoral Candidate
The George Washington University
Washington, D.C.

Page S. Morahan
Co-Director, The Hedwig van Ameringen Executive Leadership in Academic Medicine (ELAM) Program for Women
Drexel University College of Medicine
Philadelphia, Pennsylvania

Kirk A. Nooks
Dean of Student Development
Northern Virginia Community College, Loudoun Campus
Loudoun, Virginia

Lorraine Sloma-Williams
Doctoral Candidate
The George Washington University
Washington, D.C.

Rosalyn C. Richman
Co-Director, The Hedwig van Ameringen Executive Leadership in Academic Medicine (ELAM) Program for Women
Drexel University College of Medicine
Philadelphia, Pennsylvania

With Appreciation: The authors wish to thank the following for their assistance with this article: Svetlana Burdina, MA in higher education administration, The George Washington University; and Victoria C. Odhner, associate director, The Hedwig van Ameringen Executive Leadership in Academic Medicine Program for Women, Drexel University.

This article proposes a thematic framework that can serve as a window for understanding the leadership definitions of women academics, and through these how leadership is articulated, understood, and enacted within the culture of leadership in higher education. The framework was generated from analysis of 283 available leadership definitions from classes 1996–2004 provided by Fellows in the Hedwig van Ameringen Executive Leadership in Academic Medicine Program for Women. Definitions were analyzed using Atlas.Ti software by coders and discussants in an iterative process that generated, applied, and challenged findings. Beginning with Rost's (1991) framework, the project went beyond this to develop a framework derived from the voices of the women that includes: leadership as activities, relationship to followers, envisioning and strategy, traits, communication, influence, and transformation. The article closes with application to various groups, notes for future research, and conclusions.

INTRODUCTION

Individual leadership definitions provide a window into understanding the nature of leadership as it is acted, the culture of leadership, and the collective understanding of the phenomena of leadership as experienced within an organization (Clark & Clark, 1990; Hughes, Ginnett, & Curphy, 2002; Klein, Gabelnick, & Herr, 1998; McDade & Lewis, 1994). While the word "leadership" has come to mean "all things to all people" (Rost, 1991, p. 7), most individuals believe that they know "it" when they see "it." Similarly, many believe they can describe their own concept of leadership, even if they do not have scholarship-based categories and adjectives with which to report those beliefs (Rost, 1991). In particular, what can leadership definitions of women faculty who have signaled their interest in taking on advanced leadership responsibility and administrative advancement tell us about the culture of leadership in higher education? What can these leadership definitions tell us about the broader scholarship on leadership culture broadly written? This study considered leadership in the academy from a case study of women faculty participants in the Hedwig van Ameringen Executive Leadership in Academic Medicine (ELAM) Program for Women for which a comprehensive database on the participants' leadership was available for study.

CONCEPTUAL FRAMEWORK AS A STARTING POINT

The heart of any field is a definition of the phenomena under investigation. Yet, neither scholars nor practitioners of leadership use a common definition. Rost (1991, p. 6) argued that leadership studies have a "culture of definitional permissiveness and relativity." This pervades leadership studies in every field, including higher education. First, many scholars fail to provide a definition of leadership in their work, perhaps stemming from beliefs that leadership is commonly known or that it is abstract and indefinable such that definition would be foolhardy. Of the 312 studies published in the 1980s examined by Rost (1991), 202 did not provide a definition, including those written by many major scholars. Second, Rost found that often authors subsequently ignored their leadership definition in their discussion of findings. Third, with few exceptions (e.g., Kellerman, 1984; Rost, 1991), the leadership literature does not address leadership definitions or establish criteria for evaluating these. Finally, what little discussion that does exist on leadership definitions is not rooted in what those in organizations say, but rather in how scholars define the phenomena (Rost, 1991).

Rost (1991) provided the only in-depth treatment of leadership definitions found by the authors of this study. He conducted an analysis of leadership definitions offered in scholarly research written in the 1980s and drawn from many disciplines. (Bass [1990] provided the largest analysis of leadership literature as a whole, not definitions per se.) Rost's stated that he analyzed 312 "books, chapters, and articles, which by title indicated that they were primarily concerned with leadership" (p. 44). From these he distilled six themes (pp. 70–88: leadership as traits, influence, transformation, management, do the leader's wishes, and achieving organizational goals).[1] Rost acknowledged potential theme overlaps, but

1. Rost (1991) noted that he found 110 studies with definitions, but he did not provide specific definitions or definitional counts in his discussions of the themes. Instead he discussed each theme with representative quotations and references to studies. Numbers presented in this paper were established by counting citations (n = 126, the base number used for analysis) of studies listed in each thematic discussion and thus are stated as numbers of citations, not numbers of definitions. Similar to his explanation regarding overlap, some citations appeared in at least two themes, suggesting that a single definition can include elements from several themes. See Table 1.

noted that context mitigates this effect when applying to definitions themselves. Thus, Rost's analysis, seemingly unique, provides a window into how leadership is understood and discussed within leadership scholarship broadly writ, and within which the scholarly roots of leadership studies in higher education are planted (Bensimon, Neumann, & Birnbaum, 1989). As a typical strategy in qualitative research, we started with Rost's themes but expanded beyond these to understand how the women faculty in our study articulated leadership (Marshall & Rossman, 2006).

Rost (1991) found the *Leadership as Do the Leader's Wishes* theme most popular (26.2% of the studies' citations). Used in scholarship from every discipline, it was "extremely popular with many of the authors who do not define [but imply] leadership" (p. 70), and it was apparent in the media. The theme captures commands flowing downward, with leader as direction-giver. Rooted in the great man theory, most works using this theme studied presidents, statespersons, and organization heads. Coding cues in this project referred to acts of commanding and directing.

Derived from Burns' (1978) segmentation of leadership as transactional or transformational, the theme of *Leadership as Transformation* (24.5% of the studies' citations) captures definitions about leaders "transform[ing] an organization according to some criteria of excellence" (p. 85). With focus on change and how it affects people, places, and products to improve, this overlaps with "do the leader's wishes." Coding referred to change or development within a person, team, or organization.

The leadership-as-excellence movement that began in the 1980s emphasized talents or abilities associated with leadership (e.g., Peters & Waterman, 1982; Bennis & Nanus, 1985; Conger, 1989). Because this movement produced popular leadership books in the 1980s and beyond, the *Leadership as Traits* theme (15.9% of the studies' citations) was "undoubtedly the source of many people's understandings of leadership" (Rost, 1991, p. 82) who came of age in that era. Coding cues were references to traits or abilities possessed by leaders.

Popular in social psychology, organizational behavior, and education, the *Leadership as Achieving Organizational Goals* theme centers on organizations and their goals associated with "leadership to group facilitation and human relations skills of organizational development" (p. 76). This theme (13.5% of the studies' citations) can also emphasize effectiveness over quality, as related to achievable and identifiable organizational goals. If leader and organizational goals are identical, then this theme links to "do the leader's wishes." If leadership equates to management, then this overlaps with the next. Coding cues for this study were references to establishing and achieving group goals.

The *Leadership as Management* theme (10.3% of the studies' citations) equates leadership with management process, power and authority, and the superior-subordinate relationship. Coding cues referred to management or management principles and structured processes within a leadership role.

The *Leadership as Influence* theme (9.5% of the studies' citations) recognizes influence as the ability to move and inspire a group through relationships, not power. Typically, studies in this theme shunned management connections while catering to a team's human side. Coding referenced motivation, influence, inspiration, encouragement, and positive persuasion.

Together these themes speak to the expectations that society has of leaders, what leadership entails, and the resulting culture of leadership. The strengths of Rost's themes are that they were derived from an interdisciplinary and comprehensive body of scholarship based on every book, chapter, or article from a decade of leadership scholarship. It is a unique resource that needs to be considered in any subsequent treatment of leadership definitions. Weaknesses derive from issues of meta analysis of a vast range of scholarship that included varying research designs and methodologies. Means to establish definitions varied tremendously in the cited studies. Although Rost's meta analysis did not consider or note the population or sampling within the studies cited in his leadership definition analysis, since most leadership scholarship has historically had a male focus given that the majority of leaders have been men, a gendered orientation could be speculated but is not stated nor implied by any of Rost's analysis. Although Rost provided information about his analysis methodology, his thematic framework would have been strengthened if he had provided the definitions and citations for the source studies and had presented and critiqued the studies in which the definitions were embedded for population and sampling parameters so that his thematic framework would support more rigorous methodology replication. While these weaknesses signal caution, they do not lesson the unique resource or encyclopedic nature of his analysis, or the conceptual usefulness of his framework. Thus, this current project began with, but was not limited by, this thematic framework; and went beyond it in an effort to understand how women academics perceived and articulated leadership.

THE CONTEXT OF THE CASE STUDY

Data were gathered from women admitted to the Hedwig van Ameringen ELAM Program for Women. This program is notable for its large and comprehensive database about the leadership development of its alumnae. This paper's authors participated in building this database and are involved in multiple analyses from it. This drove choice of this database for answering the research questions posed in this project.

The year-long program, based in the Institute of Women's Health and Leadership at Drexel University College of Medicine (www.drexelmed.edu/ELAM), was launched in 1995. The mission of the program is "aimed at expanding the national pool of qualified women candidates for leadership in academic medicine, dentistry, and public health"[2] (ELAM Web site, 2007, ¶ 1). ELAM graduates number more than 400 and serve in numerous leadership positions—department chair through university president—at more than 115 U.S. and Canadian schools of medicine and dentistry, including 5 of the 15 women deans at U.S. allopathic medical schools (n = 125), 5 of the 11 women deans at U.S. dental schools (n = 56), and 1 of the 5 women deans at U.S. osteopathic medical schools (n = 22) (R. Richman, ELAM, personal communication, November 20, 2006). Through a rigorous screening process, it identifies senior women faculty (associate and full professor rank) in its fields of focus who are rising in leadership responsibilities and who have been deemed, by the dean of each applicant's school, as having high potential for future leadership. Applications are scrutinized through a multilevel screening process, including a committee of deans and senior leaders of the fields of focus. The application requires a personal definition of leadership.

The 283 definitions available for analysis included those of nine cohorts—23 consent from class of 25 (class of 1996), 18/29 (1997), 28/32 (1998), 28/36 (1999), 31/38 (2000), 32/42 (2001), 35/44 (2002), 44/44 (2003), and 44/45 (2004). Definitions from classes of 2005 and 2006 were not available in this dataset. At the time of application, 50% were associate and 48% full professors. In the most recent report on women academics in medicine, 38% were assistant, 28% associate, and 16% full professors

2. Fellows from public health are not represented in this study as they began admission to ELAM after the dataset for this study was completed. Dental Fellows were a recent addition to the ELAM program, and constituted only 8% of the dataset; thus, workplace statistics are provided for academic medicine as a yardstick of comparison.

(Magrane & Lang, 2006). Although the ELAM dataset oversampled in the number of full professors in ratio to associate professors compared to the actual numbers in the workplace, it is from the senior faculty ranks, particularly professor rank, that academic leaders are chosen and thus these voices are particularly important and relevant to this inquiry. As would be expected of a group of academics, education level was high: 46% had M.D./D.D.S. degrees, 17% had M.D./D.D.S. plus other medical degrees, 16% had M.D./D.D.S. degrees plus other degrees such as J.D./M.B.A./MPH, 2% had terminal degrees other than M.D./Ph.D./D.D.S., 17% had Ph.D. degrees, and 1% had M.D.+Ph.D. degrees. Based on Fellows' highest administrative career title at application, categorized by a panel of experts in the academic medicine and dental fields, 57% had low, 15% medium, and 27% high levels of administrative experience. While the ELAM coding of administrative experience includes 28 title levels condensed into these three levels and thus comprehensively captures the range and nuances of administrative experiences, these levels are roughly analogous to the Magrane & Lang's (2006) tracking of women in 19% of division/section chiefs (low), 10% of department chairs (medium) and 42% of associate, senior associate/vice deans, and medical school deans (high). This oversampling of women as division/section chiefs, the first rung in the medical/dental school administrative ladder, is in keeping with ELAM's goal to develop women with leadership experience and aspirations and is valid given that this is a first step to leadership and thus relevant as these women grapple with the meaning of leadership in the academy. Lower Fellows' representation in the associate/senior /deans category acknowledges ELAM's service to aspiring women administrators, rather than women already in senior leadership posts. In sum, the ELAM dataset consists of senior women (associate and full professors, oversampled in comparison with the medical school women faculty population) who are ascending the administrative ladder and showing aspiration to leadership advancement validated by their deans through support of their application to ELAM.

Based on the strictures of the dataset, this project has delimitations. The study does not include definitions from women who applied but were not accepted into ELAM, who did not apply to ELAM but had comparable academic and leadership experiences, male academics in medicine/dentistry, or women academics in fields outside medicine or dentistry. With these delimitations, findings are most directly applicable to senior women academics in medicine and dentistry who have at least modest administrative experience and aspire to higher leadership contribution;

with cautious application to women academics in allied health fields, disciplines that involve science and technology, and in intensive research institutions; and to the larger population of women academics in higher education institutions.

METHODS

After definitions were saved as text files and imported into Atlas.ti, data coding proceeded through several steps. Initially, two researchers, using traditional qualitative analysis techniques (Coffey & Atkinson, 1996; Marshall & Rossman, 2006), intensively addressed the definitions to find references to Rost's (1991) themes, and definitional elements outside Rost's themes (emerging themes) (Straus, 1987). The two initial coders and the lead author discussed potential cues related to fit with Rost's themes to achieve a common coding strategy. The two coders processed an initial batch of 25 definitions, flagging elements not fitting in Rost's themes for return visits, and then discussed results with the lead author, including interpretations, nuances of language, and the varying meanings of terms. For example, one coder from Ukraine challenged and provoked deeper understanding of the terms "management" and "leadership" for the U.S. citizen project members, causing the researchers to return to scholarship on these concepts for deeper understanding of their differences and similarities, yielding a refined common understanding of the meaning of cues among the researchers. Based on agreement achieved in discussions, the two coders processed two more batches of definitions (initial agreement at 85% [second batch] and 95% [third batch]), checking coding at the end of each batch of approximately 25 and resolving differences of assignment through discussion until 100% agreement was achieved. The lead author reviewed the coding process and disagreements to understand issues and nuances. Elements outside Rost were discussed with a dozen emerging themes noted for new coding cues. The coders continued with batches of approximately 25 (fit to Rost, emerging themes outside Rost), with check-up and resolution of differences for each.

Coders refined their articulation of emerging themes, tested these through discussion with the lead author and reference to the definitions, and went back through the definitions for application and coder checking until 100% agreement was achieved in these areas and no new themes or coding disagreements were found. Through this iterative process (discussion, going back to the data to find examples to support discussed themes, and testing of language choices and meaning), many possibilities of themes boiled into four: *Activities* (references to the acts or tasks carried out by leaders), *Communication* (references to communication, listening, speaking and the like, describing how the leader interacts with the group in a receiving or giving capacity), *Strategy and Envisioning* (references to the efforts of creating goals, vision, and objectives, including how leaders generate these and implement a plan toward achievement of these), and *Followers* (references to followers, team members, and the like, describing what a leader does for and to others, relates to others).

We noted overlap and interrelationships of our emerging themes with Rost's (1991) themes. For instance, within the *Activities* theme we ultimately combined articulations of what a leader does and should do regarding leadership tasks, deciding that verb tense was an applicant's stylistic choice in presenting her leadership definition. We contemplated *Communications* as a subset of activities, but definitions articulating this concept used language that went beyond stipulating simply a type of activity to the means, quality, and values of communications; and finally, we decided that this was both an action and a philosophy of leader/follower relationship and merited its own theme. We also considered combining our emerging theme of *Activities* with Rost's theme of *Traits*, but concluded that separate headings allowed stronger contrast between action (*Activities*) and ability (*Traits*) that seemed important for so many of the Fellows in their definitions. We also contrasted *Activities* with Rost's *Leadership as Transformation* where the focus is on change and how it affects people, places, and products to improve, with *Activities* not necessarily presented in any relationship to change or transformation. We found that the definitions differentiated *Strategy and Envisioning* from Rost's *Organizational Goals* in that the emerging theme focused on what the leader does to envision and implement vision, while Rost's theme referred to accomplishment of goals already in place without any action by the leader to generate those goals. In Rost's sample definitions within *Organizational Goals*, the goals simply exist and the leader pursues implementation of them.

The codes and samples of definitional elements were then shared with two other authors and the discussion expanded and challenged for understanding of coding choices and issues regarding emerging themes. These two authors reviewed the set of definitions for application of the coding scheme, flagging areas of disagreement (approximately 100 disagreements per each out of nearly 1,000 coding incidents). These were discussed with the lead author until 100% coding agreement was achieved, with explanations of the emerging themes further refined. The presentation of the counts and narrative discussion were subsequently shared with the remaining authors who challenged and probed for nuances and provided context for interpretations within academic medicine and faculty environments. No coding changed, but interpretation of coding for emerging themes was tightened in presentation and explanation.

It took 990 coding incidents to capture the nuances of the Fellows' definitions. A coding incident means the individual code applied to a phrase or definitional element. Many definitions listed items that together constituted leadership in the thinking of the author, thus each concept received a separate coding, yielding multiple codes per definition. Percentages of thematic usage yielded information cross-group comparisons on the proportional emphasis articulated by the two groups (Rost's leadership scholarship, ELAM women). (See Table 1.)

THE LEADERSHIP DEFINITIONS OF ELAM FELLOWS WITHIN THE CONTEXT OF ROST'S THEMES

The definitions provide insight into the experiences and expectations of leadership held by ELAM Fellows. All six Rost themes were found in the dataset in varying concentrations. Thematic discussions are presented in the order of importance among ELAM Fellows. All quotations are from the Fellows' definitions.

Rost Theme: Leadership as Traits

This theme ranked first for ELAM participants among Rost's themes (appearing in 50.4% of ELAM definitions and 19.1% of the coding incidents across all definitional elements) but third among the scholars cited by Rost. Four subthemes emerged from the ELAM participant definitions that Rost had not identified in his discussion: independence, insight, intellect, and integrity. Fellows identified a key trait of leadership as independence, explained as the ability to not be "unduly influenced by current environmental or financial pressures." In other words, this subtheme refers to leading with a feeling of independence, a freedom from outside influences and constraints. Independence was also explained by a Fellow as "accepting the responsibility of being a 'pioneer,' changing some very entrenched habits, so those who come after me will not have to fight the same battles."

Table 1. ELAM fellows' leadership definitions analyzed by rost and emerging themes.

Comparison of Rost Themes and How The Leadership Definitions of ELAM Women Fit Within Rost Themes (Ranked in Order of Importance Within ELAM Definitions)	Rost Counts 126 citations found		ELAM Fellows Counts 283 definitions/990 coding incidents		
	Total # of counts	/126	Total # of counts	/283	/990
Leadership as Traits	20	15.9%	189	50.4%	19.1%
Leadership as Influence	12	9.5%	105	28.0%	10.6%
Leadership as Transformation	31	24.5%	46	12.3%	4.6%
Leadership as Management	13	10.3%	27	7.2%	2.7%
Leadership as Do the Leader's Wishes	33	26.2%	4	1.1%	.4%
Leadership as Achieving Organizational Goals	17	13.5%	4	1.1%	.4%
		100%*		100%*	

Emerging Themes from ELAM Women beyond Rost Themes	Total # counts	/283	/990
Leadership as Activities	205	72.4%	20.7%
Leadership With Relationship to Followers	165	58.3%	16.7%
Leadership as Envisioning and Strategy	156	55.1%	15.8%
Leadership as Communication	89	31.4%	9.0%
			100%

Note 1: Rost did not state numbers of definitions or definitional incidents for each theme. The baseline of 126 was established by counting citations listed in theme discussions.
Note 2: Column percentages do not add up to 100% because of rounding.
Note 3: For the two columns comparing number of citations and number of ELAM definitions within the confines of the Rost themes (marked with * in the summation row), do the scholars cited in Rost have different leadership definitions from the ELAM Fellows? Yes, the Pearson $\chi 2$ is 166.568 ($p < .05$); hence, the two groups have significant differences in their leadership definitions within the confines of the Rost themes.

Second, insight was another important trait for ELAM Fellows. This was characterized as the ability to see with a "keen eye." "A leader is an individual who can see the broad picture, [and] identify strengths and weaknesses in those with whom they are working." Insight involves "the courage to look both inward and outward. The inside foundation must be solid to give one the credibility to influence others. . . . As one looks outward, it is helpful to view situations and problems from many different perspectives." A third key trait was the concept of intellect, referencing "wisdom," "intellectual rigor," and "knowledgeable." Ultimately, "a leader must possess a high degree of professional expertise."

A final important trait was integrity. This can be viewed as a leader's will to be honest and forthright with employees, team members, and others. Integrity had to do with an individual's character and the decisions he or she makes based upon a value set, inside or outside of the work environment. One Fellow noted, "Personal integrity should be maintained at all times." Another stated, "A true leader...has the personal strength and integrity to make decisions and implement them." Professional integrity was directly linked with the organization and its employees. Plainly put by one participant, "Leaders must have integrity." ELAM Fellows emphasized key traits that went beyond Rost's theme regarding traits.

Rost Theme: Leadership as Influence

Rost (1991) provided only 12 citations for this theme, making it the least used in his framework. For the ELAM participants, this ranked as the second most mentioned theme (appearing in 28% of the definitions and 10.6% of the coding incidents among definitional elements). In the language of the ELAM Fellows, leadership is a noncoercive act that should "inspire others to do things they might not otherwise" do, translating into a positive result for all involved. A leader's influence should "inspire others toward constructive teamwork that drives toward efficiency and excellence" and should be "inspiring buy-in and participation of others in the project." Combining the essence of these many comments, one participant described influence as "encouraging people around us to perform to their best abilities to realize the big picture while maintaining their own goals." Another key sentiment was that a leader should influence without being the "star" in each plan. The ELAM women gave greater attention to a wider range of concepts relating to leadership influence than did the scholars.

Rost Theme: Leadership as Transformation

Scholars and ELAM participants emphasized different aspects of this theme. This was second in ranking in Rost's analysis; the ELAM Fellows ranked this third in importance among the Rost themes (mentioned in 12.3% of the definitions and 4.6% of the coding incidents across definitional elements). Fellows mentioned two subthemes of change and innovation. The word *change* and its variations appeared 27 times (for example, "make change," "effect change," "achieve change," and "implement change"). ELAM participants reported that a leader should identify "barriers to change, and solutions for obtaining buy-in from the faculty for change" and "opportunities for enhancing the effective implementation of change." Rost also found concepts of innovation to be a subtheme within transformation definitions. The ELAM participants expressed this as "significant innovation and forward movement" or "warding off unforeseen problems by using innovative approaches." Thus, while there was difference in the emphasis placed on transformation between the two groups, word use was similar.

Rost Theme: Leadership as Management

In fifth place in Rost's (1991) analysis of the definitions from scholars, this concept ranked fourth for ELAM participants among Rost's themes (7.2% of the ELAM definitions and 2.7% of the coding incidents across definitional elements) relating to language addressing directives handed down to groups. Comments highlighted a strong "management style" and "effective management skills." Key phrases included "direct a group of people efficiently and fairly," "not a micromanager nor one who hoards authority," and how decisions "must ultimately be made unilaterally" while avoiding "micromanagement." Thus, the scholars and the ELAM participants gave roughly the same low emphasis to this theme as part of leadership.

Rost Theme: Leadership as Do the Leader's Wishes

This theme comprised the largest count among the scholarly definitions that Rost (1991) analyzed, but only four ELAM definitions or definitional elements fit this theme (1.1 % of definitions/.4% of coding incidents across definitional elements). Rost's discussion focused on the hierarchical aspect of leaders telling people in an organization (for example, a business company, a military unit) what needed to be done as directed from the top of the pyramid. The images of this type of leadership could be captured as "take that hill" or "the company will move into a new product area." The four women's definitions spoke of leadership as directing and telling followers what needed to be done to accomplish a task or goal.

Rost Theme: Leadership as Achieving Organizational Goals

Ranked fourth in count among the definitions that Rost (1991) considered, only four ELAM participants (1.1% of definitions/.4% of coding incidents among definitional elements) offered references that fit Rost's explanation of this theme. The women and scholars articulated perceptions relating to goals with such different language and context that a new theme, *Strategy and Envisioning*, was created to capture the viewpoint of the women (further discussion follows). The lack of emphasis on this form of leadership among the ELAM participants signifies a lack of buy-in to this form of leadership and a commentary as to how rarely this form of leadership may exists in the faculty culture of higher education (Massy & Wilger, 1995)

In conclusion, the six themes outlined by Rost (1991) were represented in the Fellows' leadership definitions, to varying degrees, and thus suggests that the framework was useful as a beginning tool in investigating the Fellows' leadership definitions. *Leadership as Traits* was the theme most identifiable in the Fellows' definitions with *Leadership as do the Leader's Wishes* and *Leadership as Achieving Organizational Goals* least represented.

To further understand the fit of the ELAM leadership definitions to Rost's themes as articulated by the scholars of leadership, we calculated a chi-square analysis. In answer to the research question—Do the scholars cited and categorized by Rost have different leadership definitions from the ELAM Fellows?—the Pearson χ^2 was 166.568 ($p < .05$). In other words, the two groups have significant differences in their leadership definitions within the confines of the Rost themes, with less than 5% possibility of match. This suggests that Rost's thematic framework does not adequately capture the thinking of the ELAM Fellows. Explanations could be that Rost's themes may have been skewed by studies that did not sufficiently capture the higher education environment or the viewpoint of women, in particular, women academics.

GOING BEYOND ROST'S THEMES: EMERGING THEMES REGARDING LEADERSHIP ARTICULATION

While many of Rost's themes did have resonance with the ELAM Fellows, there were four other themes important to the Fellows that went beyond Rost's framework.

Emerging Theme: Leadership as Activities

Found in 72.4% definitions (20.7% of the coding incidents in definitional elements), this was the largest of the emergent themes. This theme captured how the women talked about the actions or tasks associated with leadership. Subthemes emerged: leading by example, making difficult decisions within a context of personal values, and collaborating and teambuilding.

Leading by Example

The most referenced activity was leading by example and role modeling, in which the leader guides a group by word and action. This was expressed as "the ability to show that the accomplishment of a task or goal [is] significant enough to be undertaken by the leader" and a leader should "be comfortable working shoulder to shoulder" with the team members. Fellows embraced this concept because it "encourages participation and involvement. This is not to say that the leader needs to be the prime 'doer' in the event, but rather have the investment in the goal to complete it." Similarly, leadership "includes a strong emphasis on modeling of desired behavior by demonstrating fairness." One Fellow summarized:

> I believe role modeling is an extremely important part of leadership. You cannot expect those persons whom you supervise to grow if you are not willing to follow the same rules, work the same schedule and present the image that you believe is important for your department or your college.

Inherent in this language was the notion that leading by example is contagious.

Making Difficult Decisions

Another subtheme was that a leader must make difficult decisions. While decision-making in the normal routine of work was assumed by the Fellows, the more important concept was how "a good leader is not afraid to make a difficult or unpopular decision." The power of decision-making comes with the role of being the leader. "Leadership requires that one be willing to make the hard decisions in which no one is a winner and to take responsibility for that decision." This subtheme also captured the issues of making decisions within crisis. A leader should be able to solve "crises quickly, effectively, and fairly." In addition, a leader should be "capable of dealing with conflict and prioritize which conflicts to address based on the needs of the organization." The leader "must not be afraid to make decisions, but makes them based on facts rather than impressions."

Another aspect was the values context of decision-making. Leaders make judgments based on personal integrity. A leader needs to "ruthlessly scrutinize her own motives and performance so she does not slip her moral moorings." Another Fellow noted, "A true leader leads by example and has the personal strength and integrity to make decisions and implement them." An environment conducive to progress and success "establishes a climate of respect, trust and satisfaction that will allow individuals to achieve their best." When making critical decisions, the leader must conduct an "honest self-evaluation about core values and principles." A values context for decisions was strongly felt.

Collaborating and Teambuilding

One more subtheme was centrality of collaborating and team building. "Good leaders need the savvy of compromise and the ability to bring opposing parties together. Good leaders need patience, but resolution," noted a Fellow. The ability to create a synergistic environment "convinces others to accept and assist in making changes that will frequently be unpleasant and disruptive," stated another Fellow. This included "building collaborative programs across departmental lines" and "encourage[ing] interdepartmental alliances." While Rost (1991) did not find the scholars' definitions to focus on the activities needed to accomplish leadership, this was the most cited definitional element for the women.

Emerging Theme: Leadership as a Relationship with Followers

Evident in 58.3% of the definitions (20.7% of the coding incidents across definitional elements), this was the second most important emergent theme. Although the definitions analyzed by Rost (1991) may have implied that followers exist, the women explicitly named followers, making them central to leadership action. The women believed a relationship must exist between leader and followers so that followers will benefit and be better off at the end than they were at the beginning of the experience. This happens through "inspiring them [followers] to reach their highest potential." The leader/follower relationship must be synergistic.

> The leader should work with key individuals to assist the team in feeling that their work is worthwhile and important to the overall mission. The leader should remember that successes of individuals do not detract from his or her importance but rather are a reflection of the success of the leader.

Followers, and their importance to leadership, appeared in many ways in the women's definitions. Leaders should "enlist the assistance of others in implementing the goals" and "empower team members with responsibility and authority." Recognizing "an individual's strengths and weaknesses and mentoring to allow them to reach their full potential is a necessary skill for a successful leader." One woman summarized that leadership "will always involve working closely with other people, seeking consensus and working toward an outcome that meets or exceeds the needs of the people and institutions involved." For ELAM women, followers are so important that they must be specified in the leadership definition.

Emerging Theme: Leadership as Envisioning and Strategy

Fourth in importance to ELAM Fellows across all themes (appearing in 55.1% of all definitions, or 15.8% of coding incidents across definitional elements) was the concept of leadership as envisioning a future and strategizing to accomplish it. Although allied with Rost's (1991) theme of *Achieving Organizational Goals*, the women's language was sufficiently different to merit a distinct theme. This theme has to do with having the "vision to look to the future and confront it energetically" and "breaking down the vision into components which can be defined as a series of short- and long-term goals and projects." The references in this theme break into usage as nouns and verbs.

As nouns, "envisioning" and "strategy" relate to vision, goals, and plans as in "well defined goals," "mission and direction," and "vision and strategy." Leaders first "provide a vision for the future," then establish goals within that vision, and finally possess the "power to achieve a goal or carry out an agenda." Similarly, leaders "develop concrete achievable goals that are well-matched to visions, to accurately estimate and garner necessary resources to achieve goals, and to assure responsible and creative resource use." Leaders must "articulate a vision for their program/division/school/institute," noted one Fellow, while another stated, "a leader must have a clear vision of where the institution must move over time and a realistic idea of what it will take to achieve the goal." A Fellow summarized: "Sensing a dynamic vision for the institution is an important part of being an effective leader, and facilitates the 'graceful shedding' of selected previous roles and commitments in order to focus on achieving concrete aspects of the vision."

As verbs, envisioning and strategy related to the process of working toward a vision developed collaboratively with team members. One Fellow explained the process "to assist a heterogeneous group of individuals to find shared goals and then plan the route that will allow them to reach those goals." Another noted that a leader should "act as a focus for the group, establishing goals, promoting shared values, and facilitating goal-related activities for the group." Strategy and envisioning can be viewed as "defining a collective vision of the future and relating that vision to the mission of the institution." One participant termed this collaborative process as "enlightened leadership." Leaders were typically described as capable of getting members of their organization "to accept the vision of the organization and to be motivated to do what it takes to achieve those goals." Overall the leader should "create a clear vision and set of goals, make sure that everyone understands what those goals are, and invite all concerned to work together toward those goals." While these notions of envisioning and strategy in both their noun and verb versions overlap with Rost's (1991) theme of *Achieving Organizational Goals*, the contextual language required a new theme to capture the concepts expressed by the women.

Emerging Theme: Leadership as Communication

The fourth emerging theme was *Leadership as Communication* (appearing in 31.4% of all definitions and 9.0% of coding incidents across definitional elements). References encompassed listening as well as speaking, as a leader should be a "good listener as well as a good communicator." As a strategy it had to do with "listening to a wide range of views and ideas is essential, as well as incorporating others' ideas in developing these goals." As a process, a leader must "listen very carefully and thoroughly to all sides of an issue and to become educated about the issue" before making decisions. As a style, a leader must show "willingness to listen," because the message being conveyed is as important as the desire to convey a point to the team. Listening was also expressed as having to do with culture and environment: "It is critical to be open and listen to the ideas of others on how to improve the organization. There is a need to balance a culture that supports the open exchange of ideas."

Speaking comprised the other end of the communications spectrum. Leaders must be "as clear and precise as possible" to "translate the vision and mission into a strategic plan" for the group to understand. Hence a leader should "be a clear communicator on both conceptual and emotional levels." Leaders often represent the group or organization and must be able to "articulate the needs of one's constituency, and to create an atmosphere of shared mission and purpose." Ultimately, a strong communicator should be "leading by a combination of empathy, listening, feedback, and resource allocation" based on the needs of the organization.

While communication could be a subtheme under *Leadership as Activities*, we chose to keep it as a separate theme. First, so many Fellows used language about communications that we did not want this concept lost in the already large theme of activities. Second, the women used communication not just as an activity, but in a much richer array of language encapsulating strategy, process, and style. Finally, Fellows asserted that leadership cannot be successful unless its essence is communicated with followers in a bilateral process of listening and speaking.

A PROPOSED NEW FRAMEWORK FOR CONSIDERING LEADERSHIP DEFINITIONS FOR WOMEN ACADEMICS

A new framework can be created from the data assembled from the ELAM women. They eschew a leader who merely *dictates her wishes* upon an organization. Nor do they equate leadership with *management* or as simply *implementing goals* within an organization. For them, leadership has an equal emphasis on who a leader is (*traits*) and what a leader does (*activities*). A leader must have the intellect to analyze situations, the insight to understand conditions, and the independence to make difficult decisions. A leader must have integrity derived from a personal set of values. These women see leadership as a collaborative involvement with *followers* in a process of *envisioning* an organization's future, and cocreating goals that will *change* an organization as it accomplishes that future. To be successful in this definition a leader must *communicate* (listening and speaking) with followers and constituencies to ensure progress by all elements of the organization. See Table 2 for a presentation of this proposed framework.

APPLICATIONS

The proposed thematic framework has application on several levels. Although it could be possible to argue about relationships of the ELAM sample to various population groups addressed in this discussion, the emphasis in this discussion is not on strict sample to population transferability bur rather on consideration of conceptual transferability and questions raised by the research that relate to each application constituency (Marshall & Rossman, 2006). The following discussion lists these from most to least direct connections.

Table 2. A proposed new framework for considering leadership definitions for women academics.

Themes	Subthemes
Leadership as Activities	Leading by example, making difficult decisions, collaborating and teambuilding
Leadership With Relationship to Followers	
Leadership as Envisioning and Strategy	Vision, goals, and plans; the process of working toward a vision developed collaboratively with team members
Leadership as Traits	Independence, insight, intellect, and integrity
Leadership as Communication	Listening, speaking
Leadership as Influence	
Leadership as Transformation	Change and innovation

To ELAM Fellows and Similar Senior Women Academics in Academic Medicine/Dentistry

The most direct application of the proposed leadership definition thematic framework is to the past, current, and future ELAM Fellows if the mission of ELAM and criteria of applicant screening remain the same. This framework provides a context for the ELAM program to understand its participants. Other leadership programs could collect similar data and perform analogous analysis. Furthermore, the framework provides a window for understanding equivalent senior women faculty in academic medicine and dentistry who have had a base of leadership experience and who aspire to senior posts in dimensions and scope similar to those of the ELAM Fellows. The framework could be useful for deans and others who seek an understanding of aspiring women academic leaders in these fields, for these women to appreciate themselves and each other in their conceptualization of leadership, and for analyzing the fit of their aspirations and the environments in which they pursue these aspirations. Examined in another way, the academic ranks and administration of these fields are dominated by men (only 32% of faculty, 10% of department chairs, and 11% of deans are women in medical schools (Magrane & Lang, 2006). The proposed thematic framework may help to understand the academic environment within these fields and the viewpoint of women who work in these. This proposed framework provides a unique window into how women academics define leadership in these fields. Conversely, while the framework is derived from women's voices, it is possible to speculate that to achieve success in these fields, women have absorbed the male orientation around them, and thus the framework may say more about the gendered environments rather than unique women's viewpoint. Further study will be needed to probe these possibilities.

To Women Academics in Scientific and Professional Fields and in Research Universities

Medical and dental schools are science-based, research-oriented fields; and thus there could be immediate application of this proposed thematic framework to women who work in related fields of science, technology, engineering, and mathematics as well as to professional fields such as business and law. These fields similarly tend to be based on defined scientific principles and paradigms, prize quantitative research, fund most research through large-scale grants, are highly competitive, function mostly at the graduate level educating adult students who find jobs in the professional rather than academic realms, and are predominantly found (especially at their highest level of research generation) in research-oriented institutions. These fields, and research institutions in general, are male-dominated. Data from the National Center for Education Statistics show that women "rarely make up more than 30% of faculty at research extensive universities" (Marschke, Laursen, Nielsen, & Rankin, 2007, p. 1). The proposed framework may help to understand the academic environment within these fields, and the viewpoint of women who work in these types of male-gendered academic environments. Faculty at non-research universities or at research universities in non-science areas may experience different cultures that have impact on understanding of and articulation of leadership. Given the recent focus on needs to increase numbers and visibility of women in these fields, this framework could provide useful insight. Further probing is needed for clarification.

To Women Faculty in General

While the project happened to have data from women medical and dental school academics, it is more broadly an investigation into the leadership definitions of women faculty. Little knowledge or analysis of individual definitions of leadership exist within higher education, by faculty, from women, or from women who are rising in leadership responsibility. This study applies to this research gap and provides a strategy for understanding women faculty in general.

There are different stands as to the effect of disciplinary differences among faculty relevant to whether the proposed framework would be relevant to women faculty as a group given their disciplinary roots. Although Favero (2006) found that effects of disciplines cannot be discounted in framing studies of administrators' perceptions of their leadership context and the behavior which necessarily flows from those perceptions" (p. 281), Yakhontova (2006) found a common rhetoric across disciplines that contributes to the possibility of interdisciplinary cooperation. Being female may have greater resonance than academic discipline and rhetoric similarities or differences, institutional type, or other considerations. Thus, the proposed thematic framework may be a window to understanding how women experience and hope that the leadership environment in higher education will function. Again, more research is needed.

To Faculty and the General Culture of Leadership in Higher Education

This proposed framework may be a tentative step to understanding a faculty-oriented view of leadership in the academy. Most leadership studies in higher education look from the perspective of administrators, particularly those in senior and departmental ranks, to the rest of the organization. Faculty life was the common experience denominator among the ELAM Fellows at the time of their application to the program, with 57% having low administrative experience, thus possibly reflecting a more faculty-oriented view of leadership within higher education as they experienced and contribute to it within the smaller units in which they worked, where unit goals may be more tangible and leadership more shared, distributed, or rotated among members (Gmelch & Schuh, 2004). Thus, these findings may speak more of a faculty-centric view of leadership, but more investigation is needed.

Academics tend to live and work within their departments and schools, and relate to the larger organization through these smaller, loosely coupled units (Gilmore, 1994). Thus it may not be surprising that the ELAM women's definitions gave minimal attention to hierarchical, top-down aspects of leadership (such as Rost's [1991] themes of *Doing the Leader's Wishes* or *Achieving Organizational Goal,* which showed up in only 1.1% of the definitions and only .4% of the total coding). The proposed thematic framework may speak to the faculty experience within their smaller work units, and as such represent a less-expounded view on academic leadership than the larger organizational view that is more typically articulated.

The Fellows' definitions also contribute to understanding how leadership is conceptualized and (preferably) practiced within higher education. The definitions painted a picture in which goals and agendas are not driven by a CEO at the top of a hierarchical pyramid (Rost's *Do as the Leader Wishes*). Nor is it about *Management* (Rost), which is often ridiculed as a concept within the academy. Perhaps by shunning management language in their definitions, the ELAM women were echoing this low appreciation for management and hierarchy that is pervasive among faculty (Powers & Maghroori, 2006).

The collective definitions of this study paint a portrait of the culture of leadership within higher education. As a condition of admission to ELAM, all Fellows have served as leaders at one time or another, as heads of important committees, division chairs, and institute directors and thus seemed to ascribe vocally to a leadership culture where people are simultaneously leaders and followers (Spillane, 2006). Thus there is greater need for attention to *Followers* (emerging theme) and greater recognition of the importance of collaborating with followers in the accomplishment of any task. In this sense, the leadership culture within higher education places greater emphasis on the personal aspects of leadership (*Traits* [Rost], *Activities, Strategy and Envisioning, and Communication* [emerging themes]) than seem to be found in Rost's (1991) framework because in higher education, followers often interact and trade places with leaders. This line of investigation has relevance to Amey's (2006) metaphors of leadership and Eddy's (2003) sensemaking in higher education in that leadership definitions often use metaphors to capture abstract leadership concepts and definitions serve as the lens through which leaders make sense of and relate to the environments in which they work. All of this points to a general need for more information about how faculty define leadership, with the proposed thematic framework providing a useful initial probe for research on this topic with faculty.

To Rost's Framework in Specific and Leadership Scholarship in General

The study challenges Rost's (1991) framework. The proposed thematic framework contributes to the scholarship in leadership by considering leadership definitions from new perspectives not available to Rost for his analysis. The study also extends a methodology for examining leadership definitions. Further study is needed to investigate these potential applications and to determine consensus for definitions and cultural description.

As extensive as Rost's (1991) analysis of leadership definitions was, his themes were not sufficient to capture the full range of nuances within the definitions from the ELAM Fellows. Several reasons may contribute to explaining this lack of fit. First, leaders, leadership, and leadership scholarship may be sufficiently different between the 1980s and today to challenge Rost's framework. Second, the bulk of leadership research is situated within business, with higher education leadership scholarship a small percentage of the total leadership field. Definitional disparity may speak about higher education vs. business culture. This may launch inquiry as to whether leadership has field-specific, cultural orientations. These women were articulating leadership definitions that they had experienced and come to expect because of the culture in which they worked, thus providing credence for why their definitions did not fit with Rost's themes, which could be derived from other realms. This may contribute to an argument that effective leadership is not defined the same in all environments. Contrarily, these women work in medical/dental education, a subset of higher education. Medical/dental education has experienced profound change over the past decade resulting in a business-like university unit (Souba & Day, 2006; Souba, Mauger, & Day, 2007). This line of analysis would suggest that the definitions might have resulted in a better fit to Rost's (1991) definitions devised from a predominantly business-oriented literature. Definitions did not fit, thus challenging Rost.

Third, only recently have major leadership studies included women in sufficient numbers to merit gender comparison. Rost (1991) devised his themes from literature published in the 1980s. Since he did not specify the samples of the studies from which his definitional analysis was derived, it would be reasonable to speculate that few of the studies included women to any significant degree. Perhaps the lack of fit of Rost's themes had to do with gender differences. Gilligan (1982) found that women and men think, speak, and rationalize in different voices. Her findings may apply to perceptions of leadership, too. In the tradition of Belenky, Clinchy, Goldberger, and Tarule (1986), the ELAM women considered followers, traits, how goals are envisioned and strategized in the context of a group, and the importance of communications. Perhaps the lack of fit for Rost's definitions speaks to gender disparities in experiencing, perceiving, articulating, and valuing facets of leadership. If women indeed define leadership differently than do men, then the barriers experienced by women in their attempts to rise to senior posts may, in part, be due to a lack of congruence between their leadership definitions and the prevailing male model of leadership embedded in the culture. As Bass (1990) stated, "earlier research may need to be discounted" as more women achieve leadership posts and are included in research, making it necessary to "continue to give careful consideration to the underlying dynamics and dimensions of importance to success and effectiveness of women leaders" (p. 737). While Rost's framework was found wanting for fit in the statistical analysis, it did have resonance in the narrative analysis. Thus, Rost did serve as a useful initial lens for exploring the leadership definitions of the ELAM Fellows, even though eventually his framework needed to be extended to capture fully the perspectives of the women in the study.

Fourth, Rost's (1991) themes reflect the fact that most leadership studies look only at people who are in top leadership jobs. ELAM Fellows are selected based on already exhibited leadership within their organizations but they are not yet in senior posts. Perhaps the disparity arises from the differences between leaders who work in the middle, not the tops, of organizations. Then, the definitions, and the Rost mismatch, may speak more about how leadership is experienced and perceived by positioning within organizations, in general, and the complexity of universities and the academic fields represented therein. This study may contribute to our understanding of higher education mid-tier leaders such as department chairs, deans, and aspiring deans and academic field differences—and call for more research in these areas.

While Rost's framework did not fit with the definitions of the women in this study, most of his themes had saliency. While it is possible to speculate in many ways regarding the Rost framework, the usefulness of the newly proposed framework, and the relevance of both to leadership scholarship, none of these speculations can be resolved without further research.

CONCLUSION

The women's leadership definitions in this project speak about the culture in which they have matured and worked as well as about their individual leadership. For the most part, the Fellows launched their careers in the 1980s as medical students and new faculty members. The first leadership books they read may have been the very publications counted and analyzed by Rost. Thus, the ELAM Fellows may have been influenced by the definitions that Rost analyzed, which have become part of the current cultural understanding and societal language about leadership, arguing for the Rost framework as a launching pad for this investigation. That Fellows went beyond these understandings and language to more nuanced articulations of leadership sufficient to propose a new thematic framework for understanding leadership definitions may provide insight into the currently acceptable culture of leadership within academic medicine and dentistry, faculty, and the higher education context from the perspective of women. As McDade and Lewis (1994) noted, leadership is a cultural phenomena shaped by a culture's members while socializing members' expectations and actions in a continuously reinforcing cycle.

Admittedly, these are self-reported and possibly self-serving explanations of leadership in the pursuit of acceptance into the ELAM program. Yet, the large number of definitions provides a foundation for understanding the collective leadership culture of higher education institutions, and the socialization in these cultures that fosters and shapes the people who rise from within to become deans (McDade & Lewis, 1994). The number of definitions outbalances the self-reported nature in that they become an aggregate commentary on the community, not just an insight into individuals since the definitions reflect the culture of leadership of the community.

DIRECTIONS FOR FUTURE RESEARCH

General areas for research were identified in the above discussion about study applications. Broader research is needed with leadership definitions of other groups in higher education and to women in other contexts. Such research needs to test the proposed thematic framework for leadership definitions for applicability across gender, fields, and experience.

In specific, the ELAM database on Fellows' leadership development allows future investigation relevant to the issues raised in this study. First, insights into how these women view and experience leadership through lenses of leadership theories (such as Bolman & Deal, 2003; Sashkin & Sashkin, 2003) are possible. Second, subsamples of the women have been interviewed at 1.5-, 3-, 5-, and 8-year intervals after ELAM participation, again asked to provide leadership definitions, allowing examination of the evolution of these leadership definitions over time. Third, the ELAM database includes details about Fellows' career progress, enabling cross-analysis of leadership conceptualization at various responsibility levels. Fourth, the database includes coding for the women on topics ranging from academic rank, administrative experience, academic discipline, and Myers-Briggs score. Another line of investigation will be to parse the definitions by these and many other factors that interact with the leadership definitions.

SUMMARY

The goal of this paper was not to produce an all-encompassing definition of leadership, but rather to understand nuances and application in a generalized way for faculty in higher education and particularly for women faculty and then women academics in academic medicine and dentistry. The proposed thematic framework for leadership definitions provides a useful window for seeing leadership in higher education. To answer the research questions, the leadership definitions of women faculty who have signaled their interest in taking on advanced leadership responsibility and administrative advancement tell us a great deal about the culture of leadership in higher education with less to more application to many constituencies. The leadership definition analysis tells us that the broader scholarship on leadership culture generally written may not adequately capture the higher education experience or women, and Rost's leadership definition framework is not a good fit for these. This effort addresses Rost's (1991) lament that the field is permissive and relative in understanding and offering definitions of leadership. It opens avenues for analyzing leadership definitions using other models.

REFERENCES

Amey, M. J. (2006, Nov/Dec). Leadership in higher education. *Change, 38*(6), 5--58.

Bass, B. M. (1990). *Bass & Stogdill's handbook of leadership*. New York: The Free Press.

Belenky, M. F., Clinchy, B. M., Goldberger, N. R., & Tarule, J. M. (1986). *Women's ways of knowing: The development of self, voice, and mind*. New York: Basic Books.

Bennis, W., & Nanus, B. (1985). *Leaders: The strategies for taking charge*. New York: Harper & Row.

Bensimon, E. M., Neumann, A., & Birnbaum, R. (1989, October). *Making sense of administrative leadership: The "L" word in higher education*. ASHE ERIC Higher Education Reports. San Francisco: Jossey-Bass.

Bolman, L., & Deal, T. (2003). *Reframing organizations: Artistry, choice, and leadership*. (3rd ed.). San Francisco: Jossey-Bass.

Burns, J. M. (1978). *Leadership*. New York: Harper and Row Publishers.

Clark, K. E., & Clark, M. B. (Eds.). (1990). *Measures of leadership*. A Center for Creative Leadership Book. West Orange, NJ: Leadership Library of America.

Coffey, A., & Atkinson, P. (1996). *Making sense of qualitative data: Complementary research* strategies. Thousand Oaks, CA: Sage Publications.

Conger, J. A. (1989). *The charismatic leader*. San Francisco: Jossey-Bass.

Eddy, P. L. (2003). Sensemaking on campus: How community college presidents frame change. *Community College Journal of Research and Practice, 27,* 453–471.

ELAM (2007). The ELAM program. Retrieved August 25, 2007, from http://www.drexelmed.edu/elam/AboutELAM/home.html

Favero, M. (2006, May). An examination of the relationship between academic discipline and cognitive complexity in academic deans' administrative behavior. *Research in Higher Education, 47*(3), 281–315.

Gilligan, C. (1982). *In a different voice: Psychological theory and women's development.* Cambridge, MA: Harvard University Press.

Gilmore, T. N. (1994). *Managing loosely coupled systems.* Philadelphia: Center for Applied Research.

Gmelch, W. H., & Schuh, J. H. (Eds.). (2004). The life cycle of a department chair. *New Directions for Higher Education*, No. 126. San Francisco: Jossey-Bass.

Hughes, R. L., Ginnett, R. C., & Curphy, G. J. (2002). *Leadership: Enhancing the lessons of experience* (4th ed.) Homewood, IL: Irwin.

Kellerman, B. (Ed.). (1986). *Leadership: Multidisciplinary perspectives.* Englewood Cliffs, NJ: Prentice-Hall.

Klein, E. B., Gabelnick, F., & Herr, P. (Eds.). *The psychodynamics of leadership*. Madison, CT: Psychosocial Press.

Magrane, D., & Lang, J. (2006, October). An overview of women in U.S. academic medicine, 2005–2006. *AAMC Analysis in Brief, 6*(7). Retrieved August 25, 2007, from http://www.aamc.org/data/aib/aibissues/aibvol6_no7.pdf

Marschke, R., Laursen, S., Nielsen, J. M., & Rankin, P. (2007, Jan/Feb). Demographic inertia revisited: An immodest proposal to achieve equitable gender representation among faculty in higher education. *Journal of Higher Education, 78*(1), 1–26.

Marshall, C., & Rossman, G. B. (2006). *Designing qualitative research* (4th ed.). Thousand Oaks, CA: Sage Publications.

Massy, W. F., & Wilger, A. K. (1995, July/August). Improving productivity. *Change, 27*(4), 10–21.

McDade, S. A., & Lewis, P. H. (Eds.). (1994). Developing administrative excellence: Creating a culture of leadership. *New Directions for Higher Education*. San Francisco: Jossey-Bass.

Peters, T. J., & Waterman, R. H. (1982). *In search of excellence*. New York: Harper & Row.

Powers, C., & Maghroori, R. (2006, June 6). The accidental administrator. *The Chronicle of Higher Education 52*(40), C2-C3.

Rost, J. C. (1991). *Leadership for the 21st century*. New York: Praeger.

Sashkin, M., & Sashkin, M. G. (2003). *Leadership that matters: The critical factors for making a difference in people's lives and organizations' success.* San Francisco: Berrett-Koehler Publishers.

Souba, W. W., & Day, D. V. (2006, January). Leadership values in academic medicine. *Academic Medicine, 81*(1), 20–26.

Souba, W. W., Mauger, D., & Day, D. V. (2007, March). Does agreement on institutional values and leadership issues between deans and surgery chairs predict their institution's performance? *Academic Medicine, 82*(3), 272–280.

Spillane, P. (2006). *Distributed leadership*. San Francisco: Jossey-Bass.

Yakhontova, T. (2006, April). Cultural and disciplinary variation in academic discourse: The issue of influencing factors. *Journal of English for Academic Purposes, 5*(2), 153–167.

Welfare Women Go Elite: The Ada Comstock Scholars Program

Auden D. Thomas
Director, Center for Survey Research
The Pennsylvania State University – Harrisburg

This article traces the development of Smith College's program for returning women from 1968 through 1985. Guided by Smith's feminist president, Jill Conway, the elite women's college offered full financial aid packages to support women welfare recipients and their dependent children through a complete undergraduate education. The program garnered national attention as a model for expanding college access to one of the nation's least-well served populations. Three key aspects of the program's development are considered: Conway's top-down support of continuing education, which was crucial to the program's success; the mechanisms by which the College was able to circumvent restrictive welfare policies and implement a novel approach to educating the poor; and the broader aims of the Ada Comstock Scholars Program as a national model for both informing public policy and expanding college access. The work draws on archival sources, an interview with Conway, and secondary literature.

INTRODUCTION

The relationship between women, welfare, and higher education is salient today in light of both contemporary public policy, which favors work over education for the poor, and the ongoing access critique of American higher education. Welfare reform laws passed in 1996 aimed to reduce taxpayer burden by moving welfare recipients into the workforce. However, such policies have effectively channeled the poor into low-skill, low-paying jobs and reduced the likelihood that they would pursue postsecondary education or attain a college degree. The few low-income individuals who do elect to attend college are increasingly directed toward the most ineffective, short-term forms of training rather than higher-quality college-level education (Adair, 2001; Shaw et al., 2006).

As the majority of welfare recipients are single mothers, so called "welfare-to-work" or "work-first" laws have had a disproportionately negative impact on poor women and their children (Morgan, 2002). The numbers are staggering: in 2005, over 7.5 million, or 10%, of children under age 18 in the United States lived in a household headed by a single woman on welfare (U.S. Census Bureau, 2005). For these women, a college degree "can unlock the door to economic opportunity and thus enable disadvantaged women to live lives of dignity, supporting and nurturing their children" (Adair, 2001, p. 223).

Arguments for expanding access to U.S. colleges and universities have a long history. College access has been linked to such notions as fulfilling America's democratic potential, providing a foundation for civic participation, fostering human capital, and securing individuals' economic well-being. At the institutional level, rationales for broadening equity include attracting the most promising students, diversifying the student body, and affirming inclusiveness as a core value. Yet, despite a rhetoric of equity as well as many well-intended efforts, barriers to access continue to exist. Individuals of low socioeconomic status are at highest risk of being disadvantaged by lack of access to higher education (Bowen, Kurzweil, & Tobin, 2005).

Focused on the years 1968 through 1985, this article traces the development of Smith College's returning women's program and its experiment to educate women on welfare. Guided by Smith's feminist president, Jill Conway, the elite women's college added an innovative twist to the standard accommodations made for the nation's growing population of older and returning women students. In addition to offering rolling admission and part-time schedules, as numerous other institutions did, Smith offered full financial aid packages to support women welfare recipients and their dependent children through a complete undergraduate education. The program garnered national attention as a model for expanding college access to one of the nation's least well-served populations.

This article considers three key aspects of the program's development. First, it illuminates the personal and professional motivations that impelled President Conway to become a vigorous champion of higher education for poor and older women. Her support was crucial to the program's success. Second, the article elucidates the mechanisms by which the College was able to implement such a novel approach to educating the poor. These processes included raising foundation funds for scholarships, cleverly maneuvering around restrictive state and federal welfare regulations to avoid having scholarship students' public assistance benefits reduced, and ensuring the program's future through creating an endowment. Finally, the piece considers the broader aims of the Ada Comstock Scholars Program as a national model for informing public policy and an exemplar for expanding college access. By providing a sound example of how collegiate education could transform poverty-destined, welfare-roll women into productive members of society, the Comstock Program offered the public sector a proven money-saving strategy and created an opportunity for faculty and administrators at Smith College to contribute to the national debate about welfare as a no-exit phenomenon. This work draws on archival sources, secondary literature, and the author's 2002 interview of Jill Conway.

RETURNING WOMEN AT SMITH COLLEGE, 1968–75

Smith College initiated its program for returning women on a trial basis and without a formal title in 1968. Sometimes referred to as the Mature Women's Program, the impetus for starting a continuing education program at Smith had come from the College's own alumnae. Inspired by labor market shortages, the growth of the service professions, and the feminist movement, significant numbers of these women returned to the College in the late 1960s and early 1970s to complete degrees left unfinished when they married and had children (Chamberlain, 1988). The program as originally conceived, however, was not particularly groundbreaking for its time. Designed to enable women over age 24 to begin or continue their college educations, Smith's program for returning women was one of 375 such programs nationwide and an expression of an idea whose time had come to campuses—both coeducational and single-sex—across the country (Campbell, 1973; Chamberlain, 1988). Across the nation, programs for returning women varied from campus to campus but tended to offer special counseling programs, advocate for flexible policies and individualized programs, and provide targeted career development and placement services (Campbell, 1973).

Smith's surge in returning women's enrollment mirrored that of colleges across the United States as women and nontraditional students flocked to college campuses in increasing numbers. Nationally, the number of college-going women age 35 or older jumped from 418,000 in 1972 to 700,000 in 1976—an increase of over 67% in just 4 years. Correspondingly, the enrollment of people under age 25 dropped from 72 to 67% of the total college population (National Center for Education Statistics, 1979). In 1977 alone, women accounted for 93% of the nation's enrollment growth, with the greatest increases among women age 25 and older (Gappa & Uehling, 1979).

College administrators at Smith jumped on the bandwagon to recruit this new population. The move made good financial sense in light of these new demographics and predictions that the number of traditional college age students would continue to shrink considerably during the decade of the 1980s. In addition, Smith faced increased competition for female students from an elite cadre of formerly male colleges that were recent converts to coeducation. By 1975, Yale, Princeton, Dartmouth, Williams, Bowdoin, and Wesleyan annually accepted about 1,400 women who might have applied to Smith, had those colleges not opened their doors to women (Blake, 1975). Perhaps for these reasons, support from faculty and administrators for educating returning women was easy to garner. Those at the College were understandably nervous after watching many women's colleges across the country become coeducational or close altogether. Though Smith was unlikely to do succumb to those fates, in an era of waning demand for single-sex education, educating older women meant the College could ensure the quantity of its applicant pool without sacrificing quality.

In 1970, fewer than half of U.S. institutions made any adjustments to meet the needs of older students. Even fewer institutions had special programs for returning women (Campbell, 1973). Not surprising given their missions, women's colleges were ahead of the curve in courting and accommodating this new population (Duffy & Goldberg, 1998). They realized early on the demands of women's varying roles as wives, mothers, and paid workers and the necessity for women to interrupt their educations as part of their gendered life pattern. Smith College had a history of leadership in women's education, and its nascent continuing education program was envisioned by its planners as a contemporary expression of College founder Sophia Smith's charge to "develop as fully as may be the powers of womanhood, and furnish women with the means of usefulness, happiness and honor, now withheld from them" (Quesnell, 1999, p. 222).

After its 7-year trial period from 1968 to 1975, the limited project to educate older women at Smith was deemed a success. It had admitted 62 women to the College and boasted a higher retention rate than that of the Smith undergraduate body as a whole. Some of its graduates achieved honors, magna cum laude, and Phi Beta Kappa distinctions. In 1974, the College faculty gave formal approval for the project's expansion, definition, and launching as a specific, named program (Smith College Archives). Three groups of students were targeted for inclusion: those whose education had been interrupted (including those returning to college and those who had not previously entered); those who wished to ease the transition to graduate study at Smith or elsewhere; and college graduates who desired further course work. The program was officially named in honor of the late Ada Comstock Notestein, an 1897 Smith graduate who served the College for 11 years as dean and professor of English before becoming dean, and later president, of Radcliffe College. Her life had been devoted to widening women's educational horizons (Skarda, 2000).

A TOP-DOWN COMMITMENT TO CONTINUING EDUCATION

In 1975, Smith College celebrated its 100-year anniversary, and Jill Ker Conway became the College's first woman president. Conway was no stranger to either the impulse for educating older women or the mechanics of implementing a program to do so. She was an historian of women's experiences and an experienced university administrator with a feminist bent. Like many of her counterparts around the United States, accommodating women's particular life-cycle issues figured prominently in her vision of creating educational opportunity for all women. As Smith College entered its second century, Conway embraced the education of older women as "one of the first steps toward redefining the mission of the college as a women's institution" (Smith College Archives). She was compelled to action not only by her scholarly understanding of the importance of college education for women of all ages, but by a strong personal commitment as well.

One of Jill Conway's deepest motivations for championing the Ada Comstock Scholars Program was her own family situation, which brought the issue of older women's education very close to home. Conway reported witnessing her mother's unfortunate transformation in the years following the death of Jill's father. According to Conway, in widowhood Mrs. Ker lost the competent pragmatism and purpose that had once defined her life and sank gradually into a state of manipulative dependency exacerbated by alcoholism and prescription drug abuse. Before Jill moved from her native Australia to the United States, Mrs. Ker had counted on her daughter's nearly constant companionship and assistance. It was years later that Jill Conway realized,

> I was living with a tragic deterioration brought about because there was now no creative expression for this woman's talents. . . . Society encouraged a woman to think her life finished after her husband's death and encouraged a woman's emotional dependence on her children. (Conway, 1989, p. 195)

Conway blamed sexist Australian cultural norms for her mother's downfall and the subsequent decline of their family relations. When she wondered about the possibilities and the promise of educating older women at Smith, Conway's most compelling thought was of her "superintelligent mother" who had been denied more than a grade-school education. "I'd had to leave her to escape her rage and frustration at life, and her anger at me for having the opportunities she'd paid so dearly for missing," Conway reflected. "But she was the reason I'd never stopped trying to expand women's opportunities, and why I wanted to make schools and colleges treat older women with genuine respect for their intellect and curiosity" (Conway, 2001, p. 22).

Besides this intensely personal motivation to educate older women, Conway's academic focus on the history of women's experiences lent her insight into the significance of education in their lives. Within the large, coeducational setting at the University of Toronto, Conway had parlayed her scholarly convictions as a faculty member not only into her women-focused course content, but into her choice of students as well. She taught "by preference, at night, when the part-time women came in droves to the downtown campus. I knew what their battles were, how hard it was for them to feel entitled to take time for expansive nonutilitarian learning" (Conway, 1994, p. 242).

She continued her efforts on behalf of older women from an administrative vantage point when she became vice president at Toronto by working to establish a part-time college for returning students. "A very high percentage were women, and the dropout rate for them was the highest in the entire educational system," she recalled. "They lacked counseling, health care, [and] time to build relationships with faculty" (Conway, 1994, p. 242). Her efforts at Toronto were truncated by her departure for Smith, where the opportunity to create strong support structures for returning women beckoned. "What could be achieved if an elite college for women began to take older women students seriously, to give them financial aid and all the services necessary to maximize their talents?" she mused (Conway, 2001, p. 22).

ADA COMSTOCK SCHOLARS PROGRAM, 1975–85

Jill Conway publicly articulated her commitment to the Ada Comstock Scholars Program from the beginning of her Smith affiliation. As president-designate, she indicated in her first official address to the College in November 1974 her intent to increase the number of women involved in the College's continuing education program (Smith, 1974). Even before assuming her official duties as Smith's president in July 1975, she gave her stamp of approval to the budget for the 1975–76 academic year. She reported taking pleasure "in allocating the funds to launch an admissions program for older women, a first step along the way to creating an institution that concerned itself with educating all women, not just 18- to 22-year-olds" (Conway, 2001, p. 26). Her words and deeds echoed the actions of those at Smith who recently had ushered the program into formal existence.

In addition to the financial benefits of tapping a new student market, expanding the number of older students on campus would add what Conway considered to be much-needed age diversity to the Smith student body. An exchange between the generations was "one of the important ways for the conventional undergraduate age group to confront some of the perplexing questions that face today's woman" she said (Smith College Archives). She was not alone in expressing her concern for diversity. Smith's image as a conservative New England finishing school was hard to shake. "We're having trouble getting rid of the image of the 'nice safe school for nice safe girls," admitted Director of Admission Lorna Blake (Weil, 1975). One alumna described Smith as a place that attracted "nice young women who came from nice homes" (Nelson, 2002, author interview). Conway hoped that the campus presence of Adas, as the returning women were called, would help dispel Smith's genteel public image and infuse student life with the richness of perspective that older women could provide.

When President Conway inherited the fledgling Ada Comstock Scholars Program, it had few resources other than a budget allocation for a director's salary (Conway, 2000). In short order, Eleanor Rothman was hired to direct the Comstock Program, which she did successfully throughout the remainder of Conway's tenure at Smith. Together, Conway and Rothman were among the program's most ardent advocates. Rothman skillfully and creatively administered the program through its growth years, while Conway pushed to expand its scope and raise the necessary funds to move the program from vision to reality.

Shaping the new program meant changing both the standard Smith admissions policy and the support services offered to this new group of students. The College instituted a flexible admissions process for older women in which the student had to show she was capable of academic work, write a biography, and undergo a daylong interview (Stout, 1983). Unlike traditional applicants, no SAT scores or application deadlines were mandated. Changing the composition of the Smith student body also meant putting into place a comprehensive program to accommodate the particular needs of this population. When the older women encountered campus rules and policies inappropriate for their life stages, they gradually impressed upon the administration the need for changes (Conway, 2000). Based on feedback from the women themselves, a special dean was designated who served as the first point of contact for accepted Comstock Scholars (Smith College Archives). Also important to facilitating the education of older women was the establishment in 1975 of the Smith College Child Care Center, designed to provide the Comstock Scholars, as well as Smith faculty and staff, with high-quality, low-cost childcare (Shanahan, 1976).

A distinguishing feature of Smith's program was its full integration of older students into the fabric of the institution without distinction in status from traditional-age students. Some other women's colleges offered continuing education programs that separated older women from the mainstream student body. For example, Mundelein College and the College of Notre Dame of Maryland offered returning students weekend colleges, Marymount Manhattan College offered a day-and-night year-round curriculum for working students, and Saint Mary of the Woods offered an external degree program (Ingalls, 1985). By comparison, Smith's older students were held to the same academic requirements as its traditional students, taking the same courses and number of credits, and were granted the same degree (Rothman, 1982). No academic credit was granted for life experience, common practice in other returning student programs (Castro,

1983). The College made sure that older women did not receive a watered-down educational experience, and Smith promoted the integrated nature of its program as a mark of high quality.

Despite special support services designed for returning women, their social integration to campus life proved to be an ongoing challenge. The Adas encountered cultural and social adjustments, and many expressed feelings of isolation while enrolled (de Villiers, 1996; Skarda, 2000). Some felt like imposters. "The idea that I would go to a school like Smith was only slightly less ridiculous than the idea that I might be president of the United States," recalled Rita M. Bleiman, a member of the 1984 graduating class. "Smith was too elite. Too expensive. And probably too difficult. . . . I applied. I got accepted. Someone had made a terrible mistake" (Skarda, 2000).

Generational differences necessitated adjustment by traditional-aged students as well, who arrived at Smith to find classmates old enough to be their mothers. The maturity, motivation, and diverse perspectives Adas brought to classroom discussions was widely appreciated by the Smith faculty but sometimes intimidating to 18 year olds (de Villiers, 1996). "I was a bit confused the first time I encountered an Ada Comstock Scholar in class. . . . she really stepped on my *last* [italics in original] nerve with her nonstop questions," recalled Erin Alexander Paisan, a 1987 Smith graduate.

> And it was always a treat when you had a promising date in for the weekend whose first impression of Smith on a Friday night is a 55-year-old woman hanging out in the living room watching television in her pink poodle-puffed houseslippers and floral housecoat. . . . To top it off, the Smith faculty just l-o-o-o-v-v-v-e-d Adas. How annoying. (Skarda, 2000, pp. 272-274)

For many, though, the intergenerational diversity that Conway had predicted was ultimately positive. "Most younger students are very tolerant of Adas," recalled Edith Stenhouse Bingham, class of 1985. "After the ice is broken, they realize that we aren't going to be their mothers, that we are all in the same boat, can be wrong, say stupid things and occasionally impart brilliant insight" (Bingham, 1985).

EDUCATING THE POOR

When Smith first allowed entry into what it originally had called its Mature Women's Program in the late 1960s, the population attracted was predominantly middle-class women in their 40s and 50s who were returning to school after raising children. As the 1970s unfolded, however, a broader spectrum of women sought admission to Smith. Ada Comstock Program Director Eleanor Rothman attributes the increased interest by women beyond traditional college age to a combination of the women's movement, the growth of community colleges, and the advancing age of baby boom children (Rothman, 1988). Following national publicity in the mid-1970s that announced the newly defined and expanded Comstock Program, applications poured in from older women. Many were community college students seeking to transfer; others held jobs and sought brighter career futures. Clerks, secretaries, farmers, nurses, and switchboard operators all wanted to attend Smith College (Castro, 1983).

Federal Pell Grants introduced in 1972 provided aid to students on the basis of financial need (Geiger, 1999). Beginning in 1975, returning women benefited from federal student aid programs that extended grants and loans to half-time students (Conway, 2000; McDonald, 1979). Until that time, however, little attention at Smith had been given to the financial aid needs of the new population of returning women. As a result, one of Conway's immediate tasks was to shore up resources to enable less financially secure women to attend Smith. Soon after she assumed Smith's presidency, she wrote:

> At present, this program can be made available to students who can commute to the College or who have the resources to move to Northampton. However, one of my highest priorities will be to locate the resources to enable the College to offer appropriate scholarships and financial aid to qualified students on a nationwide basis and to provide the necessary residential facilities for older women students. (Conway, 1975, p. 4)

Though she realized the desirability of financial support for the Adas, even Conway could not have predicted the flood of applications from very poor women. By 1977, a considerable number of older women on welfare applied for admission to Smith, testing the College's financial commitment to its new undertaking (Rothman, 1988).

Conway learned firsthand of such women at a garden reception on her campus. Attending the event was a Smith student who was not only on welfare, but also living out of her car with her children. "We're not in school," the woman's 7-year-old told Conway. "Mom's on welfare, and no one will rent to us" (Caldwell, 1985). The lack of a permanent address prevented the youngsters from attending school. Smith's president was appalled. "It was the first time I realized anyone in the [Comstock] program was on welfare," she recalled (Caldwell, 1985). Conway soon discovered that three other Smith students were on welfare and that some of the best students at nearby community colleges were mothers on welfare who might have attended Smith had they the money to do so (Gudzowsky, n.d.).

Although the number of very poor applicants to the Ada Comstock Scholars Program had been unanticipated, Smith, under Conway's leadership, began seeking foundation funding specifically designated to support women on welfare and their dependent children through a full undergraduate education at Smith (Smith College Archives). Conway realized that in order to support these recipients of Aid to Families with Dependent Children (AFDC), she would have to generate new funds to avoid draining resources from the traditional student financial aid pool. After unsuccessfully soliciting a number of foundations for support, lengthy negotiations with the Charles Stewart Mott Foundation yielded tangible results: beginning in the fall of 1979 and continuing for the next 6 years through 1985, the Mott Foundation would provide Smith a total of over $750,000 to support women welfare recipients with dependent children (Rothman, 1988). Each year during this period, Smith would use the scholarship money to admit 10 new older women students on public assistance to its entering class. At the height of the grant period, Smith would enroll 40 Mott Scholars. Funds of $40,000 to $60,000 per student would be allocated to assist the women with educational costs as well as living expenses for them and their children. (The Mott Scholar designation was for internal purposes only. Publicly, recipients of Mott funding were known only as Ada Comstock Scholars.)

The aim of the grant money was pragmatic: to move women off welfare dependency and into productive roles in society. The potential for change seemed immense, as only 2.2% of women receiving AFDC nationwide were pursuing any educational program (Caldwell, 1985). Conway thought a private college like hers could lead the way in demonstrating the benefits to society of educating welfare recipients, and then share that lesson not only with other higher education institutions but also with government policymakers. Her logic was that the public sector was often slow to innovate but responsive to proven money-saving strategies.

Many of the women who received Mott funding came to Smith from nearby community colleges, where transfer counselors recommended the Comstock Program. Their backgrounds were often quite different from that of the traditional Smith student: one student had worked as an apple picker; one had returned to college after 10 years as a "beatnick;" many had blue-collar roots (Castro, 1983; Dembner, 1980). A student attending Cape Cod Community College in Massachusetts was "absolutely dumbfounded" when Smith agreed to enroll her. "When you grow up like I did, you're not really sure you're not really stupid," she said shortly after she graduated from Smith with a biology degree ("Grant helps older students at Smith," 1985).

Different in both age and socioeconomic background from the typical Smith student, the experiences of Mott Scholars were not always positive. In addition to the sense of isolation felt by many Adas, some perceived pervasive classism at Smith. An ethnographic case study of Adas conducted in 1995 found that an unconscious prejudice against the poor existed (Cohen, 1998). "We have these discussions in class about welfare and other kinds of social programs," reported one student.

> What's amazing to me is the hostility—I mean real hostility—that the students express about the welfare recipients. I become apoplectic—like they know anything at all about what it is like to raise a family without a paycheck, or how hard it is to get a job without skills, or the [lack of] childcare if you want to go back to school. With their fathers writing checks out for them every month. . . . I just sit there and fume. (Cohen, 1998, p. 363)

From the College's standpoint, there were other difficulties associated with educating the poor. Giving money to welfare mothers was not as easy as it might seem, as pursuing a 4-year liberal arts degree at Smith on scholarship meant a woman would lose her public benefits. One woman who was 18 months from attaining her Smith degree was told by her welfare caseworker that she was "overtrained" because she had an associate degree. The caseworker recommended she take a job cleaning toilets in a local mall or face losing her welfare allotment (Caldwell, 1985). "It's so illogical," complained another frustrated Comstock Scholar. "Welfare will pay for 1 year of vocational training but won't pay for you to raise yourself up. It's a double bind: they don't want you on welfare, but they won't help you get off" (Dembner, 1980).

Providing financial aid for these women required maneuvering around restrictive state and federal welfare policies. Those at Smith met the challenge by cleverly reconfiguring the way institutional scholarship aid was disbursed. In consultation with the local Department of Public Welfare, Annette Keppler, the College's director of financial aid, and Eleanor Rothman, director of the Comstock Program, devised a "rather ingenious plan" to offer vendor payments (Rothman, 1988, p. 9). "We didn't give them scholarships," Conway explained after the successful implementation of this new system. "We paid the rent. We had an account for them at the grocery store, and the dentist, and doctor and so on. Not a cent of any money passed through their bank books" (Gudzowsky, n.d.).

With the financial hurdle cleared, another potential stumbling block for educating welfare recipients appeared on the horizon. The regulations of the federally funded and state administered Work Incentive Program (WIN) required a single parent with children ages 6 and older to work 30 or more hours a week (Dembner, 1980). During the 1979–80 academic year, the first year of Mott funding, the local WIN office bent the regulations to allow half a dozen WIN-eligible Mott women to attend school without penalty. But the relief for these students was temporary. "We've been trying to go easy on them," WIN assistant supervisor Michael Morrisey explained.

> We're allowing them to be awfully fussy about the kinds of work and the hours, but there's a limit. One year is possible, but after that they are collecting welfare on false pretenses if not engaged in a full-time work search. (Dembner, 1980)

When the College learned of the jeopardy in which they inadvertently had placed the first Mott Scholars, Smith agreed to pay living expenses for any Mott recipient thrown off welfare for choosing to study rather than work. Again, the College did so by making payments directly to the student's creditors (Dembner, 1980). The Commonwealth of Massachusetts eventually changed its welfare system so that scholarship students wouldn't lose their benefits, though in 1996 federal welfare reform law unraveled the state's progressive policy (Gudzowsky, n.d.).

A MODEL PROGRAM

The Ada Comstock Scholars Program grew from enrolling 45 students in 1975 to over 400 by 1988 (Skarda, 2000). The Adas ranged in age from 24 to 85 years old. They tended to be motivated students who excelled academically, and their success stories were touted frequently by Conway as examples of the transformative powers of a solid undergraduate education. Two of the first four Ada Comstock Scholars, both recipients of Mott funding, graduated in 1982 and were elected to Phi Beta Kappa. One of these students also graduated magna cum laude and won a Herbert H. Lehman Graduate Fellowship in Social Studies and Public and International Affairs (Mott Foundation, 1982). The other was admitted to the University of Connecticut Law School. A 1983 Comstock program graduate was nominated for a Mellon fellowship by her faculty advisor (Mott Foundation, 1982). Another from that class went on to Harvard Law School (Gudzowsky, n.d.). In response to the influx of high-caliber Comstock Scholars and a smaller group of talented transfer students, the College was able to become more selective in its admissions: in 1982–83, it raised its minimum acceptable SAT score for traditional undergraduates (Conway, 1984). A comprehensive survey in 1995 of all of the 1,080 alumnae of the Ada Comstock program found that half of the graduating Adas went on to obtain a graduate degree, the same percentage as for traditional aged graduates of Smith (de Villiers, 1996).

The Ada Comstock Scholars Program received national recognition by realizing such dramatic results as these. Even the popular press tapped into the successes of Smith's older women graduates. Charles Kuralt profiled Ada alumnae on CBS's *Sunday Morning* in 1985. ABC featured graduates of the program—including the foster mother of 10 children from Hartford, Connecticut—on its widely watched program *Good Morning America* (Gudzowsky, n.d.; Rothman, 1988).

In its creative and effective modification of traditional student services to meet the particular needs of older women and welfare recipients, the Ada Comstock Scholars Program served as a model for similar programs all over the country. Even among other women's colleges, which tended to be more hospitable than coeducational institutions in their treatment of adult students and in the provision of support services, Smith's accommodations stood out (Chamberlain, 1988). Program Director Eleanor Rothman thought Smith's innovations went beyond that of other colleges: "As far as I have been able to determine, no other comparable institution has a program of this size and scope, designed to serve an equivalent population," she said as she reflected over the program's first decade (Rothman, 1988, p. 8). "There are opportunities for women to return to school almost anywhere, including other Seven Sister Colleges and the Ivy League Universities, but usually without any substantial support system similar to that which Smith's program provides" (Rothman, 1982, p. 2). Among the Seven Sisters, Barnard limited its program to its own alumnae, Radcliffe offered only nondegree programs for returning women, and Mount Holyoke's program was largely modeled on that of its nearby neighbor, Smith. Rothman cited the differences in Smith's program: the range and number of students enrolled, the type of academic requirements, and the amount of financial aid provided (Horner, 1984).

One of the original aims of Smith's strong financial aid program for older women on welfare was to enable such women to break their cycle of dependence on state and federal assistance so they could contribute productively to society (Mott Foundation, 1982). Near the close of her presidency, Conway noted with satisfaction that the reentry of Comstock alumnae into the workforce meant that "society . . . is beginning to be repaid for those welfare payments by their taxes" (Smith College Archives). The public policy implications of the successful Mott component of the Ada Comstock Scholars Program were important to Jill Conway's vision of improving the lives of women not just at Smith, but around the country. From the beginning, it had been her intent to parlay the program's innovative aspects into broader-based and more pervasive efforts to educate America's often-ignored population of poor, older women.

Turning the spotlight on policy meant sharing the program's strengths and its potential to wider audiences, which she sought to do through periodic press releases and by convening a conference of policymakers, scholars, activists, and adult educators to discuss the topic of welfare policy as it applied to education and jobs (Ackelsberg, Bartlett, & Buchele, 1988). Conway reported that she dedicated a significant amount of her time as president "on the whole subject of welfare reform, both within Massachusetts and federally. . . . I would go down to Washington and testify anytime anybody wanted me to on welfare questions." She realized some success in her own state of Massachusetts to persuade the legislature

> that they should not subtract financial aid given to a welfare mother from her welfare allocation, so that a woman could get a scholarship and go to a good university without having it take away their children's healthcare or food or lodging. (Conway, 2002, author interview)

During the final year of her presidency, Conway challenged others to take up her cause. At a convocation at the University of Toronto, she said pointedly:

> I believe that academic institutions have an obligation to respond to the educational needs of the female head of a household who is in poverty. Her life and her children's can be transformed by access to educational opportunity on terms which make it possible for her to study and reach her full academic potential. We have done relatively well in the academy in recent years for the young woman lawyer, business executive and doctor. Now we need to educate her older and less economically fortunate sister. (Smith College Archives)

At the close of her 10 years leading the College, the Ada Comstock Scholars Program was the initiative of which Jill Conway was the most proud (Gudzowsky, n.d.). She continues today to tout "the admission of older women, and a different attitude to very poor women, women in poverty and on welfare" as one of the most important causes she championed during her presidency (Conway, 2002, author interview).

Ironically, the spectacular success of the Comstock program eventually brought increasing concerns about its size. After Jill Conway's retirement from Smith in 1985, the program's growth continued throughout the late 1980s, averaging nearly 400 students per year or about 14% of the total undergraduate population. Conway's presidential successor, Mary Maples Dunn, reported hearing "negative murmurings" from students about the domination of classroom discussion by older women who brought more extensive life experience to their studies. Conversations ensued among trustees and faculty about what the "appropriate balance" should be between the traditional-aged students and Adas. There was concern that "the presence of too many women the age of their mothers" would diminish the attractiveness of the College to traditional age applicants (Skarda, 2000, p. 13). A study was undertaken in 1995 to assess the impact of the program to the Scholars and Smith College.

At the same time, the infusion of Mott Foundation funds for poor scholars ceased in 1985. The institutional resources required to provide the burgeoning group of Adas with sufficient financial aid became troublesome for the College, which during the late 1980s and early 1990s was suffering from budget deficits. Ultimately, the College intentionally reduced the size of the program in 1995 by capping the enrollment of Adas at 261 students, down from its peak of 409 in 1988 (de Villiers, 1996; Skarda, 2000).

IMPLICATIONS FOR CONTEMPORARY POLICY AND PRACTICE

The Ada Comstock Scholars Program is a prime example of how an elite college educated poor, nontraditional age women students when doing so was still a relatively new idea in American higher education. Though small in terms of numbers of students, the program was effective in expanding access to a new group of women and delivering to them a quality educational opportunity.

Despite the successes of Smith's program, its long-term public policy implications have not been realized. Restrictive welfare reform measures passed in 1996 mandated states have at least 50% of their welfare populations working a minimum of 30 hours a week, and those laws redefined education narrowly as vocational or technical training rather than broader higher education programs. Soon, the law may become even more stringent: HR 4737 passed by the U.S. House of Representatives in 2002 legislates that by 2007, 70% of a state's welfare recipients must work at least 40 hours a week. In addition, the bill cuts the maximum amount of time that education can qualify as "work" to 4 months every 2 years, and includes funding for programs that encourages poor women to marry (107th Congress; Morgan, 2002). The bill has yet to be acted on by the U.S. Senate, but if passed would further erode higher education prospects for the poor.

The majority of welfare recipients are single mothers (Morgan, 2002). Despite their glorious successes under favorable conditions at Smith in overcoming difficult life circumstances, the contemporary response to welfare reform and education continues to penalize the poor. For the moment, at least, the transformative powers of a solid undergraduate education are apparently lost in the policy arena.

Nonetheless, advocates for the democratic potential of higher education can be effective contributors to the public dialogue on this issue and innovators on their own campuses in addressing the need to educate poor women. Indeed, increased attention to at-risk populations of adult, part-time, and poor students was urged recently by both Lumina Foundation for Education and the California Postsecondary Education Commission (Ashburn, 2007; Fischer, 2007). These groups recommend that institutions of higher education take such varied actions as revamping financial aid policies, providing more robust student counseling, and opening administrative offices during evenings and weekends to accommodate students. Further, given that students from low-income families under-enroll in the most selective, most expensive institutions, some have suggested that elite colleges reconsider their need-blind admissions policies to include a preference to well-qualified applicants from modest backgrounds (Bowen et al., 2005).

All of these institutional accommodations have a familiar ring, reminiscent of returning women's programs such as Smith's. Tackling the complex relationship between women, welfare, and higher education will continue to require persistence, conviction, and, perhaps, the perspective that a look back in history offers. Over 30 years since its inception, the lessons of the Ada Comstock Scholars Program and the successes of its graduates serve as proof that strides toward creating a more equitable society are possible.

REFERENCES

107th Congress. *Legislative Archives of the 107th Congress.* Retrieved October 18, 2006, from http://www.socialsecurity.gov/legislation/legis_bulletin_051702.html

Ackelsberg, M., Bartlett, R., & Buchele, R. (Eds.). (1988). *Women, welfare, and higher education: Toward comprehensive policies.* Northampton, MA: Smith College.

Adair, V. C. (2001). Poverty and the (broken) promise of higher education. *Harvard Educational Review, 71*, 217–239.

Ashburn, E. (2007, April 13). Mapping the misunderstood population of adult students. *The Chronicle of Higher Education.*

Bingham, E. S. (1985). Coming back as an Ada. *Smith Alumnae Quarterly, LXXXVI*(4), 11–12.

Blake, L. (1975, November). Admission at Smith—1975. *Smith Alumnae Quarterly, XVII,* 15–17.

Bowen, W. G., Kurzweil, M. A., & Tobin, E. M. (2005). *Equity and excellence in American higher education.* Charlottesville, VA: University of Virginia Press.

Caldwell, J. (1985, April 7). At Smith: Education for women on AFDC. *Boston Sunday Globe.*

Campbell, J. W. (1973). Women drop back in: Educational innovation in the sixties. In A. S. Rossi & A. Calderwood (Eds.), *Academic women on the move* (pp. 93–124). New York: Russell Sage Foundation.

Castro, J. (1983, November 21). Cultivating late bloomers: Smith's Ada Comstock Scholars give more than they take. *Time.*

Chamberlain, M. K. (1988). *Women in academe: Progress and prospects.* New York: Russell Sage Foundation.

Cohen, R. M. (1998). Class consciousness and its consequences: The impact of an elite education on mature, working-class women. *American Educational Research Journal, 35*(3), 353–375.

Conway, J. K. (1975). *New responses for the second century.* Northampton, MA: Smith College.

Conway, J. K. (1984). *The report of the President 1982–84.* Northampton, MA: Smith College.

Conway, J. K. (1989). *The road from Coorain.* New York: Alfred A. Knopf.

Conway, J. K. (1994). *True north: A memoir.* New York: Alfred A. Knopf.

Conway, J. K. (2000). Foreword: The Presidents Speak. In P. L. Skarda (Ed.), *Textured lives: Celebrating Ada Comstock Scholars at Smith College* (pp. 10–11). Northampton, MA: The Smith College Press.

Conway, J. K. (2001). *A woman's education.* New York: Alfred A. Knopf.

Conway, J. K., interview by the author, March 26, 2002.

de Villiers, P. (1996). *Report of the President's Task Force on the Ada Comstock Scholars Program.* Northampton, MA: Smith College.

Dembner, A. (1980, May 28). Program for welfare women survives turbulent first year. *Daily Hampshire Gazette.*

Duffy, E. A., & Goldberg, I. (1998). *Crafting a class: College admissions and financial aid, 1955–1994.* Princeton, NJ: Princeton University Press.

Fischer, K. (2007, March 21). California commission reports on decline in ratio of part-time students and other access issues. *The Chronicle of Higher Education.*

Gappa, J. M., & Uehling, B. S. (1979). *Women in academe: Steps to greater equality.* Washington, DC: American Association for Higher Education/ERIC Clearinghouse on Higher Education.

Geiger, R. (1999). The ten generations of American higher education. In P. G. Altbach, R. O. Berdahl, & P. J. Gumport (Eds.), *American higher education in the twenty-first century* (pp. 58–69). Baltimore, MD: Johns Hopkins University Press.

Grant helps older students at Smith. (1985, July 21). *New York Times.*

Gudzowsky, N. (n.d.). Telling it straight. Retrieved July 27, 2001, from http://www.horizonmag.org

Horner, C. (1984, February 21). At Smith, women get 2nd chance. *Philadelphia Inquirer.*

Ingalls, Z. (1985, March 27). Alumnae give high marks to women's colleges in survey. *Chronicle of Higher Education,* p. 16.

Nelson, M. P., interview by the author, March 6, 2002.

McDonald, K. (1979). Women in higher education: A new Renaissance? *The College Board Review, 111,* 10–13, 21.

Morgan, R. (2002, June 21). In debate over welfare reform, work triumphs education. *Chronicle of Higher Education,* p. A24.

Mott Foundation. (1982). Fact Sheet: Ada Comstock Scholars Program.

National Center for Education Statistics. (1979). *Digest of Education Statistics.* Washington, DC: U.S. Department of Health Education and Welfare, Education Division, National Center for Education Statistics.

Quesnell, Q. (1999). *The strange disappearance of Sophia Smith.* Northampton, MA: Smith College.

Rothman, E. B. (1982, fall). In a class by themselves: The Ada Comstock Scholars. *Smith Alumnae Quarterly, LXXIV,* 2–7.

Rothman, E. B. (1988). Women, welfare, and higher education: The Smith College experience. In M. Ackelsberg, R. Bartlett & R. Buchele (Eds.), *Women, welfare and higher education: Toward comprehensive policies* (pp. 7–10). Northampton, MA: Smith College.

Shanahan, A. E. (1976, November). Never too late to graduate. *Smith Alumnae Quarterly, LXVIII,* 18–21.

Shaw, K. M., Goldrick-Rab, S., Mazzeo, C., & Jacobs, J. A. (2006). *Putting poor people to work: How the work-first idea eroded college access for the poor.* New York: Russell Sage Foundation.

Skarda, P. L. (Ed.). (2000). *Textured lives: Celebrating Ada Comstock Scholars at Smith College.* Northampton, MA: Smith College Press.

Smith, A. L. (1974, December 5). Conway meets students. *The Sophian.*

Stout, K. (1983). A 'Seven Sisters' college updates its image. *United Magazine.*

U.S. Census Bureau. (2005). *2005 American Community Survey.*

Weil, A. (1975, February 6). The student won't change until the image does. *The Sophian.*

Communities of Exclusion: Women Student Experiences in Information Technology Classrooms

Julia Colyar
Assistant Professor
The University at Buffalo
The State University of New York

Despite important enrollment gains in science and engineering majors, women students are still conspicuously underrepresented in information technology (IT) programs. Previous research has reported that women students are isolated and less confident in their IT courses and, ultimately, become discouraged by competitive classroom environments. In this article, I extend previous research on the classroom experiences of women IT students through a series of ethnographic observations aimed at understanding classroom discourses. Rather than focusing on women students' challenges, I focus on classroom spaces, interactions, and community characteristics. I argue that the four classroom contexts included in this study can be described in terms of two discourses: discourses of power and discourses of disengagement—discourse patterns the women students in this study have limited access to and utility with. These understandings can be beneficial to faculty and student affairs professionals as they seek to improve classroom communities for all students.

INTRODUCTION

When I arrive to Room 205 in the Applied Sciences and Arts building, several students are already in their seats. Geoff plays solitaire on his laptop computer; Steve flips through his textbook; Jason asks Mark when the next assignment is due. These students are enrolled in a junior-level networking course offered by the Department of Information Systems and Technology. Students stream in steadily, filling up the rows of desks. When Brenda, the only woman student in the class, walks through the classroom doorway, Jason yells a greeting: "Brehehehnndaaa!" Brenda smiles and takes her seat next to him in the second row.

Brenda is accustomed to these exaggerated greetings. She is often the only woman student in her information technology (IT) courses. And her experience reflects a larger trend: Since 2000, institutions have seen steady decreases in the percentage of women IT graduates (Carlson, 2006). While women students currently make up approximately 58% of undergraduate students (Wilson, 2007), only 17% of IT graduates are women.

Women are underrepresented in science, technology, engineering, and mathematics (STEM) disciplines in not only the United States, but also in most other countries around the world (Blickenstaff, 2005; Clegg, Trayhurn, & Johnson, 2000). Recent research has looked at various aspects of women students' experiences in order to understand this enrollment and achievement gap, including institutional environment, disparity in financial aid awards, campus support services and mentoring programs, and individual students' background characteristics and preparation (Kondrick, 2003; Sadker & Sadker, 1994; Seymour & Hewitt, 1997; Astin & Astin, 1993). National and local support programs have helped women students make small gains in the STEM disciplines, but IT programs continue to attract and graduate more men than women (Carlson, 2006). And of women students who do choose IT majors, more leave their programs than their male counterparts (Cohoon, 2001). At the same time, IT is one of the fastest growing sectors of the U.S. economy (Bureau of Labor Statistics, 2000). Technology is integral to academic work, commerce, and communication; in many ways, technology is integral to who we are as citizens and students. Within this context, however, male students are benefiting most from new programs that prepare them for careers in the field (Sadker, 1999). Women students in IT programs are often considered "untraditional" or "pioneering" (Nelson, 2005); women students are still concentrated in traditionally "female" majors: education, psychology, nursing, social work, and the liberal arts (Sadker, 1999; Engle, 2003). When women students like Brenda walk into many IT classrooms, they find themselves outnumbered and conspicuously alone.

In this article, I explore the experiences of IT students at a large, public university. In particular, I examine the characteristics of IT classroom communities through a series of ethnographic observations. My goal in this study is to more completely understand IT classroom environments. In doing so, I seek to understand and describe the academic spaces women students enter when they walk into these classrooms. In the next section, I outline the research related to women IT students, and I provide a rationale for my approach.

REVIEW OF THE RESEARCH: WOMEN STUDENTS IN TECHNOLOGY PROGRAMS

Research related to women student experiences in computer-related courses has provided important understandings for addressing the achievement gap between male and female students. Researchers have looked at women students in a variety of disciplines, including IT and computer science. IT and computer science have much in common, but they have different academic foci: Students in IT study the technical processes that drive information systems for businesses and organizations. While computer science students focus on the principles of computing and how computers solve problems, IT students apply technologies to business settings. Despite these differences, research related to women students reports similar findings across the fields. For this reason, my review includes research related to IT as well as computer science students and classrooms.

Like K–12 classrooms, as well as larger social and cultural spaces, undergraduate technology-related classrooms are dominated by "traditionally male" communication patterns, role models, and pedagogical strategies (Beyer et al., 2003; Dryburgh, 2000; Clegg & Trayhurn, 1999). As Margolis and Fisher (2002) note, cultural norms associate "interest and success with computers" to boys and men (p. 4). From as early as middle school, guidance counselors advise more male students into computing courses and careers, and female students in computer courses are considered "geeky" or "nerds" by their peers (Carlson, 2006); in many cases, women students themselves consider computer work to be "uncool" (Thomas & Allen, 2006), or worse, "unnatural" and "unfeminine" (Hughes, 2000). Women students also tend to have more negative expectations regarding job prospects in IT (Thomas & Allen, 2006). In some cases, even parents discourage their daughters from careers in computing (Carlson, 2006).

Outnumbered in undergraduate computer-related classrooms, women students often feel "lost, unsupported, and unconnected" to the course material as well as other students (Margolis & Fisher, p. 83). Many researchers attribute this discomfort to the learning environment: While women students are drawn to cooperative learning opportunities and cross-disciplinary perspectives, computer-related classrooms are typically competitive in nature and focused on technical programming (Margolis & Fisher, 2002; Smithson, 1990; Barker & Garvin-Doxas, 2004; Baxter Magolda, 2001; Abrahams & Sommerkorn, 2004; Belenky, Clinchy, Goldberg, & Tarule, 1986).

Researchers have also noted that faculty in technical courses call on male students more often and praise male students more often than female (Huang & Brainard, 2001; Conefrey, 2000). Huang and Brainard (2001) noted that compared to male students, female students are more likely to be interrupted by faculty, and less likely to be called on by name. Given these classroom interactions, it is not surprising that women students in technology majors more often report feeling discouraged by their faculty and peers (Hughes, 2000). Moreover, women students perceive themselves as less competent and less well prepared than their male peers (Barker & Garvin Doxas, 2004; Margolis & Fisher, 2002). This sense of insecurity has also been expressed in survey research, which notes that women students report lower self-confidence in mathematics and science (Margolis & Fisher, 2002; Huang & Brainard, 2001), as well as lower self-confidence in IT-related content areas such as networking, programming, and cryptography (Colyar & Woodward, 2007).

Researchers have proposed important recommendations for addressing the gender disparities outlined in their research. Margolis and Fisher (2002), for example, argue for a "curricular and cultural revolution" that will "change computer science so that the valuable contributions and perspectives of women are respected in the discipline" (p. 6). They describe the ways in which parents, teachers, and advisors can encourage female students; and they suggest curricular and pedagogical strategies that can engage female students toward empowerment and confidence. Most importantly, they argue that any effort at improving the experiences of female students in computer-related programs must look at institutional and classroom practices, not at the individual characteristics of women students that need to be "improved." Likewise, Huang and Brainard (2001) suggest curricular and programmatic changes to improve the educational experiences of female students in science and technology majors. Their study, however, also posits that more information is needed in order to fully understand women students' self-confidence in male-dominated fields. They call for "further research into the dynamics of the classroom and student interactions with faculty members as well as with fellow students" (p. 336).

Taken together, these studies provide important foundations for understanding women student experiences, as well as suggestions for further research. As is evident in the research, many studies have focused on the set of characteristics women students "lack;" women students are less confident, less competitive, and less independent. When research is framed in this manner, male experiences and attitudes become normative—male students embody the "correct" attitudes and behaviors that will ensure success. If researchers, practitioners, and faculty locate the problem of women student experiences in the women themselves, there may be no urgency to examine the institutional environment, course curriculum, or student support programs; institutions may never worry about how they might respond or be engaged in the problem. This study seeks to focus attention on the classroom environment rather than on students themselves.

This project, then, is aimed at extending previous research efforts in the area of women student experiences in postsecondary IT classrooms. In particular, in this study I seek to understand classroom contexts in terms of faculty and student interactions and behaviors, and the community created in these classroom spaces. My goal is not to redefine differences based on gender by focusing on the individual attributes of female students (Wolfensperger, 1993), but to think more broadly about educational context as created and expressed in classroom discourse. I use the term "discourse" generally, to refer to classroom communication, social relationships, and activities that are enacted (and normalized) through language and behaviors (Cazden, 1988; Biklen, 1995). Classroom discourse refers not only to what is said, but also the context in which the utterance is embedded.

Understanding classroom discourse requires extensive observation. In this project, I utilized ethnographic observations of four IT classrooms: two classrooms with female instructors, and two with male instructors. Classrooms were second- and third-year IT courses. My research questions included the following: What discourse patterns are evident in IT classrooms? How do these discourse patterns shape community and the learning environment?

METHODOLOGY: ETHNOGRAPHIC OBSERVATIONS

I used an ethnographic approach to better understand classroom community as articulated in discourse patterns. In keeping with ethnographic tradition, my primary research tool was observation (Wolcott, 1999). Wolcott (1999) further specifies that observation is a means of gaining "experience." He notes "we are . . . overwhelmed by how much we can take in through looking and listening, from the subtleties of body language to the organization of cultural space" (p. 46). Because I am not a student of IT and have only a consumer's general experience with computers, I did not define myself as a "participant observer," a label that suggests interaction within the setting. Wolcott (1999) defines a role like mine as "non-participant participant observer," one who makes "no effort to hide what they are doing or deny their presence," but unable fully to "avail themselves of the potential afforded by participant observation to take a more active or interactive role" (p. 48). In many ways, because I could not engage with the content of the course, I was more able to attend to the culture and community of the classroom.

During the summer and fall semesters of 2006, and during the spring semester of 2007, I observed four IT classrooms. Though all of the courses were designed for second- or third-year students, they varied in terms of content and organization. Two of the courses met during the summer session of 2006: "Information Systems and Technology" and "WAN Network Installation and Administration." "Information Systems and Technology" was a lecture-based course designed to provide an overview of office and business information systems. In the course, students learned about hardware devices, software programs, database design, and networking technologies. In particular, students discussed the many computing choices business administrators negotiate in developing office systems. This class met in a traditional classroom, not in a computer lab, and was taught by a woman instructor. Two women students were enrolled.

"WAN Network Installation and Administration" was a hands-on laboratory course in which students learned to install and configure networking systems across a Wide Area Network (WAN). In particular, students worked with networking protocols designed for business applications. This course was taught by a male instructor and included only male students. During the fall semester of 2007, I observed another section of this course, which was taught by a woman instructor and enrolled one woman student. Unlike the more introductory course, this course required that students manipulate hardware and input networking commands. Much of the class time in each semester was spent in laboratory assignments.

The course I observed during the spring semester of 2007 was "Network Security." This course was taught by a male instructor and enrolled one woman student. During the semester, students focused on the design and implementation of network security solutions intended to protect the privacy of individual and business data. Like the networking course, this class included a great deal of hands-on laboratory work.

Classrooms for this project were selected with the assistance of a faculty member in IT. The faculty member recommended particular instructors that were likely to welcome me in their classrooms over the course of the semester; I contacted the instructors and met with them to discuss the project. I assured them that I would not be evaluating their teaching styles or their students, but I would be looking more generally at classroom community. My selection of classrooms was, therefore, based on instructor approval rather than on criteria such as class size, class demographic, or course content.

I observed most sessions of each course, with the exception of exam days and when scheduling proved difficult. In total, I observed more than 160 hours of class time. Each class was audiotaped, and I recorded detailed fieldnotes. I listened to the audiotapes following the class meetings and transcribed selected sections of dialogue. Five meetings from the "Network Security" class were also videotaped; as with the audiotapes, I viewed the videotapes and transcribed selected sections.

One of the challenges of this project was finding IT classrooms with female students. Of the four courses observed for this study, including 60 students, only four (6%) were women. This is significantly lower than the program average, which has women students enrolled at approximately 14%. In one of the courses, I was the only woman present in the room; in two of the courses, only one woman student was enrolled. This enrollment disparity sets up a male dominance by sheer number, without even factoring in the concerns indicated in the literature. While ideally I sought classrooms with more women students enrolled, finding available classes, with faculty willing to be observed throughout the semester, proved difficult. Ultimately, I believe that classrooms with few (or no) women students were useful sites for exploring classroom community and discourses. My focus is not limited to women students, but more generally located in classroom discourses. Indeed, for many women IT students, classrooms populated mostly by male students are environments women students must negotiate as they pursue their undergraduate degrees.

In addition to classroom observations, I also completed interviews with each of the instructors and two of the women students. The interviews were helpful in triangulating the data gathered in observations. In particular, interviews with the instructors were important for understanding if my interpretations were consistent with instructors' perceptions. Interviews with the two women students were also essential in understanding how they interpret the environment. Because of the small number of women in this study, I do not intend that these data are generalizable to all IT classrooms, women students' experiences generally, or even to IT classrooms at this University. Instead, I offer these findings as suggestive toward understanding the four classrooms in this study and this research approach.

Data generated from my observations were significant, including more than 300 pages of fieldnotes—as Wolcott (1999) suggests, the data were often overwhelming. My analytic process began early and continued throughout the data collection process, an approach Bogdan and Biklen (2007) label "analysis-in-the-field" (p. 160). To begin, I listened to audiotapes and reviewed fieldnotes for each class meeting; I initially focused on patterns of behavior (for example, in my initial reviews, I began by looking at interactions between students during lecture and lab times). I read and reread my notes, looked for overlapping ideas or incidents in my descriptions, and then reviewed my notes again, looking this time at interactions between faculty and students, and between students before and after class started. From my descriptions and transcriptions, I developed categories that helped organize and summarize the data. I then used these categories to examine and interpret the data I was continually collecting, and I used the data to refine the emerging categories. I completed interviews throughout the process—at the conclusion of each course—and used the interview data to further refine and define my interpretations.

DATA PRESENTATION: IT CLASSROOM DISCOURSES

Each of the classes observed in this study had its own personality and character. One of the classes was largely lecture, while three were lab-based and included group activities. One of the summer courses was very small—eight male students—while the others averaged 15 students. At the same time, however, I noted many similarities in terms of discourse and classroom community. I identified two types of discourses that can be used to describe the various classrooms: discourses of power and discourses of disengagement. These are outlined below.

Discourses of Power

After 45 minutes of lecture, Ms. Jackson folds her hands and instructs the class to begin their lab projects: "Get your routers to talk," she says. The small group seated in the third row of desks jumps immediately to work, but Brenda's group, in the second row, is distracted. Brenda stands awkwardly behind Jason and Mark as they talk about a recent parking ticket; Geoff continues his game of solitaire on a laptop computer. Brenda puts her hands in her pockets, looks around, and finally calls Ms. Jackson over. Geoff closes his solitaire window. "We want to use the standard ACL, right?" Brenda asks. Before Ms. Jackson can answer, before Brenda can even get the full question out, Geoff calls out the answer. Brenda raises her eyebrows and looks at Ms. Jackson as Geoff, Jason, and Mark begin working. Ms. Jackson pauses, turns to Brenda, and tells her: "I know . . . just be patient." As Ms. Jackson moves to the group in the front row, Brenda turns and smiles at me. Then she rolls her eyes. Later, Ms. Jackson pulls me aside and tells me that Brenda calls her after almost every class meeting and asks the central question: "Should I drop this course?"

The primary element of the discourse of power is technical talk. My observations support the literature that notes the privileging of technical knowledge and technical talk; my observations, however, also suggest that technical talk is connected to the power structures of the classroom, to identifying those most competent and confident. Technical talk is the voice of authority. Most students in these classrooms, and in particular male students, spent the available class time in technical talk. Before classes started, for example, male students like Geoff and Jessie often talked about games, programs, or troubleshooting on their home computers. Frank often spent the few minutes before class talking about software he found access to without purchasing a license. One morning, after describing a new program he found online, he turned to me, pointed to the tape recorder, and said: "But you didn't hear any of that!" Many days, Frank wore technical talk on his T-shirt, literally embodying his knowledge of technology. For example, one day, his T-shirt read:

C:/DOS
C:/DOS/run
Run/DOS/run

Not only did Frank embody the discourse of power, he was also playful with it. He was a student who "gets" the technical joke—not just in an abstract way that recognizes the connection to children's books, but as someone who knows to what "DOS" really refers.

Many students in these classes also had IT-related jobs on campus, so even as they talked about work, their conversation centered on computers and computing. Aaron, a student who works in the student recreational center, told Jason about the security system he was designing. Jason was obviously impressed with Erik's work, and he complained about his own: "I have the [worst] computer at work," he said. "If I had a better computer," Jason continued, "I could build a much better security layer." The two carried on their conversation loudly as they finished their lab assignment and packed their bags. While students sat finishing their work, they continued their conversation outside the classroom; theirs were the only voices I could hear.

Another morning, two male students talked about the operating system each had downloaded onto their home computer the night before. When the conversation began, one described the downloading process as a "challenge"; however, by the time they finished talking about the process, and going back-and-forth about how difficult it "wasn't," the process was actually "easy." Whatever the actual process entailed, these students negotiated an "easy" answer. In this way, not only did students' conversations center on technical topics, they also subtly competed with one another: Students negotiated the level of difficulty, each trying to sound more confident and carefree about their work; Jason was envious of Aaron's work at the recreation center and complained about his work computer; they talked loudly about IT topics, providing evidence to others about their level of mastery and knowledge. Again, these can be viewed as examples of their power negotiations and expressions. However, these examples also suggest that power was constructed in conversation, not simply in their in-class computer work. These students did not simply express power in actions—in elegant programming—but also through casual technical talk.

Technical talk was also evident in classroom content—after all, students were learning about technology. Classroom talk was full of jargon, acronyms, and various series of letters and numbers. In addition to abbreviated speech because of acronyms, when students answered questions, they typically responded with specific technical points, usually a word or two, sometimes a string of letters: ISBN, DCE, PHP, OIS, WAN, VLAN, RIP, T_3, configs, docs, and interfaces. Rarely did these students respond with conceptually driven answers; they almost never responded to classroom questions in complete sentences.

Technical talk, with its various acronyms and terse expressions, provided an easy marker for identifying who belonged to the "IT haves," and who belonged to the "have-nots." "Haves" were able to use technical talk; they responded in class when instructors asked questions, and they talked with peers before and after class about computing topics. Some students had this vocabulary, and some did not. Indeed, some male students did not have this vocabulary. Technical talk was expected when students answered questions, and it was rewarded with praise from instructors. It was often the language instructors used in asking questions. Students' ability to use this technical language was an expression of their power, their knowledge of the topics, and it provided a simple means of dividing students without actually tracking them into different groups.

The discourses of power were accompanied by a set of behaviors that reinforced student assertions of power and signaled their nonchalance toward the material and the classroom experience. I identified these behaviors and discussed them as articulating a discourse of disengagement.

Discourses of Disengagement

At 2:05 p.m., 5 minutes after the class is scheduled to begin, Mr. Robertson walks into classroom drinking a Diet Coke. He pauses in front of a bright pink sign that reads: "No Food or Drink Allowed." He looks around, notices the several empty desks, and asks: "Where is everybody?" Of the eight students, only three are in class. The three are working on the computers that sit on their desks: Brian is updating his MySpace page; Derek stares intently at a series of codes on his computer screen—he occasionally hits "enter" and more codes appear; John is playing a computer game involving a space ship. Three more students walk in a few minutes later as Mr. Robertson loads the PowerPoint slides for the day; the slides outline the lab project they will work. Mr. Robertson turns around to start his lecture, still holding his Diet Coke, and counts heads. "Has anyone seen Mario?" he asks the group.

Colby, who typically sits next to Mario in the second row, asks, "Who?"

"Mario," Mr. Robertson explains. "He sits right there," pointing to Mario's seat. Colby shrugs his shoulders. It is the sixth week of the summer session, and Colby does not know Mario's name.

Perhaps the most unexpected finding from these observations was the notable lack of community evident in the various IT classes. I found it very difficult to locate a sense of classroom community outside of technical talk, that voice of authority, in which students engaged. The discourses of power were about distinction; I was looking for community. A lack of community was evident in various ways, mostly as a kind of hyper-individualism: classes often did not start on time, students came and went in the middle of class without announcement, students played video games in class, sent text messages, and read the newspaper or surfed the Internet. One student, during the lab portion of his class, had his laptop in front of him with two instant messaging windows open; he worked on the assignment on the classroom desktop, exchanged instant messages, and took calls on his cell phone, all during the class lab time. In another class, a student's cell phone rang, and everything stopped while he turned it off. The instructor reminded the student that, as a consequence of his ringing phone, all students would have to take a quiz. In response, the student put his feet up on the desk in front of him and said: "Oh well."

The absence of community in these classes was perhaps most evident in the fact that, even in small classes of eight or so, students often did not know one another's name. Colby, in the above example, didn't know the name of the student who sat next to him 6 weeks into the intensive summer session. This finding echoes the literature that notes that IT classrooms tend to be impersonal. Because students sometimes did not know one another, it was likely easier for them to work largely individually, sometimes even at cross purposes, even when they were assigned a group project—even when the topic was, ironically, networking. During one class meeting, I observed three young men working on a networking project. Each was settled at a separate computer, inputting codes that would allow the computers to "talk." The three did not speak to one another; instead, they checked each other's computer screens to see if they were ready to test the network. Rather than conversation or technical talk, I heard only the sound of chairs rolling across the linoleum floor as they checked the computers. The students approached the topic at the same time, but separately, talking only through the commands on their computer screens. When Derek, a "have not" in terms of technical talk, evidenced signs that he was struggling, one of his group members rolled his chair over to Derek's computer—essentially moving Derek out of the way—and, with one key stroke, solved the problem. Neither said a word.

In many ways, the classrooms themselves enabled this discourse of disengagement. It was built into the infrastructure of the community. The computers that sat on students' desks in three of the classrooms offered many distractions. The instructors, when I asked them about this, expressed frustration, but also understanding. Ms. Jackson noted: "Well, it's annoying, and I try to walk around to make sure they are on task, but it's what they are passionate about. It is hard to tell them, 'Hey guys, stop using the computer during class.'" Ms. Smith noticed a mismatch between course content and student experience. She said: "I mean, we're talking about software, and this is a required class, and most of these kids have already built a computer from scraps at home." Here, Ms. Smith excuses student disengagement, and she even provides a rationale. Even in the classroom that was not equipped with desktop computers, students found ways to disengage from their classmates and classwork. Steve, who sat near the back of the room, completed the school newspaper's crossword puzzle each day in class. Jack read science fiction novels and occasionally shouted out correct answers to his instructor's questions. Ultimately, disengagement was an expression of students' knowledge; it was, in fact, part of the discourse of power, which instructors, perhaps in spite of themselves, seemed to admire.

The discourse pattern between instructors and students, as well as between students, also reflected a kind of disengagement—and this overlaps again with the discourses of power. The majority of class interaction was unidirectional: Instructors asked questions related to content, and students provided answers, usually in a few words or letters. If there happened to be more than one answer to a question, students answered serially, sometimes repeating one another because they hadn't listened to their peers' answers. Instructors did not typically ask open-ended questions, or questions that might lead to discussion or disagreement. Of course, the fact that students provided answers was evidence of a kind of engagement. But students were not necessarily engaged in the learning process or the community of learning. In fact, their answers were often examples of the discourse of power—they answered because it is evidence of their mastery of the subject matter.

For IT students, classroom time and space is different than in other majors and courses. The fact that most of the classes I observed had no formal ending or beginning was likely a reflection of the fact that the coursework was not bound within the four walls of a classroom. In many cases, for example, lab time continued after class at home. While students like Jason and Erik spent class time talking about their jobs, they also spent a number of hours after class working on lab projects. Students often arranged to meet at the lab early in the morning or late in the evening to complete their assignments. It seems little wonder that these IT classrooms appeared to be spaces of disengagement; traditional notions of schoolwork, class time, and group work were redefined in these settings.

DISCUSSION: WOMEN STUDENTS' EXPERIENCES

The discourse patterns evident in these IT classrooms help describe their community and environment: These IT classrooms were spaces in which students construct and negotiate power, and students' knowledge of the subject matter was often articulated in seeming disengagement. These discourses were evident in all of the classrooms observed in this study, those with women students and those without. In this section, I discuss the ways in which the women students interacted within these discourses. These findings are presented cautiously, not to generalize across all women students; these findings only present the observed experiences of women students present in these classrooms.

The women students in this study typically did not engage in technical talk; in fact, they rarely talked in class. One notable exception was Laura, a student in the lecture-based course. However, her classroom conversations were with her instructor (also a woman) about Laura's photographs in the school newspaper. Laura never offered answers to in-class questions. In the example above, when Brenda asked a question and Geoff interrupted to answer, she was essentially talked *through*. I use the descriptive term "through" purposefully; Brenda was not talked "over," which assumes at least a minimal recognition of her presence. Talking through her, Geoff offered a subtle dismissal, an insistence on his authority. It's not simply that Geoff interrupted and answered; he also made her question unnecessary. With his response, the group could get to work.

In my observations, these few women students did not often talk with male students about home computers or gaming or routers or operating systems. In fact, Marcia sat in the front row of the classroom, an empty seat between her and Robert. I never saw them talk together. Brenda, on the occasions when she spoke to her classmates, usually asked them about recent postings to the class Web page. When male students talked to her, it was to ask about assignment due dates. During one of the group projects, Brenda was assigned the task of recording the steps the group used in creating a network. She stood behind her group members, who were huddled around the computer screen essentially blocking her view, and tried to keep up with them. She then typed out the steps and uploaded the information to the class Web page, evidence that the group completed the project. In this instance, Brenda acted as secretary to the rest of her group members, all male. Her access to technical talk was as a recorder, not as one who had the authority to speak or input code—she was not even physically included in the circle of students seated around the keyboard. Brenda also never volunteered answers in class; in fact, only one of the women in this study, Marcia, ever volunteered an answer (twice in the course of the semester). In this way, Brenda and her women colleagues were literally and figuratively on the margins of technical talk.

Brenda and her women peers also did not exhibit the behaviors of disengagement as their male peers did. The few women observed in this study did not arrive to class with laptop computers or obvious cell phones. They did not play computer games during class or read the newspaper in the lecture course, and I did not witness them sending instant messages from desktop computers. In fact, the women students in this study did not often use the computers located on their desks except to work on lab projects; and in most of those instances, they were not allowed to act as the principal coder. Brenda, in fact, often seemed anxious about the lab assignments. She called Ms. Jackson over to ask her a question because her lab group was not making progress. Calling Ms. Jackson over was the catalyst that finally got the group working. And unlike many of their male peers, the women students tended to take notes during class, communicating engagement with the material.

For these women students, the discourses of power and disengagement worked together to present a larger discourse of exclusion. However, this exclusion was very subtle. Exclusion in this setting had the superficial appearance of *in*clusion: Brenda was the group member who recorded their work; when she entered the room, her classmate called out to her, welcoming her in an exaggerated way. She was the only student everyone knew by first name. Brenda could not be just a student in the class; she was always conspicuous. Her experience in classrooms started from this obvious point, from the point of being obvious. She was always at once part of classroom discourse even as she stood at the margin.

In thinking through the discourses of power and disengagement, Brenda was in these discourses even as she was subtly, or not so subtly, *not* part of classroom conversations. These discourses did not depend on her presence—that is, male student power was not directed at Brenda or the other women students specifically; male students were not trying to "one-up" their women colleagues. But in these classrooms, the women students negotiated the various ways power was played out, and the various ways disengagement was enacted, from more marginal positions. This is not to say that the women students did not have technical knowledge. Brenda did use technical talk when she asked Ms. Jackson about the "standard ACL." Rather, it is to suggest that, unlike many of their male peers, these women students did not express and negotiate power as often or in the same ways that the male students did. As the group recorder, for example, Brenda ultimately had power over the group's project grade. But this power was not the same—and in this context, does not have the same currency—as the power expressed by her male peers as they configured a router.

CONCLUSIONS AND NEXT STEPS

These findings are not intended to generalize to all IT classrooms or women students. Indeed, these findings best describe the four classrooms observed in this study. However, these findings point to an investigative strategy that recenters the research gaze on classroom spaces rather than on the attributes of individual students. Studies that look at women students have tended to reify male characteristics, to note the characteristics and skills that women students lack. A research approach that focuses on understanding classroom discourses has two benefits: A study of discourses allows researchers to better understand the community in which all students operate; and this approach provides a means of anchoring efforts toward retaining women students. If researchers, faculty, and student affairs professionals better understand IT classrooms, we can think through the support programs that may be most useful to all students. If students—male or female—report feeling "lost" or "unconnected" in classrooms, findings like these help provide information around these emotions. The student development literature asks faculty and administrators to think about the ways in which students balance academic and social lives, and the ways students engage in academic and social experiences. If IT classrooms are characterized by disengagement, faculty and administrators who work with IT students may think about how engagement may be fostered either in classrooms or cocurricular settings.

Faculty in IT programs might think about classroom infrastructure and pedagogical styles. For example, computer desks may be rearranged to situate students in circles rather than rows. This would allow students to sit face-to-face (though still behind computer screens), and may encourage more interaction as they work on projects. Alternatively, faculty may reconfigure classrooms so that in addition to rows of computer tables, the classroom may also contain more traditional desks. During lecture and discussion, the class can use the more traditional space—perhaps with desks arranged into a circle rather than in rows—then retreat to the computers to work on lab assignments. Discussion may be easier if students and instructors are arranged in spaces that encouraged interaction.

Faculty may also mediate students' reliance on technical talk in classrooms by asking them to narrate their answers rather than offering a few words or letters. Instead of asking "what" questions in class, they could ask "why" questions—or follow "what" questions with "why?" Faculty and administrators in IT could also develop learning communities specifically for IT students. These communities may be academic or largely social. Either approach would bring students into contact outside the classroom setting, and may help students get to know one another and develop self-confidence that can be carried into classroom situations.

Though these suggestions are aimed at all students, this research is ultimately aimed at decreasing the achievement gap between male and female IT students. The question of student persistence to graduation, of course, is not as simple as describing classrooms. This work is situated within larger institutional and cultural frameworks that create, influence, and reflect the discourses of dominance and disengagement evident in these classrooms. The complexity of the problem must be met with research from a variety of approaches. This research points toward other areas for exploration. For example, additional research should explore other institutions and institution types, including all-women colleges, and including classrooms with more women students enrolled. Perhaps classroom discourses are different in other environments.

While this research cannot single-handedly change social constructions of gender and work, it can help us think about curriculum, classroom spaces, and teaching strategies. We can worry about what happens in our university classrooms and ways that classroom communities can be reimagined to increase success rates for all students. We can think about the development of professional skills that all students can carry into workplaces.

These efforts can be far reaching. With classroom communities that are supportive for all students, more women students can be retained. When a proportionate number of women faculty exist in IT departments, women students will have access to more IT role models and mentors. Similarly, when more women are hired into IT jobs, women seeking careers in IT will have more role models and mentors. Women IT students must be supported, retained, and recruited into faculty positions as well as into the profession. Higher education classrooms are important places to begin this support and recruitment.

REFERENCES

Abrahams, F. F., & Sommerkorn, I. N. (2004). Promoting gender awareness in the classroom: An example from Germany. Retrived from http://www.waxmann.com/fs/abrahams.pdf

Astin, A. W., & Astin, H. S. (1993). *Undergraduate science education: The impact of different college environments on the educational pipeline in the sciences.* Los Angeles, CA: Higher Education Research Institute, UCLA.

Barker, L., & Garvin-Doxas, K. (2004). Making visible the behaviors that influence the learning environment: A qualitative exploration of computer science classrooms. *Computer Science Education, 14*(2), 119–145.

Baxter Magolda, M. B. (2001). *Making their own way.* Sterling, VA: Stylus Publishing.

Belenky, M. F., Clinchy, B. M., Goldberg, N. R., & Tarule, J. M. (1986). *Women's ways of knowing: The development of self, voice, and mind.* New York: Basic Books.

Beyer, S., Rynes, K., Perrault, J., Hay, K., & Haller, S. (2003). Gender differences in computer science students. Paper presented at the 34th SIGCSE Technical Symposium on Computer Science Education, Reno, NV, February 23–27.

Biklen, S. K. (1995). *School work: Gender and the cultural construction of teaching.* New York: Teachers College Press.

Blickenstaff, J. C. (2005). Women and science careers: Leaky pipeline or gender filter? *Gender and Education, 17*(4), 369–386.

Bogdan, R. C., & Biklen, S. K. (2007). *Qualitative research for education.* Boston: Pearson Publishers.

Bureau of Labor Statistics. (2000). Monthly labor review. Washington, D.C.: BLS. Retrieved August 4, 2006, from http://www.bls.gov/opub/mlr/welcome.htm

Carlson, S. (2006). Wanted: Female computer science students. *The Chronicle of Higher Education,* v. LII, no. 19 (January 13, 2006), A35-A38.

Cazden, C. (1988). *Classroom discourse: The language of teaching and learning.* Portsmouth, NH: Heinemann Publications.

Clegg, S., & Trayhurn, D. (1999). Gender and computing: Not the same old problem. *British Educational Research Journal, 26*(1), 75–89.

Clegg, S., Trayhurn, D., & Johnson, A. (2000). Nor just for men: A Case study of the teaching and learning of Information Technology in higher education. *Higher Education, 40*(2), 123–145.

Cohoon, J. M. (2001). Toward improving female retention in the computer science major. *Communications of the ACM, 44*(5), 108–114.

Colyar, J. E., & Woodward, B. (2007). Women Students' Confidence in Information Technology Content Areas. Paper submitted for review to ISECON annual meeting, Pittsburgh, PA, Nov. 1–4, 2007.

Conefrey, T. (2000). Laboratory talk and women's retention rates in science. *Journal of Women and Minorities in Science and Engineering, 6*, 251–264.

Dryburgh, H. (2000). Underrepresentation of girls and women in computer science: Classification of 1990s research. *Journal of Educational Computing Research, 23*(2), 181–202.

Engle, J. (2003). "Fear of success" revisited: A replication of Matina Horner's study thirty years later. Paper presented at the annual meeting of the American Educational Research Association, Chicago, IL, April 21–25.

Huang, P., & Brainard, S. (2001). Identifying determinants of academic self-confidence among science, math, engineering, and technology students. *Journal of Women and Minorities in Science and Engineering, 7*(4), 315–337.

Hughes, W. J. (2000). Perceived gender interaction and course confidence among undergraduate science, mathematics, and technology majors. *Journal of Women and Minorities in Science and Engineering, 6*, 155–167.

Kondrick, L. C. (2003). *What does the literature say about the persistence of women with career goals in physical science, technology, engineering, and mathematics?* Paper presented at the annual meeting of the Mid-South Educational Research Association, Biloxi, MS, November 5–7.

Margolis, J., & Fisher, A. (2002). *Unlocking the clubhouse: Women in computing.* Cambridge, MA: The MIT Press.

Nelson, D. J. (2005). A National Analysis of Diversity in Science and Engineering Faculties at Research Universities. Norman, OK: Diversity in Science Association.

Sadker, D. (1999). Gender equity: Still knocking at the classroom door. *Educational Leadership, 56*(7), 22–26.

Sadker, M., & Sadker, D. (1994). *Failing at fairness: How America's schools cheat girls*. New York: Macmillan.

Seymour, E., & Hewitt, N.M. (1997). *Talking about leaving: Why undergraduates leave the sciences.* Boulder, CO: Westview Press.

Smithson, I. (1990). Introduction: Investigating gender, power, and pedagogy. In S. Gabriel & I. Smithson (Eds.), *Gender in the classroom* (pp. 1–27). Urbana, IL: University of Chicago Press.

Thomas, T., & Allen, A. (2006). Gender differences in students' perceptions of information technology as a career. *Journal of Information Technology Education, 5,* 165–178.

Wilson, R. (2007). The new gender divide. *The Chronicle of Higher Education*, pp. A35–A39.

Wolcott, H. F. (1999). *Ethnography: A way of seeing*. Walnut Creek, CA: Altamira Press.

Wolfensberger, J. (1993). 'Science is truly a male world': The interconnectedness of knowledge, gender and power within university education. *Gender and Education*, *5*(1), 37–55.

The Impact of Childhood Abuse on University Women's Career Choice[1]

Rosemary C. Reilly
Assistant Professor
Concordia University
Montréal, Québec

Miranda D'Amico
Associate Professor
Concordia University
Montréal, Québec

A study is discussed that describes a link between childhood abuse and career choice for 12 university women. Purposive sampling was used, and the study employed a cross-case comparative approach with an emphasis on feminist principles. An interactive, collaborative interview was developed, prompting stories that reflected career choice processes. A general framework for processing the naturalistically obtained data was constant across the cases and was subjected to criteria to insure trustworthiness. Three basic themes emerged: (1) for women who were still enduring a cycle of pain and fear as a result of long-term child abuse, safety was a dominant concern; (2) women who had managed to transform their experiences approached career choice as a "mission" in order to right the wrongs of their past; and (3) negative cases that did not fit the general trend provided an opportunity to reexamine the data and the theme of distance. These results have important implications for vocational counseling and academic advising.

1. This research was supported through a grant from the General Research Fund from the Social Science and Humanities Research Council, Concordia University.

INTRODUCTION

Violence has long been a specter that haunts the human experience. The psychological impact of violence on individuals and family relationships is well known; however, the long-term impact on life choices is not. Researchers (Browne & Finkelhor, 1986; Finkelhor & Browne, 1985; Newberger & DeVos, 1988) have implied that the impact on the future of an abuse survivor would be feelings of powerlessness to act on wishes and beliefs, self-destructive behavior, loneliness, poor self-esteem, and revictimization. These patterns might extend themselves into the career choice context.

This study arose out of our observations from a pilot qualitative study on the effects of violence on the learning of university women (Reilly & D'Amico, 2002). A majority of the participants disclosed to us that their child abuse experiences influenced their choice of a university major leading to a professional career. The purpose of this study, conducted as a follow-up to the previous research, uses a feminist research design to describe the impact abusive experiences may have had on career choice, in order to further clarify the societal cost of family violence.

RELEVANT LITERATURE

Recent investigations have shown that adult abuse significantly impacts women's ability to find work and maintain employment (Moe & Bell, 2004); women's job performance as measured by absenteeism, tardiness, job leavings, and terminations (Swanberg & Logan, 2005); and their ability to concentrate on the job (Wettersten et al., 2004). Chronister and McWhirter (2004) found that battering could create barriers to pursuing educational goals. However, violence can extend its influence before gainful employment is attained, and it can be rooted in childhood abuse experiences. In one pilot study (Reilly & D'Amico, 2002), participants mentioned that their past abusive experiences influenced their choice of career, either in choosing a helping profession, or in seeking departments that were populated mainly by women. However, little research has been done in this area (Dickinson, 1991).

Most research in the vocational domain has been an effort to rebalance women's presence in traditional and nontraditional careers. Therefore, much has focused on the variables that influence women in choosing a career. The concepts of self-efficacy (Betz & Hackett, 1986; Hackett &

Betz, 1981; Rotberg, Brown, & Ware, 1987), attribution (Fiorentine, 1988; Luzzo, Funk, & Strang, 1996), self-concept (Betz & Fitzgerald, 1987; Love, 1986), psychological influences (Roundtree & Frusher, 1991), social and cultural factors (Hackett & Byars, 1996; Reis, 1995), sexual orientation (Fassinger, 1996), and family patterns (Goldwasser, 1992; Whiston, 1996) have all been the subject of investigation.

The literature on sexual harassment of high school girls demonstrates that a long-term effect of harassment is to limit the educational and vocational opportunities for young women. Levels of sexual harassment determined girls' selection, attendance, and success in courses that were mainly populated with boys (Larkin, 1994; Yewchuk, 1994). Sexual harassment also influences women's ability to stay and succeed in nontraditional jobs or in male-dominated fields (Benson & Thomson, 1982). Sexual harassment has been described as the single most widespread occupational hazard women face in redressing the gender imbalance in many fields (Betz & Fitzgerald, 1987; Mansfield, Koch, Henderson, Vicary, Cohan, & Young, 1991; Swerdlow, 1989; Tangri, Burt, & Johnson, 1982; Working Women's Institute, 1980). Personal histories of childhood abuse may play a similar role in limiting women's career choice.

Abuse has been seen to have far-reaching effects in the realm of epistemological processes and self-concept, salient dimensions in career development. Belenky, Clinchy, Goldberger, and Tarule (1986) found that 38% of the women in school or college, and 65% of the women contacted through social service agencies, experienced incest, rape, or sexual seduction. Many survivors perceived themselves to be mindless and voiceless, subject to the whims of authority. They did not cultivate representational thought and believed knowledge to be a magical process beyond their grasp. Sexual violence, in particular, functioned as an effective technique of silencing. Violation and shame undermined the process of gaining and valuing subjective knowledge (Belenky et al., 1986), and many women began to conceive of themselves as "invisible." This dynamic may exert a similar effect on a woman's ability to make career choices and to function within certain professions.

PURPOSE OF STUDY

This study explored the significance of the relationship between childhood abuse and career choice in university women. The researchers developed an inquiry process that attempted to detail the impact of these events on career choice.

THEORETICAL FRAMEWORKS THAT GUIDE THIS INQUIRY

Though there is a major debate about whether we as researchers can, and indeed should, identify a distinct feminist methodology (Ramazanoglu & Holland, 2002), we have conducted this inquiry guided by feminist epistemological and methodological frameworks. A basic assumption of our approach is that family violence is a patriarchal process, whose casualties are women, men, and children. We view gender as an organizing principle in this research, and we seek to understand how a gendered social order has shaped women's lives, their consciousness, and career choice. Our aim is to render visible the distortion that abuse has on the female experience in order to illuminate and end women's unequal social position. We do this by integrating women's knowledge and experiences with a multiplicity of women's own voices. Our approach to research is informed by the following principles (Fonow & Cook, 1991; Meis, 1991; Reinharz, 1992; Stanley & Wise, 1993):

- The research relationship should not be a hierarchical relationship but a collaborative one.
- Emotions of the researcher and the participant are valuable aspects of the research process.
- Objectivity is not an ideal stance; researcher subjectivity is a powerful asset.
- The researcher's intellectual autobiography informs the framing of the conclusions.
- The researcher must effectively blend the different "realities" held by the researcher and the participant.
- The researcher must be aware of issues surrounding authority and power.

Methodologically, we employed techniques and processes that established collaborative and nonexploitative relationships with participants, emphasizing trust, reciprocity, and empathy. We avoided objectification of the participants and their experiences by adopting shifting situational identities (Angrasino & Mays de Perez, 2000) that were harmonious with the social interaction and context (as women, teachers, learners, mothers, and as a survivor). We negotiated the meanings of the results with the participants and were self-reflexive about what we ourselves were experiencing and learning. And we are disseminating these results in order to produce research that is educationally and vocationally transformative.

In terms of the actual career choice processes that were under investigation, a grounded theory approach was used (Strauss & Corbin, 1998). We developed a rough definition of the career choice phenomena to be explored. Dimensions of this definition were: present course of study, long-term plans for employment, and the self-construction of a "dream career" from the participant's perspective.

We then formulated a tentative hypothesis to explain the phenomenon on the basis of the cases reported in the study and our own insight into the data. Based on the data generated from the first case study, we conducted a comparison with the case participant regarding the fit between the hypothesis and the data. We reformulated the hypothesis and redefined the phenomenon in response to the comparison with each succeeding comparison case. We then delimited the hypothesis by comparing it with the negative cases, reformulating or redefining as necessary with the case participants.

METHODOLOGY

Research Design

This study employed a cross-case comparative study approach (Merriam, 1998). We selected this methodology on the basis of (1) its flexibility and adaptability to the description of multiple realities, (2) its potential transferability to other participants and age groups in order to build a foundation of description, (3) its susceptibility to a self-reflexive and empowerment process, and (4) its congruent positioning with our ethics and values as researchers in regard to social change and the research process (Lincoln & Guba, 1985).

Interviews were a cooperative and interactive process, minimizing hierarchical relationships in favor of a joint enterprise approach (Oakley, 1981). Using an open-ended conversational format to facilitate the development of trust, rapport, and maximum exploration of the phenomenon, we, as interviewers and collaborators, attempted to elicit stories from the participants, since stories reflect human consciousness (Vygotsky, 1987). Interview questions were designed to prompt reconstructions of the reasons for their choice of courses and majors, past experiences with childhood abuse (being aware of psychological boundaries and privacy issues), and the here-and-now self-constructions of the participants as career choosers and emerging professionals. Questions also attempted to elicit feelings, thoughts, intentions, and meanings. Some examples of the questions posed are:

1. What is your major?
2. What career do you aspire to enter?
3. What are some of your motives for this career choice?
4. What past experiences led you to this choice?
5. Tell me about how you see yourself in this career in the future.
6. For how long have you aspired to this career?
7. Do you see any links between your childhood experiences and your career path? What specifically? If not, describe why not.

Participants

The focal points of the cross-case comparative study were 12 women participants who experienced physical, sexual, or emotional (including verbal and psychological) childhood abuse (as defined by the Intergovernmental Committee on Family Violence, 1991). The women belonged to various age, racial, class, and ethnic groups; and they were enrolled in a university undergraduate program.

Sampling

Since this project was concerned with university women who have had previous child abuse experiences, we used purposive sampling. Lincoln and Guba (1985) suggested this method in order to increase the scope or range of data exposed, since random sampling may not produce the kind of sample that the project concerns. We recruited volunteers from the campuses of two large universities in a major Canadian city through advertisements and flyers distributed in classes. We established various methods for contact (voice mail, e-mail, and a letter box) that allowed prospective volunteers various degrees of anonymity before consenting to participate. Prospective participants could then self-select out of the study. Though this might have biased the sample, we believe that, ethically, due to the sensitive nature of the research topic and our feminist stances, participants should exert maximum control and freedom over their own participation.

Phases of Inquiry

We conducted all interviews in person, and each interview was audiotaped, while maintaining ethical considerations of confidentiality and emotional distress. We used the format of the three-interview series (Seidman, 2006).

1. **Orientation and overview.** The first interview addressed issues of informed consent: an explanation of the motives and intentions in the research process, the purpose of the inquiry, the protection of the participants, the discussion of the collaborative nature of the analysis, logistics, and the consent form (Bogdan & Biklen, 1998). The interview then proceeded to a focused life history, in which the participant's reasons for course and career choice were placed in context. This session accentuated reconstructions of reasons for course concentration selection and past experiences with violence (with appropriate privacy and psychological boundaries being maintained).

2. **Focused exploration.** The purpose of the second interview was to concentrate on the concrete details of the participants' present experiences, including their here-and-now self-constructions as career choosers and emerging professionals. This interview took place approximately 2 weeks after the first one.

3. **Member check phase.** In this interview, participants reflected on the meaning of their experiences, in light of the data generated. They were asked to comment on its accuracy, analyze its meaning and implications, and clarify any ambiguities or inconsistencies. This phase took place approximately 3 to 4 weeks after the second interview.

Analysis Procedures

We created a general framework for processing the data, and we used it consistently and continuously across the cases (Strauss & Corbin, 1998). Our research design and analysis was an interactive, reiterative one (Maxwell, 1996), whereby we analyzed the data in a current case while continuing to collect data from additional cases. We performed a provisional categorizing of the data (units that seemed related to the same content) and formed propositional statements to characterize a category. Each case participant reviewed the categorizations and propositional statements; and she was able to clarify, revise, and add elements (Miles & Huberman, 1994).

We developed rules for categorizing the data (i.e., the inclusion of units with similar meaning into the same category) in order to keep the category internally consistent (Dey, 1999). We checked the coherence of these rules with each participant to maintain the integrity of the representation of her experience. We gave each category a metaphoric title, which attempted to capture the essence of the rule for inclusion of units into the category. We reviewed the data to check for consistency and relevance, and we proceeded with this process until the four criteria proposed by Lincoln and Guba (1985) were fulfilled: exhaustion of data sources, saturation of categories, emergence of regularities, and overextension. We then created clusters of categories and formalized their relationship to other clusters in order to facilitate the development of theory. We subjected the data to various criteria and procedures to ensure trustworthiness (Lincoln & Guba, 1985; Merriam, 1998), including credibility, transferability, dependability, and confirmability.

RESULTS

Three basic themes emerged from the interview data. The following are illustrations of the patterns that emerged. We have selected passages from the words of some of the participants that most aptly describe the theme.

"I Want To Be Safe Now": Issues of Physical and Psychological Safety

For those four women who were still enduring a cycle of pain and fear as a result of devastating long-term effects of chronic child abuse, safety was a dominant theme. Choices concerning course work and fields of study were determined by levels of safety, which was defined by them as the *presence* of women and the *absence* of men.

Louise,[2] a 54-year-old woman, disclosed being sexually assaulted at the age of three by a male relative. This abuse occurred frequently until she was 9 years old, at which time she was able to report these events to her parents. Though her parents stopped the abuse, they never acknowledged the effects it may have had on her, and the abuse was shrouded in silence. In her interview, Louise described that she felt more comfortable and safer in smaller classes that had a majority of women students; in fact, her future career plans were based on the fact that the department in which she was

2. All names are pseudonyms.

enrolled had a majority of female faculty and students. Louise said, "It was very hard for me to come back to school. I really checked things out so that I'd know I'd be okay." She revealed that she felt safer in that department than elsewhere in the university. Watching others in order to keep herself safe was a major thread to her reconstructions. According to Louise, "With one classmate [a man], I felt very intimidated by him when we had to work together. I would watch him to see if he was judging me . . . to size him up."

She disclosed that her biggest challenge in university was to open herself up to "men's viewpoints," particularly in the context of family studies. She stated that often she would find herself being overly anxious when "too many men were in class." She would purposely sit next to groups of women and would only take courses that were offered during the day, because she felt at risk at night. She reported experiencing particular difficulty in the process of forming learning partnerships with men; she often had to seek out the help and support of her therapist in order to construct appropriate boundaries for these situations. She insightfully summed up her understanding of her patterns by stating in a clear though wavering voice, "It's hard when you've experienced something [sexual abuse] and you've learned the wrong way to cope [avoiding men], but you've *survived*."

For other participants whose career choice fit this theme, safety was also psychological; freedom from manipulation or "hidden agendas" by professors, especially male professors, was seen as very important. These women were extremely sensitive to power hierarchies. Rosalyn, an immigrant woman of color in her mid-30s who experienced extreme physical abuse at home and at school, said, "Female professors generally are very approachable. With male professors, you have to watch out for power dynamics. . . ." When asked about what kind of power dynamics, "Power trips," she added formidably, "especially since I'm Black."

Trust issues both inside and outside the classroom were extremely salient within this category. This issue was particularly resonant for Elaine, a 20-year-old woman who was physically, psychologically, and emotionally bullied by peers:

> Because of her [a female professor], I have a 'voice' in the classroom. I knew then I'd have a 'voice' in [her chosen field]. In other courses I'd taken in other [male-dominated] departments, there was a lack of authenticity. . . . You couldn't trust that what they said was what they really thought and felt.

These women then used the presence of female faculty to determine their course concentration and subsequent career path.

"I Want To Make Things Right:" Career as Mission

Another major theme that emerged was from six women who had managed to transform the pain and fear of chronic physical and sexual abuse into a career-as-mission in an effort to right the wrongs of their past. This sense of duty often took them into the realm of social services careers or vocations that involved work with women, children, or families. Choices concerning coursework and fields of study were less influenced by the context than the focus: The transformation of past abusive experiences was facilitated by a new career path and compelled the desire to effect transformative social change.

Isabella, an eastern European immigrant woman in her mid-50s, described her early paternal relationship with undertones of sexual imagery, though she does not have any recollection of incest. Rather, her father tended to react as if male figures around the family would molest her and, therefore, kept her fairly isolated from others. She disclosed being sexually abused at the age of 11 by a male teacher who would regularly fondle her intimately during school assemblies. This sexual abuse lasted until she was 13, at which time the teacher lost interest in her. When he began to exhibit attention toward her younger sister, Isabella told her father about the abuse. The teacher was driven from the town, but silence prevailed as a coping mechanism for the family. This pattern of acting in defense of others was further demonstrated when Isabella spoke about leaving her physically abusive husband. "I decided that I had to stop the cycle when my daughter became pregnant. I made a gift to the girl child, a promise that she would not endure what my daughter had."

Isabella retreated to a women's shelter and was encouraged there to return to school in an effort to rebuild her self-concept and find satisfaction on a new path. While still living at the shelter, she began working with other women who were experiencing domestic violence and had also endured childhood abuse. She discovered that helping others facilitated her own healing. By connecting with others, she was able to engage in a two-way process in order to overcome the isolation of lifelong abuse. As well, Isabella wanted to effect social change, an exceptionally strong theme with survivors of domestic abuse.

> I want to give a voice to women. For so long, I didn't have a voice. I want to create a safe place for women to come to. Not only physical, but mental, psychological . . . and I do this in my healing circles which I have facilitated since I got my certificate. I also want to understand why I became a battered wife. All my papers and assignments help me to understand what happened to me.

Other participants for whom this was a dominant theme related that taking action through a career was a major part of their survival process. Monica, a 24-year-old woman who was a first-generation Canadian, recalled:

> I remember when I was 12 years old, after being beaten by my [parent], I vowed I would never let anyone else suffer the way I had. That's when I decided I would be a counselor to work with others . . . to stop this cycle. This [vow] was the only thing that kept me sane.

For others, the impact did not need to be so dramatic. Christina, a mature student in her mid-40s who was in the process of completing a certificate in a helping profession, extended this sense of mission to her current job. "Even as a secretary, it is important to be able to make a difference . . . to make things better. What I learn in my classes allows me to put a human face on my job: to be and to act human, even in a big organization." Transformation through career choice of past painful experiences for the good of others was a crucial process for these women.

"Distance:" The Negative Cases

Negative cases are cases that do not seem to fit the general trend and, therefore, provide researchers with opportunities to re-examine the data in order to explain why those cases have happened in such an untypical way (Glaser & Strauss, 1967; Seale, 1999). Re-examination of the data allows for the modification of ideas and assumptions, and eventually a richer and more complex theory and explanation. In the context of this inquiry, a negative case was defined as a participant who did not base her career choice on her past childhood abuse experiences. Two women fit this criterion, and they were women who experienced emotional abuse. These women had a more cognitive than affective basis for their career choice. These women were attracted and connected to the content of the field. They spoke of past influences on their present choice, but these influences were always described with images that evoked distance and kept issues, their past, and people at "arm's length." Their main concern was to increase awareness, while leaving change up to other individuals or organizations.

Anya, a 20-year-old woman, disclosed verbal abuse concerning her weight and intellectual abilities by family members and peers. This abuse occurred on and off during her preadolescence and adolescence. Anya had wanted to become a teacher since she was 4 years old. Unlike Isabella, who spoke passionately about effecting personal and social change, Anya talked about wanting to make people aware without necessarily affecting their lives in a serious way. She was adamant about not working with preschool or elementary school age children, but preferred to focus on becoming a high school teacher. Focusing on having a one-way impact on adolescents, she used images of the teacher-as-convincer. "I'm interested in opening up people's perspectives. Making people aware of 'invisible minorities' [e.g., gays and lesbians], getting them to think about all these hidden messages. . . . That's important. You can't change things. . . . You can only make people aware."

The other participant who fit the profile of a negative case was a 26-year-old woman of color majoring in an environmental science. Jenny, the product of an alcoholic system in which emotional abuse was present, related that, for her, the career came first and wanting to make a difference came second.

> I think my interest in the environment came from my spending so much time in the ravine and the woods near my home when I was a kid . . . especially when my parents' drinking was really out of control. I liked being alone, out of the turmoil. I still like it.

Though she would like to effect change, she was not looking for "monumental change." Jenny stated:

> I don't have the strength . . . the stamina . . . to do that. But I would like my work with the environment to serve as a point [of change] for others. My dream is to advise an environmental group in a major city that would take my data and work for environmental change.

A limiting component to the influence of childhood abuse seemed to be the type of abuse: women who had experienced a component of physical or sexual abuse elaborated the categories of safety or career-as-mission; those who used metaphors of distance had experienced emotional abuse.

Boundaries of the Inquiry

Since this inquiry occurred in a particular time and place, under particular circumstances with unique individuals (Wolcott, 1990), the emergent themes and dynamics should be viewed as atypical; however, limited transferability may be warranted. At the very least, these cases expanded and enriched the repertoire of social constructions about childhood abuse shaping university course selection and subsequent career paths for some women. Certain trends, especially regarding the selection of courses or perceived career options, could be formulated into working hypotheses and carried over to new situations (Donmoyer, 1990), assessing a degree of fit with a changing context with different constituents.

As well, given the sample size and the nature of the sampling procedure, it is important to note that a causal connection cannot be drawn. However, this project has revealed some important themes that were salient for the women who were interviewed. Future research is needed to more thoroughly investigate abuse survivors of both genders in traditional and more nontraditional fields (e.g., engineering and the pure sciences) and with those whose abusers were female.

DISCUSSION

The results of this study have far-reaching implications counseling women for career choice in higher education. A portion of the women interviewed felt anxiety and fear when making life choices. These states of emotional arousal appeared to decrease career-related self-efficacy (Hackett & Betz, 1981), and these women used safety rather than interest or ability to determine their career path. Therefore, childhood physical and sexual abuse functioned as a limit to circumscribe perceived career options (Gottfredson, 1981) to a reduced range of appropriate alternatives, that is, fields dominated by women. Sexual abuse, in particular, may be a dimension that supports occupational sex segregation. Fear of revictimization seemed to interact with fear of success and reduced risk-taking behavior, substantiated barriers for women's career aspirations (Farmer, 1976).

The impact of devastating abuse on the self-concept of these survivors also tended to restrict choices (Betz & Fitzgerald, 1987). All of the women in this theme category spoke about personal qualities (lack of education or intelligence and an inability to concentrate on or learn concepts) that limited the range of fields that were open to them. These results may serve to partially explain the pattern of underutilization of abilities demonstrated by women in career achievement (Betz, 1994). In addition, vocations dominated by men were perceived as filled with the potential for sexual harassment, which further served to circumscribe these women's career alternatives (Farmer, 1976).

For another group of women, childhood physical and sexual abuse also had an impact on their career choice, though toward a different end. These women were trying to eliminate the conditions that supported these kinds of abuse. Through their career choice, they would become an instrument for social change. This sense of future purpose was a crucial element to their healing. However, their career options were still circumscribed, in that they were drawn to the "helping professions," many of which are dominated by women and are within the stereotypical female professional career sphere (Betz, 1994). Though based on proactive choice, the end result was much the same: the continued occupational segregation and limitation of career alternatives for women, and the reinforcement of occupational stereotypes.

Therefore, child physical and sexual abuse may function as a determining influence for established variables that have been linked to career choice for women. These experiences may function on many levels, either as a "debilitating" or "precipitating" factor (Sobol, 1963 as cited in Betz & Fitzgerald, 1987), dependent upon the woman survivor's cognitive construction of the events and the meaning made of the experiences. These patterns of abuse may play a profound impact on tailoring a woman's sex role attitude, fear of success, academic and performance self-esteem, and risk-taking behavior, or, as an environmental barrier by heightening sensitivity and vulnerability to the potential of sexual harassment (Betz, 1994; Farmer, 1976). For some women a career within a traditional sphere that addressed the physical and psychological "survival" needs of safety (Astin, 1984) was a preferable option to one that embodied potential danger in a nontraditional one.

Being in university departments populated by women also restricted the participants' exposure to female role models in nontraditional fields, thereby cultivating lower career self-efficacy in nontraditional occupations (Betz, 1994; Hackett & Betz, 1981). Sensitivity to potential power dynamics with male professors prevented some women from even taking courses with them, let alone developing mentoring relationships. This blueprint for relationships with female and male faculty might serve to seriously restrict the range of career options and success within male-dominated fields.

The key difference among the women who expressed the major themes of safety and transformation is the cognitive construction of past experiences coupled with the kind and strength of the emotion and arousal to the career "barrier" of past child abuse experiences. This link between thought/ emotion interaction and barrier perception has been seen as a fundamental key to coping with barriers (London, 1998). For women still caught by the fear and anxiety, who re-experienced these emotional states, safety was primary. For those women who transformed their fear and anxiety into righteous anger and action toward "a wrong committed," career served as a constructive vent to these feelings.

Given the established link between "acceptable" career aspirations for women and a woman's self-concept along with perceptions of occupations (Gottfredson, 1981), it is important to consider the long-term effects of child abuse as part of the career assessment process, and in the context of university academic advising. Chronister, Wettersten, and Brown (2004) have called on researchers to include the vocational experiences and needs of battered women so that vocational research can contribute to the liberation of battered women. This inclusion must also extend to childhood survivors of abuse. Considering the number of women who have experienced childhood violence (Herman, 1997; Meichenbaum, 1994; Root, 1996; Terr, 1991), abuse can be considered a critical incident, which may affect the career development of a survivor (Hackett & Lonborg, 1994). Childhood violence is a gender issue, which has long been neglected in the assessment process (Brown, 1990; Hackett & Lonborg, 1994). As well, abuse may influence a woman's gender-role socialization, a key element in career assessment (Brooks & Forrest, 1994).

IMPLICATIONS FOR PRACTICE

The main function of this project was to offer insight and illuminate meaning. Streaming into limited career paths is now shown to be another possible long-range effect of child abuse. We offer some suggestions to practitioners about the implications of these themes in a higher education setting.

In a Higher Education Institutional Context

Everyone within a higher educational setting needs to become familiar with the long-term signs of early abuse. Understanding some of these behavioral patterns as attributable to early abuse, rather than irrational anxiety or sex role stereotypes, creates climates, which help women realize their full potential. Horsman (2000) emphasized that the only way to adequately transform educational programs is to shift consciousness of the connections between violence and learning, and consequently career choice, to the forefront; it is the only way that changes in educational programs can begin to be pictured. "Shifting conceptions will require constant vigilance because it is all too easy to slide back into taken-for-granted conceptual frameworks [of violence]" (p. 329). More resources, therefore, must be allocated to support women's career processes. As with any change, institutional change can only occur if all levels are involved, such as program administrators, program advisors, instructors, support staff, and other students. At the same time, additional resources need to be allocated. Tutors, vocational skills and career options workshops for women, career fairs exploring traditional and nontraditional careers for women with living representatives of those careers, and mentoring support within disciplines would go a long way to sustain the widening of career alternatives for women survivors of childhood abuse.

Horsman (2000) also emphasized a holistic approach to the educational experience, where the focus is on exploring, taking charge, and enabling the whole person to support life choices and learning. This approach would empower women to make career choices based on possibilities, desires, and dreams, rather than on safety, mission, or distance. There must be a priority in creating safe environments, real and perceived, in all departments and classrooms within higher education. Safety is created by the policies that we implement, by the language that we use and the actions we take, and by being continually aware of the impact of trauma on career choice.

In Student Advising and Career Counseling

Vocational counseling cannot be divorced from psychological counseling when working with women who have experienced abuse. Part of the intake interview should address a client's experience of violence, and the consequences of silence and shame associated with it. Counselors working in university settings need to be aware of the pervasiveness of students who have experienced violence and the way that it impacts educational choices. The damage from abuse needs to be considered when assessing course selection, major declaration, and career counseling; the psychic damage from abuse needs to be considered when forming relationships with students and in discussing how women survivors form learning relationships with peers. As Horsman (2000) stated, "It is not just the mind that goes to school—it is the whole person" (p. 334).

As some participants in this inquiry reported, the fear of revictimization causes high anxiety, which interacts with fear of success, creating substantiated barriers for women's career aspirations. It is within this context that counselors need to listen and provide a therapeutic venue that addresses not only the psychological needs of the client, but also her vocational future.

REFERENCES

Angrasino, M., & Mays de Perez, K. (2000). Rethinking observation: From method to context. In N. Denzin & Y. Lincoln (Eds.), *Handbook of qualitative research* (2nd ed.) (pp. 673–702). Thousand Oaks, CA: Sage Publications.

Astin, H. (1984). The meaning of work in women's lives: A sociopsychological model of career choice and work behavior. *The Counseling Psychologist, 12*, 117–126.

Belenky, M., Clinchy, B., Goldberger, N., & Tarule, J. (1986). *Women's ways of knowing: The development of self, voice, and mind.* New York: Basic.

Benson, D., & Thomson, G. (1982). Sexual harassment on a university campus: The confluence of authority relations, sexual interest and gender stratification. *Social Problems, 29*, 236–251.

Betz, N. (1994). Basic issues and concepts in career counseling for women. In W. B. Walsh & S. Osipow (Eds.), *Career counseling for women* (pp. 1–41). Hillsdale, NJ: Lawrence Erlbaum.

Betz, N., & Fitzgerald, L. (1987). *The career psychology of women.* New York: Academic Press.

Betz, N., & Hackett, G. (1986). Applications of self-efficacy theory to understanding career choice behavior. *Journal of Social and Clinical Psychology, 4*, 279–289.

Bogdan, R., & Biklen, S. (1998). *Qualitative research in education: An introduction to theory and methods* (3rd ed.). Boston: Allyn & Bacon.

Brooks, L., & Forrest, L. (1994). Feminism and career counseling. In W. B. Walsh & S. Osipow (Eds.), *Career counseling for women* (pp. 87–134). Hillsdale, NJ: Lawrence Erlbaum.

Brown, L. (1990). Taking gender into account in the clinical assessment interview. *Professional Psychology, 21*, 12–17.

Browne, A., & Finkelhor, D. (1986). Impact of child sexual abuse: A review of the literature. *Psychological Bulletin, 99*(1), 66–77.

Chronister, K., & McWhirter, E. (2004). Ethnic differences in career supports and barriers for battered women: A pilot study. *Journal of Career Assessment, 12,* 169–187.

Chronister, K., Wettersten, K., & Brown, C. (2004). Vocational research for the liberation of battered women. *The Counseling Psychologist, 32,* 900–922.

Dey, I. (1999). *Grounding grounded theory: Guidelines for qualitative inquiry.* San Diego, CA: Academic.

Dickinson, J. (November, 1991). Toward a cognitive developmental understanding of child sexual abuse: Clinical interviews with adult women sexually abused in childhood. *Dissertation Abstracts International, 52*(5-A), 1687.

Donmoyer, R. (1990). Generalizability and the single-case study. In E. Eisner & A. Peshkin (Eds.), *Qualitative inquiry in education: The continuing debate* (pp. 175–200). New York: Teachers College Press.

Farmer, H. (1976). What inhibits achievement and career motivation in women? *The Counseling Psychologist, 6*, 12–14.

Fassinger, R. (1985). A causal model of career choice in college women. *Journal of Vocational Behavior, 27*, 160–175.

Fassinger, R. (1996). Notes from the margins: Integrating lesbian experience into the vocational psychology of women. *Journal of Vocational Behavior, 48*, 160–175.

Finkelhor, D., & Browne, A. (1985). The traumatic impact of child sexual abuse: A conceptualization. *American Journal of Orthopsychiatry, 55*(4), 530–541.

Fiorentine, R. (1988). Sex differences in success expectancies and causal attributions: Is this why fewer women become physicians? *Social Psychology Quarterly, 51*, 236–249.

Fonow, M., & Cook, J. (1991). Back to the future: A look at the second wave of feminist epistemology and methodology. In M. Fonow & J. Cook (Eds.), *Beyond methodology: Feminist scholarship as lived research* (pp. 1–15). Indianapolis: Indiana University Press.

Glazer, B., & Strauss, A. (1967). *The discovery of grounded theory: Strategies for qualitative research.* Chicago: Aldine.

Goldwasser, S. (1992). *Relationships, mothers and daughters, fathers and daughters: A key to the development of competence?* (ERIC Document Reproduction Service No. ED361 618)

Gottfredson, G. (1981). Circumscription and compromise: A development theory of occupational aspirations. *Journal of Counseling Psychology, 28*, 545–579.

Hackett, G., & Betz, N. (1981). A self-efficacy approach to the career development of women. *Journal of Vocational Behavior, 18*, 326–339.

Hackett, G., & Byars, A. (1996). Social cognitive theory and the career development of African American women. *Career Development Quarterly, 44*, 322–340.

Hackett, G., & Lonborg, S. (1994). Career assessment and counseling for women. In W. B. Walsh & S. Osipow (Eds.), *Career counseling for women* (pp. 43–85). Hillsdale, NJ: Lawrence Erlbaum.

Herman, J. (1997). *Trauma and recovery: The aftermath of violence from domestic abuse to political terror*. New York: Basic Books.

Horsman, J. (2000). *Too scared to learn: Women, violence, and education.* Mahwah, NJ: Lawrence Erlbaum.

Intergovernmental Committee on Family Violence (1991). *Woman abuse protocols*. St. John, NB: Government of New Brunswick.

Larkin, J. (1994). *Sexual harassment: High school girls speak out.* Toronto: Second Story Press.

Lincoln, Y., & Guba, E. (1985). *Naturalistic inquiry*. Beverly Hills, CA: Sage.

London, M. (1998). *Career barriers: How people experience, overcome, and avoid failure*. Mahwah, NJ: Lawrence Erlbaum.

Love, R. (1986). "I'm really different": Difficulties in balancing a business career with a liberal arts self-concept. *Journal of American College Health, 34*, 210–215.

Luzzo, D., Funk, D., & Strang, J. (1996). Attributional retraining increases career decision-making self-efficacy. *Career Development Quarterly, 44*, 378–386.

Mansfield, P., Koch, P., Henderson, J., Vicary, J., Cohan, M., & Young, E. (1991). The job climate for women in traditionally male blue-collar occupations. *Sex Roles, 25*, 63–80.

Maxwell, J. (1996). *Qualitative research: An interactive approach*. Thousand Oaks, CA: Sage Publications.

Meichenbaum, D. (1994). *A clinical handbook / practical therapist manual for assessing and treating adults with post-traumatic stress disorder (PTSD).* Waterloo, ONT: Institute Press.

Meis, M. (1991). Women's research or feminist research?: The debate surrounding feminist science and methodology. In M. Fonow & J. Cook (Eds.), *Beyond methodology: Feminist scholarship as lived research* (pp. 60–84). Indianapolis: Indiana University Press.

Merriam, S. (1998). *Qualitative research and case study applications in education*. San Francisco: Jossey-Bass.

Miles, M., & Huberman, A. (1994). *An expanded sourcebook: Qualitative data analysis* (2nd ed.). Thousand Oaks, CA: Sage Publications.

Moe, A., & Bell, M. (2004). The effects of battering and violence on women's work and employability. *Violence Against Women, 10*, 29–55.

Newberger, C., & DeVos, E. (1988). Abuse and victimization: A life span developmental approach. *American Journal of Orthopsychiatry, 58*, 505–511.

Oakley, A. (1981). Interviewing women: A contradiction in terms. In H. Roberts (Ed.), *Doing feminist research* (pp. 30–61). Boston: Routledge & Kegan Paul.

Ramazanoglu, C., & Holland, J. (2002). *Feminist methodology: Challenges and choices.* Thousand Oaks, CA: Sage Publications.

Reilly, R. C., & D'Amico, M. (2002). The impact of sexual and physical violence on women's' learning processes: Implications for child and youth care workers in educational settings. *Journal of Child and Youth Care, 17,* 166–186.

Reinharz, S. (1992). *Feminist methods in social research.* New York: Oxford University Press.

Reis, S. (1995). Talent ignored, talent diverted: The cultural context underlying giftedness in females. *Journal of Secondary Gifted Education, 6*, 162–170.

Root, M. (1996). Women of color and traumatic stress in "domestic captivity": Gender and race as disempowering statuses. In A. Marsella, M. Friedman, E. Gerrity, & R. Scurfield (Eds.), *Ethnocultural aspects of post traumatic stress disorder: Issues, research, and clinical applications* (pp. 363–388). Washington, D.C.: American Psychological Association.

Rotberg, H., Brown, D., & Ware, W. (1987). Career self-efficacy expectations and perceived range of career options in community college students. *Journal of Counseling Psychology, 34*, 164–170.

Roundtree, J., & Frusher, S. (1991). Fear of career development success among women: Implications for community college educators. *Community-Junior College Quarterly of Research & Practice, 15*, 203–209.

Seale, C. (1999). *The quality of qualitative research.* Thousand Oaks, CA: Sage Publications.

Seidman, I. (2006). *Interviewing as qualitative research: A guide for researchers in education and the social sciences* (3rd ed.). New York: Teachers College Press.

Stanley, L., & Wise, S. (1993). *Breaking out again: Feminist ontology and epistemology.* New York: Routledge.

Strauss, A., & Corbin, J. (1998). *Basics of qualitative research: Techniques and procedures for developing grounded theory* (2nd ed.). Thousand Oaks, CA: Sage Publications.

Swanberg, J., & Logan, T. (2005). Domestic violence and employment: A qualitative study. *Journal of Occupational Health Psychology, 10*, 3–17.

Swerdlow, M. (1989). Men's accommodations to women entering a nontraditional occupation: A case of rapid transit operatives. *Gender & Society, 3*, 373–387.

Tangri, S., Burt, M., & Johnson, L. (1982). Sexual harassment at work: Three exploratory models. *Journal of Social Issues, 38*(4), 33–54.

Terr, L. (1991). Childhood traumas: An outline and overview. *American Journal of Psychiatry, 148*, 10–20.

Vygotsky, L. (1987). *Thought and language.* (A. Kozulin, Ed.). Cambridge, MA: MIT Press.

Wettersten, K., Rudolph, S., Faul, K., Gallagher, K., Trangsrud, H., Adams, K., Graham, S., & Terrance, C. (2004). Freedom through self-sufficiency: A qualitative examination of the impact of domestic violence on the working lives of women in shelter. *Journal of Counseling Psychology, 51,* 447462.

Whiston, S. (1996). The relationship among family interaction patterns and career indecision and career decision-making self-efficacy. *Journal of Career Development, 23*, 137–149.

Wolcott, H. (1990). *Writing up qualitative research.* Newbury Park, CA: Sage.

Working Women's Institute. (1980). *Sexual harassment on the job: Questions and answers.* New York: Author.

Yewchuk, C. (1994). *Gender issues in education.* (ERIC Document Reproduction Service No. ED371 553)

She Fears You: Teaching College Men to End Rape

Keith E. Edwards
Director of Campus Life
Macalester College
St. Paul, Minnesota

Troy Headrick
Independent Consultant
Burlington, Vermont

The authors share a pedagogical approach to engaging college men as allies for social change as a tool for sexual assault prevention. Once college men understand that they too are harmed by men's violence against women, they can be motivated not only to examine their own socialization and behaviors but also to join with women to speak out against the rape culture that encourages, condones, and teaches men's violence against women. The authors share prominent examples from popular culture and everyday campus life to illustrate how the rape culture can be identified, deconstructed, and confronted with college men and women in an effort to end rape.

INTRODUCTION

The authors of a recent national survey by the U.S. Department of Justice concluded that the rates of rape and attempted rape in college "might climb to between one-fifth and one-quarter" (Fischer, Cullen, & Turner, 2000, p. 10). A previous study found that one in four college women report surviving rape (15%) or attempted rape (12%) since their fourteenth birthday (Koss, Gidycz, & Wisniewski, 1987). These studies not only support each others findings, but also provide evidence of a sad lack of progress over the past 25 years in ending rape on college campuses. Although it is important to recognize that rape happens between people of the same gender and that women can rape men, men are the perpetrators in 99% of sexual assaults reported on campus (Greenfeld, 1997). Although some men do rape, not all men are rapists. In fact, a significant portion of college men show a strong desire to be allies with women, particularly on issues of sexual assault, but are inhibited from doing so by their expectations of peer norms and lack of concrete strategies (Fabiano, Perkins, Berkowitz, Linkenbach, & Stark, 2003).

The authors of this article have more than 25 years of combined experience developing a social change approach to sexual assault prevention both as student affairs professionals on our individual campuses and speaking regularly to college students on campuses across the country. In this article, we share the conceptual approach and specific strategies that we have used to engage college men in sexual assault prevention. This pedagogical approach helps men see how both men and women are harmed by the rape culture, which encourages, condones, and teaches men to rape women, and how men can join with women to change the culture toward ending rape. First we discuss how student affairs professionals and faculty in higher education can help college men recognize how their own humanity is diminished by violence against women. This realization can motivate men to not only examine their own socialization about rape and consensual sex, but also to join with women in working to end rape. Next, we examine the construct of informed consent and its critical role in preventing many of the perpetrators of sexual assault on college campuses. We then discuss how examples from popular culture and everyday campus life can be dissected to illustrate with students how the rape culture can be identified, deconstructed, and confronted.

A NEED FOR A PROACTIVE APPROACH TO PREVENTION

Colleges and universities have traditionally responded to rape on campus by implementing risk reduction approaches for women despite recent efforts to emphasize the role of men in primary prevention (Yeater & O'Donohue, 1999). When we speak to college students across the country, vast majorities share that they have heard messages directed at women such as *carry this whistle, take this mace with you, don't wear that, don't go there, if you do—go with friends, or come home with those same friends.* These messages are prominent, important for the safety and survival of women on campus, and firmly planted in the consciousness of the college students we speak with, even if they are not always heeded. However, it is an incomplete message. When campus responses to rape are focused only on this risk reduction approach, the message conveyed really is, "Rape happens here. Here's how you women need to deal with that." This places the responsibility on individual women to not be rape victims, but does nothing to protect women as a group.

This reactive approach to violence against women persists because rape continues to be seen primarily as a women's issue. However, if men are overwhelmingly the perpetrators of sexual assault, it is clear that rape is primarily a men's issue. In addition to educating men about consent, individuals and institutions can promote a more proactive message, focused not only on men as potential perpetrators, but also on men as potential change agents as allies with women to end rape on campus. As bell hooks (2004) explained, "Men have a tremendous contribution to make to feminist struggle in the area of exposing, confronting, opposing, and transforming the sexism of their male peers" (p. 563).

Over the past 25 years, a number of interventions directed at men's role in ending sexual assault against women have been developed (Berkowitz, 1994; T. L. Davis, 2000; Foubert & McEwen, 1998; Katz, 1995, 2006; Kilmartin, 2001; Kivel, 1992; Men Can Stop Rape, 2002). Although the literature on the evaluation of these rape prevention programs is still growing, the current evidence indicates that engaging men as partners to prevent violence and capitalizing on the role of male peer influence toward positive change is more effective than using blame and approaching men only as potential perpetrators (Berkowitz, 2004). The way this content is conveyed, or what Davis (2000) calls "program process," is also important. The pedagogical approach outlined here shares the approach we have found useful in encouraging men to take responsibility and understand that rape and other forms of violence against women are men's issues and illustrate the concrete actions men and women can take to create meaningful social change toward ending rape.

HOW MEN TOO ARE HARMED BY VIOLENCE AGAINST WOMEN

The uncomfortable reality is that men do rape. Although not all men are rapists, the overwhelming majority of rapists are men. For college men, acknowledging this fact calls into question their own behaviors and the behaviors of their male peers. Acknowledging this reality also validates women's concerns and fears of men, fears men's male privilege (McIntosh, 1988), and allows men to ignore or dismiss. As long as some men rape, many women's fear of men as potential rapists is not irrational or paranoid, but informed. When we ask college men, "Do you think you have ever been feared?" most men pause to think and then answer, "No." When we then ask college women to raise their hands if they think a particular man in the audience who has said that he isn't feared has ever been feared on campus, all but a few rare hands go up in the air. This is a shocking yet important realization for many college men, especially those who have never considered that they might be feared simply because they are men. The frustration of this recognition can trigger anger and a desire to work toward change. We have found that showing men what they personally can gain from working to end rape can be an effective strategy to engage men as allies, particularly men who have never before considered men's responsibility in ending rape.

As men, we will never know what it is like to be a woman on a college campus or in society in general, but we do know exactly what it is like to be feared as potential rapists. As men who have lived and worked on college campuses for many years, we notice it when walking alone across campus, particularly at night. A woman walking alone will often hold her keys to use as a weapon, dial 9-1-1 on her cell phone and wait to hit send, pull the mace out of her purse, or cross the street to avoid us all together. In that moment we are being feared as potential rapists. We are not being seen for our intelligence, our caring, or our humanity. We have also struggled with how to let women know that we are not men who need to be feared and reclaim our humanity in the process. We could try crossing the street, or will she wonder if he is just circling around? We could put our hands in our pockets, or will she wonder what is he grabbing for? Should we slow down, or will she wonder what is he plotting? Should we speed up or will she think he is attacking? Should we say, "Hi, I'm not a rapist. I'm just trying to get home," as we pass each other? Unfortunately, as long as some men do rape, our efforts to reclaim our humanity and prove that we need not be feared will be futile.

Men's loss of humanity does not begin to compare to the very real and very direct physical and sexual violence that women experience in a rape culture. But men are also being hurt by men's violence against women and a culture that permits and even encourages men's violence. As long as some men rape, all men will lose the freedom to not be feared and be perceived as who we really are. For the authors personally, being feared does not leave us feeling powerful, in control, or masculine in any way. Instead we feel angry, powerless, and sad. However, we do not blame the women who fear us. Despite our frustration, we actually encourage women to fear us if that is what is required for them to take the precautions necessary to protect themselves. Instead, we blame the men who do rape and the rape culture supporting their behavior for our loss of humanity. It is because of the violence of some men that women's fear of us is nothing more than necessary, informed, and rational. And we personally also share some responsible for this violence because we have not confronted our male peers or spoken up against the rape culture as often as we could. By working to end rape, men are not only seeking to keep women safe from violence, men are also working to gain their own freedom to be perceived as who they really are, in their full humanity. Recognizing men's own self-interest may not be the most important reason for men to work to end rape, but it can be an effective starting point from which to engage many college men for the first time and a powerful tool for sustaining our efforts. Fostering men's self-interest in addition to the altruism to help women can lead to men being more consistent, sustainable, accountable, and effective allies with women (Edwards, 2006).

INFORMED CONSENT

To be effective in ending rape, college men must first be clear about their own behavior and their own conceptualization of consent to be sure they themselves are not and will not be rapists. Men are often misinformed about what constitutes rape and what constitutes consensual sex by the rape culture. By clearly explaining informed consent and accurately defining the differences between rape and sex, those seeking to prevent sexual assault on campus may not only prevent men from becoming what Berkowitz (2005) described as "unintentional perpetrators" but may also empower men and women to confront their male peers and the rape culture.

Most college men we speak with eagerly agree that rape is a bad, terrible, immoral thing, but they do not see the point of rape prevention education for themselves because they personally have never raped and would never rape a woman. These men have often bought into myths and misperceptions about men who rape. Many men and women conjure up the image of the rapist as a shady, smelly, often racialized (Brownmiller, 1976; Mann & Selva, 1979) predator lurking in the bushes. Although stranger rape is an issue, 84% of women who experienced rape or attempted rape knew the male perpetrator (Koss et al., 1987). The fact that people racialize this image of the perpetrator is a myth not supported by data, as perpetrators overwhelmingly tend to target victims within their own racial group, (A. Davis, 1981; Greenfeld, 1997; Hirsch, 1981) and is purely a manifestation of individual racism and the racism in our culture. Of the 1 in 12 college men who admitted on a survey to acting in a way that met the legal definition of rape, 84% of these men did not view their actions as illegal (Koss et al., 1987). College men must begin asking themselves about their own behavior and whether or not they are one of those men who are raping women and don't know it. These unknowing rapists have been "mis-educated" about the difference between rape and sex. They have been taught by our culture, through media, sports, peers, parents, and so on, that their behavior is acceptable and normal, not rape.

Consent is generally an informed verbal or nonverbal "yes." If she says "no," she has not given consent. It is also important to note that consent is not the absence of a "no," it is the presence of a "yes" and assumes that a question has been asked (Domitrz, 2003). Rape also happens when women are unable to give informed consent. Generally, in the following situations, informed consent cannot be given: if the victim is under the age of consent (often defined as younger than 16 or 18 years old), developmentally disabled, asleep or unconscious, drugged, or drunk. When we speak with college audiences, the only questions we get are about informed consent when alcohol is involved. These questions arise because students recognize that the sex scene and the alcohol scene on campus are deeply intertwined.

Generally, the legal question of sexual assault is whether or not the perpetrator knew or should have known if "the victim" or "the woman" was intoxicated to a point where she could not give informed consent (Sokolow, 2004). Students often want a blood alcohol level or number of drinks with which to gauge informed consent, but there is no magic number. Students also want to know how others will decide if the alleged perpetrator knew or should have known if she was unable to give informed consent. These are questions for a jury. More importantly, why would any man want to risk it? The legal consequences are significant, but more important are the very real damages done to another human being. In fact, it is rare when we meet college men who do not already know and empathize with a survivor of sexual assault. There is significant scholarly support for cultivating empathy in men as a means of addressing sexual assault (Berg, Lonsway, & Fitzgerald, 1999; Berkowitz, 2004; Dietz, Littman, & Bentley, 1984; Foubert, 2000; O'Donohue, Yeater, & Fanetti, 2003).

Because so many men who rape don't consider their actions rape, effective prevention programs must clearly define informed consent. Doing so not only helps men avoid becoming unknowing perpetrators, but also empowers men to confront their peers beyond the immediate audience. These participants can also be encouraged to identify, recognize, and confront the rape culture that continues to mis-educate us all about rape and sex.

RAPE CULTURE

Once men are motivated to end rape, they must not only understand informed consent and their own behavior, but also identify and confront the rape culture (Buchwald, Fletcher, & Roth, 1993) around us everyday. The rape culture is complex and hard to describe concretely, but four main components of the rape culture include objectifying women (Kimmel, 2004; Plummer, 1999); subordinating women's intelligence, capability, and humanity (Johnson, 1997); associating masculinity with sexual conquest (Brod, 1987; Capraro, 1994; Kivel, 1992; Marx, 2003; Plummer, 1999); and supporting other intersecting forms of oppression such as racism, homophobia, and classism (Connell, 1987). Through these messages the rape culture not only impacts individual men's behavior, but also blinds men from the realities of rape and especially men's responsibility and role in ending rape.

Rape Culture in Society

Using prominent examples from popular culture, we illustrate how the prevalence of these messages can make it easy to overlook the powerful messages that foster a rape culture. If students have never noticed the rape culture around them, we explain that is because it is *everywhere,* not because it is *not there.* We have found success with college students deconstructing powerful examples such as Kobe Bryant's statement about his rape trial, Janet Jackson and Justin Timberlake's Super Bowl halftime show, and a Fetish perfume magazine advertisement.

Kobe Bryant

The national dialogue on Los Angeles Lakers basketball star Kobe Bryant and his recent trial for rape offers a prime example about how the culture sends messages that contradict clear definitions of informed consent. After his criminal case had been dismissed with prejudice, meaning that it could not be retried, Bryant released a public statement stating in part, "Although I truly believe this encounter between us was consensual, I recognize now that she did not and does not view this incident the same way I did."

According to Bryant's own statement, he raped the woman. In this statement, Bryant is reflecting back and acknowledging that at the time intercourse occurred it was not consensual for her. Yet, at the time Bryant thought this was sex and not rape. It is important to consider how Bryant was mis-educated about what is rape and what is sex. It is important to acknowledge that issues of gender, celebrity, class, and race are all at play here. It might be valuable for the media to consider Bryant's education as a man in society; the way the society treats athletes of Bryant's stature as celebrities; or what he learned about sex, sexual conquest, and manhood in the hypermasculine environment of professional sports. It is also important, especially for White men such as the authors of this article, not to ignore the racial dynamics of this situation in a sociohistorical context and the ways in which accusations of rape, almost always from White men not White women, have historically been used as a tool of racism against Black men. Unfortunately, these are not the conversations that took place in the mainstream media.

The discussion on television sports talk shows, such as ESPN's *Sportcenter* or FOX's *The Best Damn Sports Show Period,* the night Bryant released his statement was not about Bryant's shocking admission of rape and the implications for our culture. Instead the sports pundits' conversation was about Bryant's *vindication* and whether or not this charge would give him "street cred" and actually garner him more lucrative endorsements (which it did) as his status rose among young men, especially young Black men in the views of these talking heads.

When one man's admitted rape is portrayed as vindication and "street cred" by the combination of two powerful cultural influencers, sport and media, what message does that send to men and women? As a society we can all be concerned about Bryant's mis-education and the tragic consequences for at least one woman we know about. But a more pertinent issue is what the media's coverage of this incident is teaching a whole generation of young men and what this could mean for a whole generation of young women. By using this example to illustrate how men are routinely mis-educated about informed consent and definitions of rape and sex, sexual assault prevention educators can help men and women recognize these false messages.

Super Bowl Halftime

The halftime show of the 2004 Super Bowl offers another prominent case study with which to deconstruct the rape culture. It is rare that any of the college students we have spoken with did not see the incident either during the Super Bowl or in countless replays since then. Students often have described what happened as "wardrobe malfunction" or "Janet exposed herself." This is indeed how the mainstream media has discussed the incident almost universally. However, Janet Jackson did not expose herself. Justin Timberlake reached over and removed clothing from Janet Jackson, exposing her breast as he sang the lyrics, "I'll have you naked by the end of this song." Assuming that they both planned what happened beforehand, this was a staged sexual assault in front of a national television audience of 81 million people who watched it live and many millions more who watched it in replay since.

There was a national outcry in the following weeks about Janet Jackson's obscenity and nudity. Unfortunately, this victim blaming is all too common (Bell, Kuriloff, & Lottes, 1994; Bridges & McGail, 1989; Dietz & Byrnes, 1981; Dietz et al., 1984; Krahe, 1988; Luginbuhl & Mullin, 1981) and also contributes to a rape culture by condoning or ignoring the actions of men who rape and attributing the responsibility for the attack on the woman being raped. Is sexual assault so common for a man that we do not even pay attention to his actions, even when we see it replayed over and over? How do men watching the mainstream media coverage of this incident not learn the lesson that if they tear the clothes off a woman, thus exposing her breast, that society will discuss how obscene she is and ignore him all together?

Even in this staged sexual assault there were consequences for the victim but not the perpetrator. Both Janet Jackson and Justin Timberlake were scheduled to perform at the Grammy Awards a week after the Super Bowl in preparation for new albums being released. Despite the fact that both apologized and that Justin Timberlake was the "perpetrator" in this staged assault, it was Janet Jackson who was pressured out of performing and even attending the Grammy's. Justin Timberlake, on the other hand, attended and performed with little concern from anyone in the mainstream media.

There also has been little discussion of the role of racial dynamics in this situation either. As two White men, we suggest that the mainstream media might have discussed the incident differently if Sean P. "Diddy" Combs, a Black man, ripped off clothing exposing the breast of Jessica Simpson, a White woman. By carefully deconstructing this incident, educators can help students learn how to see the subtle, yet powerful messages, that foster a rape culture by encouraging or condoning victim blaming, abdicating men's responsibility, and ignoring the context of race and racism.

Fetish Perfume

An ad for Fetish Scent perfume offers a final case study illustrating the rape culture in society. The ad has been part of Jean Kilbourne's (2000) critique of objectifying images of women in advertising. In the ad, a woman is pictured from the chest up wearing a small bikini top, her blonde hair disheveled, eyes dark and puffy, and she is touching her cheek with two fingers as though she has just been hit. Although airbrushed perfection and unrealistic expectations of beauty are problematic, this desensitization has its cost as well. This glamorized view of women as victims socializes men and women to believe that women looking like victims of violent acts are normal or even worse, beautiful and sexy. If the victimization of women becomes normal, men and women may stop asking if a woman is okay when she is walking across campus looking disheveled in the early morning. When we look further at this ad we see that the tagline is "cleverly" placed over the top of her cleavage. The tagline reads "fetish #16: Apply generously to your neck so he can smell the scent as you shake your head 'no.'" This ad contradicts even the problematic and incomplete message of "no means no" and replaces it with "no means maybe," or "no means yes," or directed specifically at men, "no means try harder."

This type of advertising is all too common. Victoria's Secret recently ran an ad for their new product, Basic Instinct perfume. This ad, for a perfume named after a movie with sexualized violence and violent sexuality, features a model with disheveled hair on the floor with her hands apparently tied behind her back as her little black dress falls off (Janson, 2005). Not only is the perfume named after a movie known for violent sex, but the ad also includes the slogan, "As daring as fragrance gets."

These prominent examples illustrate the regularity with which society sends messages that confuse sex with rape, blame the victim, and make violence against women sexually alluring. When men and women learn to recognize how these messages contribute to a rape culture, they can be motivated to take a stand against these messages in our society. Individuals can identify and deconstruct these messages to friends and family or confront them more directly by calling, writing, emailing, or boycotting the magazines, radio and television programs, and corporations who either create or distribute these messages.

Rape Culture on Campus

Not only can college men and women identify and speak-up about these messages in our culture at large, the rape culture is also prominent in everyday life on college campuses. If educators are to be successful addressing rape on campus, they must teach students to be just as savvy about their own campus culture as they are about the society at large. By recognizing the subtle, but powerful, messages fostering a rape culture in their own personal sphere of influence, individual students can be empowered to create social change within their own communities large and small. Offensive T-shirts are a useful as a way of illustrating, dissecting, and discussing how to address the rape culture on campus because they exemplify the kinds of messages that are common on college campuses because they are viewed as acceptable, cool, or funny.

Big Johnson T-shirt

The Big Johnson series of T-shirts and others like them that can often be seen on college campuses perpetuate violence against women through their messages. These T-shirts are a series of surf shop T-shirts depicting a "dweeby" little man with two or more large-breasted women with some "clever" reference to the size of his penis, using the phrase "Big Johnson." These T-shirts and others like them are problematic for three reasons: they define masculinity by penis size and sexual conquest, they objectify women, and they subordinate women's intelligence.

First, these T-shirts measure masculinity by penis size. The traditional definition of masculinity in the mainstream society often defines masculinity by penis size or sexual conquest rather than qualities such as intelligence, integrity, an ability to recognize in oneself and express to others a wide range of human emotions, the capability to foster meaningful human relationships, or commitments to causes greater than oneself. As men, we are offended when more complex versions of masculinity emphasizing men's humanity are dismissed and men are instead measured simply by penis size or their sexual conquests. We have too much faith in men to settle for that. Second, these T-shirts objectify women. The women drawn in these T-shirts are portrayed as little more than a pair of breasts. When men see women portrayed as parts and mere objects over and over again in movies, television, magazines, music lyrics, and other aspects of popular culture, sooner or later it can get a little bit easier for some men to treat women as objects. Finally, these T-shirts portray women as unintelligent.

The message of the T-shirts is that these women are only with this dweeby guy because he has a Big Johnson. In addition to objectifying men, it also sends a message that a Big Johnson is a good reason to stay with even a dweeby guy. That is not so different from a message that says, "Maybe he's not so nice to me but since he's good in bed, so I should stay with him." Or perhaps, "Maybe he hits me but he's the captain of the football team so I should stay with him." Messages like these send poor messages to both men and women about what women seek and tolerate in relationships.

Because these T-shirts contribute to the rape culture, men and women can be encouraged to confront people wearing these T-shirts and make it clear that these shirts are not funny or cool. College men and women can be encouraged to do this by simply saying, "I don't like your T-shirt." It is remarkable how often this simple statement leads to conversations with those wearing these T-shirts, overwhelmingly men in our experience, about definitions of masculinity and the objectification of women. However, even if the person wearing the T-shirt isn't interested in this discussion, if others join together to confront people wearing these shirts, men and women can change the culture on campus that says that wearing these shirts and the messages they communicate is acceptable, funny, or even popular.

Party Scene

When talking with college students, we often use a short quote, based in part on the Big Johnson T-shirts, to foster realistic conversations about the party scene on campus and how it promotes a rape culture. The quote states, "You talk to me at a party, with your beer breath, in your Big Johnson T-shirt, and tell me I should have another drink. Gimme a sec while I swoon, Okay? . . . You're so transparent."

For many women, this quote is such a realistic depiction of the party scene that they find it funny and get a very clear visual image. College women asked to explain the visual image the quote conjures up often tell us what the man *smells like*. For these women this is not an imagined or hypothetical situation that they can relate to because they've heard about it or seen it on television. They can tell us what the man smells like because it is their very real experience of the party scene on campus. These women almost always tell us that the scene this quote describes is taking place at a "frat party" or the hockey, soccer, football, rugby, or lacrosse house party. Nevertheless, it is almost always an exclusively all-male living environment hosting these events. Many college men on the campuses we visit who are a part of these groups are angry that this is how they are perceived. Their anger is a good thing. Too often men's anger has been associated with violence; instead men's anger can be connected to a sense of social justice and serve as a guide to social change (Kivel, 1992). This stigma of all-male groups is another way sexual assault hurts men, in this case particularly the public image of fraternity men and male college athletes. Despite their anger with this stigma, men in these groups will often admit that the stigma is actually an accurate reflection of what goes on in these all male groups and the events that they hold. Men can be encouraged to use this anger as motivation to be leaders to change the culture of their fraternities, athletic teams, and the overall campus community.

Only members of these groups can change the perception and the stigma. Men in these groups can begin by having different kinds of parties, by saying "I don't like your T-shirt" while wearing their chapter letters or team jersey, and by publicly confronting the behavior of other all-male organizations fostering a rape culture. This kind of leadership is at the heart of what we believe it should mean to be a male college athlete or in a fraternity and the kind of leadership that is all too often missing.

These are some of the examples educators can use to make explicit links between common campus events and the rape culture. By role modeling concrete strategies to confront the rape culture on campus, educators can give men and women tools to work against the rape culture.

SUMMARY

Most college men want to be allies working against sexual assault and are uncomfortable with the overtly sexist behaviors of their male peers (Fabiano et al., 2003). Despite this discomfort, many college men fail to confront this sexist behavior or even engage in it themselves. The pedagogical approach to working with college men to end rape seeks to motivate men to change individual behavior, speak out against the sexism of their male peers, and confront the rape culture.

When men, who are often blinded by male privilege, recognize that because some men rape, perhaps all men are feared as potential rapists, they begin to see how men's violence against women takes away men's humanity as well. Acknowledging men's loss in a rape culture does not compare men's loss of freedom, authenticity, and humanity to the physical and sexual violence women experience. However, those aspiring to prevent sexual assault on college campuses should not overlook that for many men this recognition can be an initial motivation for them to begin to examine their own socialized behavior.

It is critical to encourage men to examine their own socialization because of the ways men have been mis-educated about rape and sex. Most college men who have engaged in behavior that meets the legal definition of rape do not see anything wrong with what they have done (Koss et al., 1987). With a clear definition of informed consent, college men can better avoid becoming unknowing perpetrators and positively influence their male peers.

Mis-educating men about rape and sex is just one way the rape culture encourages, condones, and teaches rape. Men may also be motivated to speak out against aspects of the rape culture to work as allies with women for social change. By carefully examining prominent examples from popular culture and common campus occurrences, student affairs and faculty educators in higher education can use this approach to illustrate for college men and women how to identify and deconstruct the rape culture. Furthermore, by role modeling concrete strategies to confront these messages that support violence against women, college student educators using this pedagogical approach can encourage men and women to create a new campus culture in which aspects of the rape culture are unpopular and unacceptable. Once college men realize that they too are harmed by violence against women and the culture that supports it, men can be motivated to work with women as social change agents to end rape.

REFERENCES

Bell, S. T., Kuriloff, P. J., & Lottes, I. (1994). Understanding attributions of blame in stranger rape and date rape situtation: An examination of gender, race, identification, and students' social perceptions of rape victims. *Journal of Applied Social Psychoogy, 24*, 1719–1734.

Berg, D. R., Lonsway, K. A., & Fitzgerald, L. F. (1999). Rape prevention education for men: The effectiveness of empathy-induction techniques. *Journal of College Student Development, 40*, 219–234.

Berkowitz, A. D. (1994). A model acquaintance rape prevention program for men. In A. D. Berkowitz (Ed.), *Men and rape: Theory, research, and prevention programs in higher education* (vol. 65). San Francisco: Jossey-Bass.

Berkowitz, A. D. (2004, October). *Working with men to prevent violence against women: An overview*. Retrieved December 1, 2004, from http://www.vawnet.org/DomesticViolence/Research/VAWnetDocs/

Berkowitz, A. D. (2005, October). *The state of men's programming: Where have we been, where are we now, and where are we going?* Paper presented at the National Conference on Sexual Assault in Our Schools, Orlando, FL.

Bridges, J. S., & McGail, C. A. (1989). Attributions of responsibilty for date and stranger rape. *Sex Roles, 21*, 273–286.

Brod, H. (1987). *The making of masculinities: The new men's studies*. Boston: Allen & Unwin.

Brownmiller, S. (1976). *Against our will: Men, women and rape*. Harmondsworth, England: Penguin.

Buchwald, E., Fletcher, P., & Roth, M. (Eds.). (1993). *Transforming a rape culture*. Minneapolis, MN: Milkweed Editions.

Capraro, R. L. (1994). Disconnected lives: Men, masculinity, and rape prevention. In A. D. Berkowitz (Ed.), *Men and rape: Theory, research, and prevention programs in higher education*. (vol. 65, pp. 21–34). San Francisco: Jossey Bass.

Connell, R. W. (1987). *Gender and power*. Palo Alto, CA: Stanford University Press.

Davis, A. (1981). Rape, racism, and the myth of the Black rapist. In *Women, race, and class* (pp. 172–201). New York: Vintage Books.

Davis, T. L. (2000). Programming for men to reduce sexual violence. In *Powerful programming for student learning: Approaches that make a difference* (vol. 90, pp. 79–89). San Francisco, CA: Jossey Bass.

Dietz, S. R., & Byrnes, L. E. (1981). Attribution of responsibility for sexual assault: The influence of observer empathy and defendant occupation and attractiveness. *Journal of Psychology, 108*, 17–29.

Dietz, S. R., Littman, M., & Bentley, B. J. (1984). Attribution of responsibility for rape: The influence of observer empathy, victim resistance, and victim attractiveness. *Sex Roles, 10*, 261–280.

Domitrz, M. J. (2003). *May I kiss you? A candid look at dating, communication, respect, and sexual assault awareness*. Greenfield, WI: Awareness Publications.

Edwards, K. E. (2006). *Aspiring ally identity development: A conceptual model*. Unpublished manuscript, College Park, MD.

Fabiano, P. M., Perkins, H. W., Berkowitz, A. D., Linkenbach, J., & Stark, C. (2003). Engaging men as social justice allies in ending violence against women: Evidence for a social norms approach. *Journal of American College Health, 52*, 105–112.

Fischer, B., Cullen, F. T., & Turner, M. G. (2000). *The sexual victimization of college women.* Washington, D.C.: U.S. Department of Justice, National Institute of Justice.

Foubert, J. (2000). The longitudinal effects of a rape-prevention program on fraternity men's attitudes, behavioral intent, and behavior. *Journal of American College Health, 48*, 158–163.

Foubert, J., & McEwen, M. (1998). An all-male rape prevention peer education program: Decreasing fraternity men's behavioral intent to rape. *Journal of College Student Development, 39*, 548–556.

Greenfeld, L. A. (1997). *Sex offenses and offenders: An analysis of data on rape and sexual assault.* Washington D.C.: U.S. Department of Justice, Bureau of Justice Statistics.

Hirsch, M. F. (1981). *Women and violence.* New York: Van Nostrand Reinhold.

hooks, b. (2004). Men: Comrades in struggle. In M. S. Kimmel & M. A. Messner (Eds.), *Men's lives* (6th ed., pp. 555–563). Boston: Allyn and Bacon.

Janson, L. (2005). The many faces of Victoria's Secret. *Proteus: A Journal of Ideas*, 25–30.

Johnson, A. G. (1997). *The gender knot: Unraveling our patriarchal legacy.* Philadelphia: Temple University Press.

Katz, J. (1995). Reconstructing masculinity in the locker room: The mentors in violence prevention project. *Harvard Educational Review, 65*, 163–174.

Katz, J. (2006). *The macho paradox: Why some men hurt women and how all men can help*. Naperville, IL: Sourcebooks.

Kilbourne, J. (Writer) (2000). Killing Us Softly 3: Advertising's image of women [Videorecording]. North Hampton, MA: Media Education Foundation.

Kilmartin, C. T. (2001). *Sexual assault in context: Teaching college men about gender*. Holmes Beach, FL: Learning Publications.

Kimmel, M. S. (2004). Clarence, William, Iron Mike, Tailhook, Senator Packwood, Spur Posse, Magic . . . and us: A second look. In M. S. Kimmel & M. A. Messner (Eds.), *Men's Lives* (6th ed., pp. 565–579). Boston: Allyn and Bacon.

Kivel, P. (1992). *Men's work: How to stop the violence that tears our lives apart.* Center City, MN: Hazelden.

Koss, M. P., Gidycz, C. A., & Wisniewski, N. (1987). The scope of rape: Incidence and prevalence of sexual aggression and victimization in a national sample of higher education students. *Journal of Applied Social Psychology, 19,* 1182–1197.

Krahe, B. (1988). Victim and observer characteristics as determinants of responsibility attributions to victims of rape. *Journal of Applied Social Psychology, 18,* 50–58.

Luginbuhl, J., & Mullin, C. (1981). Rape and responsibility: How and how much is the victim blamed? *Sex Roles, 7,* 547–559.

Mann, O. R., & Selva, L. H. (1979). The sexualization of racism: The Black as rapist and White justice. *Western Journal of Black Studies, 3,* 168.

Marx, J. (2003). *Season of life: A football star, a boy, a journey to manhood.* New York: Simon & Schuster.

McIntosh, P. (1988). *White privilege and Male privilege: A personal account of coming to see correspondences through work in Women's studies.* Wellesley, MA: Wellesley College Center for Research on Women.

Men Can Stop Rape. (2002). *Visible allies: Engaging men in preventing sexism and sexual violence.* Unpublished Manuscript, Washington, D.C.

O'Donohue, W., Yeater, E. A., & Fanetti, M. (2003). Rape prevention with college males: The roles of rape myth acceptance, victim empathy, and outcome expectancies. *Journal of Interpersonal Violence, 18,* 513–531.

Plummer, D. (1999). *One of the boys: Masculinity, homophobia, and modern manhood.* Binghamton, NY: Harrington Park Press.

Sokolow, B. A. (2004). *Understanding campus sexual assault: The consent construct.* Paper presented at the Association for Student Judicial Affairs, Clearwater, FL.

Yeater, E. A., & O'Donohue, W. (1999). Sexual assault prevention programs: Current issues, future direction, and the potential efficacy of intervention with women. *Clinical Psychology Review, 7,* 739–771.

A Man's Academy? The Dissertation Process as Feminist Resistance

Jennifer R. Wolgemuth
Research Fellow
Charles Darwin University
Darwin, Australia

Clifford P. Harbour
Associate Professor
Colorado State University
Fort Collins, Colorado

The academy is a gendered institution that promotes and requires the adoption of a particularly masculine way of learning and producing knowledge. Commonly accepted notions of what constitutes a successful academic devalue emotions, vulnerability, and dependence in interpersonal relationships. Using Bourdieu's concept of the habitus, our analysis focuses on a collaborative narrative of a critical incident between a graduate student working on her dissertation and a faculty member pursuing tenure. In our analysis we critique the masculine bias of the academic habitus, revealing how graduate student and faculty interactions can replicate gendered power relations in the academy and shedding light on avenues of resistance. We conclude by explaining how the practice of co-mentoring within a feminist framework may help conceptualize a new kind of successful academic—one who sees the rationality in emotions and the emotions in rationality, as well as the strength in vulnerability and the vulnerability in strength.

INTRODUCTION

The process of academic socialization begins in graduate school and extends through the tenure and promotion process. It is reinforced as faculty refine and then pass along their values and practices to others (Leonard, 2001; Tierney & Bensimon, 2000). However, the doctoral student phase is where the academic community does some of its most rigorous work to produce successful academics. This socialization process is revealed, at least in part, by the multitude of texts advising students how to navigate Ph.D. programs (Fitzpatrick, 1998; Graves & Varma, 1997; Phillips & Pugh, 2005; Tinkler & Jackson, 2004), including special guides for women (Leonard, 2001), Latina/os (Castellanos, Gloria, & Kamimura, 2006), and African Americans (Farmer, 2004).

Despite these reports, however, the literature on doctoral study has been slow to acknowledge what feminists in higher education have known for decades: the academy is gendered. And, it is gendered in a way that promotes and frequently requires the adoption of a particularly *masculine* way of learning and producing knowledge. As Leonard (2001) states, the academy:

> in both its old, professorial and new, managerial forms, and the entire Enlightenment project of Science, is gendered. . . . [Members of the academy] have embedded within them an antagonism, a project of masculinity, of (super) rationality, of scientism, of independence which attempts to keep safe and secure and strong by keeping or driving out or denying elements associated with femininity (emotions, bodies, acceptance of the diversity of humanity, personal interconnections). (p. 43)

Because academic culture is masculine, successful academics are often those who learn to become manlike (Martin, 2000; Reay & Ball, 2000). Yet, we want to be clear. We neither assume academic culture is monolithic nor do we assume the masculine subject touted by academic cultures is coterminous with individual men in academe. Rather academic culture produces masculine and feminine subjectivities that are taken up and enacted by individuals.

This article concerns a "critical incident" between a male professor and a female graduate student. Similar to Ng (2000) and others (e.g., Chapman & Sork, 2001; Reay, 2004), we focus our analysis on autobiographical narratives of salient interactions between a faculty member and a graduate student to illustrate how masculine ways of doing education are privileged over feminine ones. Yet, a paradox emerged. Both the male professor and the female graduate student claim "feminist" identities. In our everyday interactions we seek to undermine the academy's hierarchical gendered structure. Using Bourdieu's (1977, 1990, 2001) concept of *habitus*, this article analyzes a critical incident to understand how feminists with the best of intentions can serve as conduits and reinforcers of a masculine academic culture.

To accomplish this task we have organized our discussion in the following manner. First, we provide an explication of our theoretical framework. This framework is grounded on Bourdieu's *habitus* and the belief that human action is often based on values that have been uncritically internalized in cultural settings. Our framework also includes insights gained from literature regarding the academy's masculine academic culture and implications for feminine ways of doing scholarship. In particular, we focus on three distinct, but overlapping areas associated with femininity that are overtly and/or covertly devalued in academe. These are emotions, vulnerability, and dependence in interpersonal relationships. Second, we discuss the standpoint and method that guided our study. Third, we present excerpts from our narratives constructed as a part of our work to analyze our critical incident. Fourth we present our interpretation of the incident and make meaning of our interactions. Then, we reflect on our experiences and offer suggestions on how faculty and graduate students can resist the masculinity of the academy in their work. Finally, we conclude with reflections and recommendations for further research.

THEORETICAL CONTEXT

Bourdieu's Habitus

For Bourdieu (1990), *habitus* is the system or systems of "durable, transposable dispositions. . . . which generate and organize practices and representations" that guide human action (p. 53). These dispositions lead people to act strategically in ways that accept the fundamental circumstances of the society along with existing systems that allocate social opportunities. However, to say individuals act strategically is not to say that human action is simply a consequence of calculated decisions based on the application of external rules or norms. To be sure, individuals may behave in ways that are consistent with certain external rules or norms. But, substantive human action is better understood as being guided by social structures that have been internalized over time. As one of Bourdieu's well regarded commentators has observed, "*habitus* results from early socialization experiences in which external structures are internalized" (Swartz, 1997, p. 103). When these external structures are internalized, "broad parameters and boundaries of what is possible or unlikely for a particular group in a stratified social world develop" (Swartz, 1997, p. 103). For us, the significance of this concept is that it explains why individuals may act in ways that conform to social structures directly contradicting the actor's social or economic interests.

For example, a student may appear to accept a grade from a professor, even if she believes it is incorrect, because of an institutional rule or norm that assigns faculty authority for evaluating student work. However, a better understanding of this behavior would be gained from examining how the external structure of the university is internalized by students and faculty. This external structure might include the unconscious or unexamined belief that faculty are not only content experts in the respective disciplines but endowed with a certain wisdom or judging power that privileges them in discerning the exact and proper grade for an assignment. This structure would be validated, for example, when a student chooses not to appeal a grade because "it wouldn't be right." Alternatively, this structure would be validated when a grade is affirmed by departmental authorities even when the basis of the grade cannot be adequately justified by the professor. This is to say, both students and faculty may act on dispositions that are a consequence of internalizing external social structures. Of course, *habitus* exists in other dimensions of society.

Bourdieu's (2000) treatise on masculine domination (developed from his study of the Kabyle society) demonstrated how *habitus* shaped gender relations. He explained how dispositions regarding gender assigned women to certain societal functions (those that were an extension of their domestic work—specifically, care, service, and education). These dispositions also placed women in positions subordinate to men and constrained their employment opportunities in secular society. Men, on the other hand, were given primary responsibility for work that involved machines and technical artifacts.

As we explain below, our use of *habitus* in this setting permits us to explain how a faculty member and a graduate student can both inadvertently reify the masculine values in the academy while intending to challenge such values in their work. Our understanding of this behavior follows a conflict that, in turn, led us to more closely examine the literature concerning how the academy regards emotions, vulnerability, and dependence in interpersonal relationships.

Emotions

In most disciplines, academics learn to emphasize rationality and limit emotionality. Consider the following description of a successful academic:

> successful postgraduates emerge with a new identity as competent professionals, able to *argue* their viewpoint with anybody *regardless of status*, *confident* of their knowledge but also aware of its boundaries. This new identity permits them to ask for information when they are aware that they don't know something and to express a lack of understanding when this is necessary, instead of pretending that there is no difficulty for *fear* of being thought stupid. To arrive at this point is what being a postgraduate research student is really all about. (Phillips & Pugh, 2005, p. 5, emphasis added)

The successful academic is rational, adept at argumentation, and unemotional. These qualities often preempt a feminine approach to academic work. As Boler (1999) laments, the prototypical emerging academic is "the rational, curious, engaged, 'balanced,' well-behaved white male student" (p. 140). This kind of professional need not develop a keen sense of empathy or an ability to relate to others with compassion. Boler asks, "Why, in our fear and resistance, do we 'lock out' the possibility of an emotional literacy regarding, for example, our vulnerabilities as well as systems of denial with respect to the pain and joy we necessarily experience in each of our globalized private and classroom lives?" (p. 140).

It is also telling that Phillips and Pugh (2005) mark the ultimate achievement of an academic as reaching a place where s/he can, without fear, express ignorance. Presumably then, the process of getting to this point is characterized by anxiety and fear at "being thought stupid." Indeed, fear is one of few emotions available to academicians so long as it is not expressed (Boler, 1999). Many men may lose this sense of fear while constructing a professional identity. But, it remains for many women because this new professional identity is always already a masculine one. Even if women unquestioningly adopt the habits of the masculinized successful academic, they must negotiate the contradiction of living a feminine life while working in a masculine culture.

One aspect of this contradiction is that women in higher education are "repositories of irrationality" (Boler, 1999, p. 42). Accordingly, to be successful *as women*, they are often expected to do the "emotional labor" and "smile work" associated with their genders (Tierney & Bensimon, 2000). This work places women in a double bind: if they fulfill the expectations of their genders, they fail to meet the criteria of the rational successful academic. As Boler (1999) succinctly notes, "Emotions are assigned as women's dirty work, and then used against her as an accusation of her inferior irrationality" (p. 43).

It is important to note that, despite this dichotomy between (male) rationality and (female) emotion, academic culture is far from unemotional. As Reay (2004) tell us, "…academia relies upon desire, greed, ambition, pride, envy, fear, betrayal, and inequality within an increasingly privatized, competitive market" (p. 35). It is not that rationality is emotionless; rather it is constructed in such a way that emotions associated with women (e.g., sadness, empathy, and love) are excluded in favor of those that are either easily concealed (e.g., desire, envy, fear) or easily harmonized with the values of masculine academic culture (e.g., ambition, pride, inequality). So-called masculine emotions are accepted as the energy and focus needed to succeed. Feminine emotions are rejected as those believed to cloud objectivity and bias research.

While feminine emotions are devalued and their expression interpreted as a sign of weakness, dissertation supervisors are now being encouraged to give effective feedback with a balance between appreciation and criticism (Phillips & Pugh, 2005). Despite this positive development, many disciplines and departments resist efforts to acknowledge feminine emotions in scholarly endeavors. Women or others in "feminized" positions remain the academy's "emotional laborers;" and when they attempt to explain the relevancy of emotions in research or teaching, they are often devalued as academics (Tierney & Bensimon, 2000).

Vulnerability

While expressing certain emotions is indicative of an "emotional" vulnerability, academic culture also frowns upon expressions of rational vulnerability. In an academic setting rational vulnerability is reflected by an ability to say, "I don't know" or "I don't feel capable." As Phillips and Pugh (2005) point out, successful graduate students are expected to emerge with a new identity and confidence that lets them express this kind of vulnerability. However, it is also the case that the expression of rationale vulnerability may come at a cost for some graduate students. They may be perceived as ignorant or lacking intellectual promise. Faculty on the other hand, having established their intellectual credentials, are permitted to express a wider range of not knowing, especially when the matter is outside their area of defined expertise. It is ironic students are made to feel this way at a time when they should be allowed to express their ignorance. However the process requires that graduate students "fake it 'til you make it." And, as we discussed earlier, the point at which one is perceived to have "made it" is partially determined by gender.

Some women (and men) never feel they've "made it" and report that even when tenured, they feel like an outsider in academia (Tierney & Bensimon, 2000). Even when women have earned the right to say, "I don't know," they are more likely to be negatively judged for not knowing (Jamieson, 1995). Therefore, many women employ the fake it 'til you make it strategy throughout their academic careers.

The problem of rational vulnerability comes partly from the definition of a successful academic as "expert." To be an expert means to be all the things we have talked about as associated with masculinity: logical, unemotional, and confident. In this way, women are at a disadvantage when it comes to being perceived as experts. Jamieson's (1995) femininity/competence bind means that a woman seen as feminine "cannot be mature or decisive" (p. 120). To say, "I don't know," reifies her femininity, her incompetence, even if her ignorance concerns a matter beyond her current scope of knowledge.

Dependence

Here we use the word "dependence" because it is placed in opposition to traditional masculine "independence." However, what we mean by dependence is the recognition of the interconnectedness of social life and the value of positive interdependence. Yet, in the independent/dependent binary, reaching out for help or seeking approval are deemed acts of weakness. Phillips and Pugh (2005) talk about the doctoral student experience as one of moving from dependence to independence:

> As students become more involved with their work, so there is a lessening of the need for external approval. In fact your supervisor should be engaged in a kind of a "weaning process" to enable you to become more independent. (p. 74)

To become a successful academic, graduate students must demonstrate an ability to independently synthesize knowledge, construct new concepts, and critique scholarly work at an abstract level. This inevitably tempers the importance assigned to collaboration. Although collaboration may be important in some disciplines, it must always follow independent analysis that reveals the graduate student is entitled to be a part of the community. This pattern of expectation continues as graduate students make the transition to faculty. Sole author publications, for example, are typically accorded more weight in tenure and promotion than multiple authored publications. Leonard (2001) points out:

> Academia also supposedly involves a cooperative search for knowledge, with rewards for honesty and collaboration, but it is in fact often duplicitous, competitive and exploitative. It does not often reward, indeed it sometimes does not even allow, collaboration, as is evident in the Ph.D. itself. (p. 230)

As independence is associated with masculinity, once again we see how qualities associated with femininity are devalued in the academy. Women who work alone may be seen as "independent," but they may also pay the price of challenging the norms of their gender. Women who work collaboratively conform to the expectations of their gender, but their work is sometimes seen as less scholarly or valuable.

STANDPOINT AND METHODS

As feminists we work to expose, challenge, and resist the masculine academic culture and reward "alternative" ways of being a successful academic. We believe that working in collaboration with others we can change academic culture. But, we also work to remain self-critical and evaluate how our actions and unexamined assumptions sometimes reify, rather than resist, oppressive gender structures in the academy. Most importantly, we must acknowledge that our actions often challenge and reify simultaneously. It is from this desire to be reflexive that we analyze a critical incident in an attempt to understand how we reinforced and then resisted traditional academic culture. Given that critical incidents like these will happen, we also seek to highlight spaces of resistance where we can learn to advance an understanding of academic success that includes emotions, vulnerability, and dependence.

To construct a collaborative account of the critical incident under examination, we followed a procedure Ellis and Berger (2003) have identified as an "unmediated co-constructed narrative" (p. 171). They note, "In unmediated co-constructed narratives, the focus turns directly to the self, as researchers examine their own relationships rather than the relationships of others" (p. 171). After we agreed on our tasks of writing about "what happened," we began by composing our narratives alone.

Next we exchanged our stories and discussed them face to face and then via e-mail to create a collaborative version that maintained our perspectives and writing styles. We quickly realized our approaches to composing narratives differed. Jenni employed Ellis's (1991) strategy of emotional recall, which involves evoking "a response in oneself in order to create a more powerful and convincing scene for others to engage" (Tillman-Healy, 2001, p. 176). Cliff wrote his narrative with its academic and gender implications in mind and with less attention to how he felt about the incident. Although both narratives were thorough, we worried that our contrasting styles might reify gender stereotypes that locate women as emotional and men as rational.

We took care to avoid construction of a narrative that might inadvertently reify the masculine academy by discounting the dynamics of our relationship, our vulnerability, and especially our emotions. We agreed with Boler (1999) that emotions tend to be "invisible because neither emotions nor women's and student's daily experiences have been foregrounded" in organizational settings (p. 36). Therefore, Cliff revised his narrative, adding adjectives describing how he had felt at the time, while Jenni added some evaluative statements to her composition. The result was a coconstructed narrative we believe resists the binary of male/logical vs. female/emotional, emphasizing the necessity of emotion in logic and the logic of emotions.

Overall, writing the scholarly personal and co-constructed narratives was a process of reflection: self-reflection, other-reflection, and intersubjective reflection (Richardson, 2000). Our writing helped us learn about ourselves and connect with one another. Yet our analysis brought us to another level where we came to understand how our "selves" were arbiters, enforcers, and ultimately resisters of masculine academic culture. A cultural analysis of our critical incident narratives helped us identify the academy's gendered scripts and hegemonic ideals. This approach also provided us with the opportunity to inscribe our story within the higher education community where members may create, enact, and resist similar gendered scripts. It is our hope that our narrative and its analysis will inform and open up spaces for dialogue about how we perpetuate and resist the gendered scripts that define a "successful academic."

CRITICAL INCIDENT

Since Cliff first agreed to be on Jenni's committee in spring 2003, we had carried on a roaming conversation about the relationship between academic power relations and gender. We each were engaged in our own respective challenges (Jenni was collecting and analyzing her dissertation data, and Cliff was on the tenure clock). But we had established some trust between us; and we each saw in the other a colleague who shared common values, interests, and perspectives. This was checked, however, by a conversation we had in March 2006. The context for this conversation was Colorado State University's School of Education and concerned Jenni's work on her dissertation, a narrative study of masculinity in higher education.

The Question

Jenni: *Having just begun my interviews I was feeling uncertain. This was an unusual feeling for me. I'd always been successful at the university and was confident in my abilities. However, over the past 3 weeks I'd sent out 3 e-mails to my committee asking them about participant selection and interview techniques. As an independent learner I also wasn't accustomed to asking for help. But, I'd chosen and organized my committee as a response community and typically addressed questions to all four members. This was a strategy supported by my advisor, Brian Cobb, and the other three members. So I sat down and typed another question that had been bothering me.*

I wrote, "A participant suggested we should have an interview 'over beers.' I don't think it would be a good idea, and told him so. I don't know what his motives are, but I think he might want to make the interview more casual. The feminist and postmodern interviewing texts I've read all talk about the importance of attending to power in the interview relationship. It's complicated, of course, as a woman interviewing men my gender would have me as less powerful. But as an interviewer I do inhabit a position of power. So I would like the interviews to be casual, but 'over beers' certainly wasn't part of the human subject protocol. I just wondered what you have done in situations like this. Any thoughts?"

Cliff: *I was rushing to prep for my seminar and finish up my list of external reviewers for my tenure portfolio. As I paused to check my "to do" list, Jenni's e-mail popped up on the screen. "Hmmm" I thought, "Jenni always has something interesting to say. . . ."*

The message was to her committee members and reported on her dissertation research. She explained that her participant interviews were proceeding as she had expected. But, the message ended with a request for advice on conducting her next interview. I winced at this last part.

"Don't ask that kind of question!" I thought, "You know what to do. This is your project. Just do it!" I thought about calling Jenni but decided to let it go. "Heck, it was her dissertation," I thought. "She's certainly welcome to ask for suggestions. And besides, Jenni had a very talented and supportive committee. They won't see this as a negative reflection on her ability." I burrowed back into my notes for class. After another half hour, however, I wasn't so sure this approach was best. "OK, Jenni's committee may not raise an eyebrow at her request. But, then again, she may end up at an institution with colleagues that expect her to demonstrate her skills independently. And, they may not tell her they have such expectations. Hmmm, should I jump into this or not?" I dashed off an e-mail, "Jenni, can we talk?"

The Call

Cliff: *We exchanged e-mails and then traded voice mail messages. When we finally connected at the end of the day, I hurriedly asked: "Why did you ask your committee about having drinks at your next interview? You'll soon be a methodologist on dissertation committees! You know what to do! Don't ask. Just do it!"*

Jenni responded with silence and then offered a frank, "I don't see where you're going with this. Can't I ask my committee for advice? Isn't that what they're there for?"

"Well, sure," I replied, "You can ask them for advice. No problem. But, do you really need it? And, wouldn't it be better to decide on a course of action and then notify them so they see you leading your research." "You know," I added, "in a while you'll be out there and your peers may expect you to take a more directive approach. They may expect you to be more independent in your work."

"Well, yes," she responded, "but I'd like some feedback and maybe start a discussion about how others have handled similar situations. That's why I'm asking for advice."

"Oh," I replied.

Jenni: *When I called Cliff, perched on the edge of my desk, I was in for a shock.*

He was direct and measured and said, "Jenni, part of your responsibility as a doctoral student is to demonstrate you know what you're doing." He went on to say, "When you send out these kinds of e-mails, you're inviting doubt and questions about your skills. You need to prove yourself."

Frustrated and angry, I muttered terse one-word responses for the remainder of our conversation. In a quick turn of events I no longer felt safe letting Cliff know how upset I was. Hanging up the phone, I sunk back into my office chair. I was hurt, angry, sad, and confused all at the same time.

"What is the purpose of a dissertation committee?" I wrote in my dissertation journal. "Am I not supposed to ask them questions? Apparently not because I'm hearing I have to prove myself to my committee. I'm confident that I'm a good student and in my ability to make decisions on my own. But on some things I feel less confident. Shouldn't I be able to gather opinions from others? Isn't that what making good decisions is all about? Maybe I'm making a mistake by admitting I don't know. Maybe this is an unacceptable acknowledgement of my vulnerability.

I retreated and Cliff and I did not speak for several months after our conversation. I hoped my silence demonstrated I was working well on my own and had everything "under control."

The Follow-Up

Cliff: *Jenni and I didn't connect later that week or later that month, for that matter. We spoke briefly at a conference, and she said her work was going well. But neither of us reached back to address "the conversation that went awry." By the beginning of the fall semester, however, I wanted to settle past accounts. I sent Jenni an e-mail, apologized for pushing her to be more independent, and suggested it might be better if I stepped off her committee.*

Jenni: *Waiting for me one morning was an e-mail from Cliff, apologizing for causing me any "heartburn." He offered to leave my committee if that's what I wanted. I knew I didn't want him off my committee; his contributions to my work had been invaluable. I realized we had to talk because I could tell from his apology that he didn't understand how much that conversation had affected me. It wasn't heartburn; it was heartache.*

Cliff: *Jenni responded to my e-mail message with a telephone call. "You know," she began, "I've been thinking about that conversation we had back in March. I'd like to process our communication, and share with you how I felt. I also think there may be a gender issue to explore."*

"Sure," I replied. "Let's talk."

Jenni and Cliff: *The meeting was better than we both expected. We met and shared our recollections, feelings, and thoughts. Our discussion affirmed McKenna's (1991) claim that faculty and students are "the starting point for analyzing how our educational practices are both constituted by and constitutive of ongoing relations of power" (p. 118). So, why not dig into this and see what turns up?*

Sharing our stories we worked to understand each other both rationally and emotionally. But, we also recognized that we had reinforced some of the more subtle elements of masculine academic culture. This paper is a result of our desire to understand how two self-identified feminists, collaborating as graduate student and faculty member on a dissertation challenging masculinity in higher education, perpetuated aspects of the academy we both opposed. Our hope is that we have made progress in developing a better understanding of academic work in ways that will facilitate resistance and positive change.

MAKING MEANING

After constructing our narratives, we recognized a good interpretation would need to simultaneously address our interactions; the relevant values of our academic culture; and perhaps most importantly, how these are transmitted, accepted, and challenged in exchanges like the one we discussed above. After reviewing our narratives we concluded that Bourdieu's *habitus* provided the best conceptual framework to begin an explication of our interpretation.

Our focus on *habitus* helps us understand two critical aspects of our interactions. First, at a general level of inquiry, *habitus* explains how we replicate power relations in the academy, especially within relationships between graduate students and faculty. Second, we believe *habitus* explains how a masculine perspective in dissertation research is systematically reproduced at the university. This, in turn, provides a point of transition to our third observation that concerns how Jenni and Cliff transformed their roles as graduate student and faculty member to resist the *habitus* of the masculine academy.

Replicating Power Relations in the Academy

Our replication was discouraging but, we believe, a necessary step to understanding how deeply we had ingrained our academic dispositions. We had tried to develop a collegial relationship that, although influenced by the academic hierarchy, was also independent of it. We had shared our respective accomplishments and setbacks. We were determined to become a part of an emerging feminist community that embraced emotions, vulnerability, and interdependence. Instead, our analysis confirmed that Cliff's attempt to help Jenni develop her academic survival skills had missed the mark and instead pressured her toward a more independent approach to her work—an approach that she had initially decided to set aside. Concurrently, Jenni's hurt was revealed as part incredulity that Cliff had not *already* assumed her independence. Jenni's attempts at collaboration were only permissible to her under the assumption she didn't *really* need the help. Jenni handled her hurt by retreating from Cliff in an "act of independence;" an attempt to demonstrate to Cliff and to herself that she could do it on her own. Cliff and Jenni came to understand that, despite her attempts at collaboration, Jenni largely accepted the proscriptives of the masculine *habitus*. They were essential to her sense of self as a successful academic. When this self-definition was threatened, Jenni retreated, an action that had her deferring to the masculine *habitus*.

These interactions reified the power relations in the academy. They affirmed the authority of faculty over graduate students in ways that could not be justified by a more informed understanding of learning and research. They also replicated the dominance of a masculine approach to dissertation research. We had not succeeded in finding a way to collaborate that allowed for an expression of our emotions and vulnerabilities. As we will explain, however, we were fortunate to realize how we had stumbled and made a commitment to learn from our missteps and analyze them, in a way that we hoped would help others in similar situations.

Our account of these interactions is also consistent with analyses by Leonard (2001), Reay (2004), and Phillips and Pugh (2005). That is, we replicated the power relations of the academy in ways that discounted the importance and relevancy of emotions, vulnerability, and the tension between independence and dependence. Our narratives reveal how both of us struggled to express and hear our emotions of frustration. And, our exchange also showed how this work can be emotionally intense (Leonard, 2001). Jenni experienced feelings of betrayal. Cliff acknowledged a fear that Jenni's success could be undermined if she did not adopt a more independent approach to her work (Reay, 2004). Finally, we each wrestled with finding the right balance between development of dependent and independent approaches to dissertation research (Phillips & Pugh, 2005).

The Masculinization of Dissertation Research

Our analysis and interpretation affirmed that the dissertation process, as a systematic method of "standardizing" graduate students and their research, also played a critical role in replicating masculine dispositions and their associated power relations in the academy. At an abstract or cognitive level, this is evidenced in the common dissertation practice that social science research must "fit into" an existing body of scholarship and explicitly establish relevance to this corpus. Yes, new research can challenge previously reported research findings, theories, and methods. But this challenge must be posed in the language and in the conceptual framework of previous work. Yet, in what now has become a truism, we know "the master's tools will never dismantle the master's house. They may allow us temporarily to beat him at his own game, but they will never enable us to bring about genuine change" (Lorde, 1984, p. 112). Accordingly, we should not expect change when research findings, theories, and methods threaten the persistence of dominant values and behaviors in a masculinized academy.

We contend this is especially true in doctoral research, where masculine assumptions about epistemology and method frequently reinforce the hierarchy that orders relationships between faculty and graduate students in their work (Hesse-Biber, Leavy, & Yaiser, 2004). These assumptions implicitly identify the conditions that must be met in order to determine who "is authorized to tell the truth of the social world" (Bourdieu & Wacquant, 1992, p. 71). Over time, they become internalized through a rigorous socialization process with academic rewards and punishments that ensure dissertation research will be either synthesized with research generated within existing paradigms or excluded from serious consideration because of its failure to establish relevancy to them.

But dissertation research is masculinized in ways that are much more immediate, personal, and emotional. We found that masculine assumptions also operate at an emotional level. For example, Jenni's decision to embrace a more collaborative approach in her relationship with committee members followed many years of success as an independent, high-energy graduate student. Stepping back to consult others before forging ahead was a conscious decision that when practiced seemed to backfire. Similarly, Cliff's suggestion that Jenni adopt a more independent approach to her work was intended to appeal to her sense of ambition and pride.

The reification of masculine assumptions, operating in cognitive and emotional registers, results in a dissertation process that forces graduate students to adhere to established practices and values—even when this counters their desire to honor their identity and move in a new direction. The outcome is not surprising. As we saw in our narratives, Jenni's work began to feel decontextualized because it did not align with the values and beliefs she held at the beginning of her work. Yet we both saw how the academic *habitus* influenced her enactment of "feminine" scholarship. It was only after she'd come to view herself as a successful academic, an independent and logical thinker, that she felt free to pursue more collaborative, emotional, and vulnerable ways of doing scholarship. Even as she challenged them, Jenni continued to reify the values of the masculine *habitus*.

Our interpretation highlights a powerful dimension of how dissertation research is masculinized. Although much academic research is pursued in collaboration with others, either formally or informally, graduate students are led to believe their committees are the best authorities for their work, and they are told that this faculty group is the sole arbiter of the quality of the research. So, graduate students practice collaboration. But, this is done in a setting where recognition and respect for the hierarchy are required.

Resisting the Reproduction of the Masculine *Habitus*

Three insights helped us transform our roles from conduits to resisters. First we recognized, as Tierney (1997) has observed, that a methodical analysis of our interactions would not enable us to see beyond the masculinization that we recognized but were struggling to disarm. Instead, we transformed our discussion into a shared acknowledgement of how our emotions, vulnerabilities, and dependencies pushed each of us into a mindset dominated by competing claims and conflicting interpretations. Second, rather than abandoning these feminine attributes, we used them as a guide to focus a conversation about our experiences in the academy. This discussion became a first step to collaborating in developing a shared perspective that could serve as the beginning of a new understanding of resistance. Finally, we agreed that this resistance would be most meaningful if it could be framed in terms that might offer help to others caught up in the masculine *habitus* of the academy.

We concluded that a return to Bourdieu (1990) would serve as the best conceptual framework to present these thoughts. Beginning with Tierney's (1997) observation that good methods and good thoughts are incapable of dissolving a masculine bias, we rejected a more typical effort to "reason our way" toward a resolution. Instead, we sketched out the kind of principled resistance that we would want to follow in our work with each other and then with others in the years ahead. This approach provided the opportunity to envision a form of critical resistance that would not be limited by its relevancy to the existing masculine values accompanying dissertation research. This is not to say we would ignore those aspects of the academy's *habitus* that limit our thought and action. We agree with Bourdieu that this is not an option. But, we would begin with positing a feminist framework for dissertation research that offers independent grounds for critical resistance.

After further discussion, we agreed that our framework would be guided by the following considerations. First, in our work, we would privilege and search for opportunities to recognize our emotions. Second, we agreed to read acknowledgements of our vulnerability as a "new" strength that reflected our inner confidence and acceptance of the challenges of our work. To understand how this feminist framework might manifest itself in dissertation student-faculty relations, we turned to the literature on feminist mentorship.

Rather than advocate a traditional hierarchical mentoring relationship, we adopted "feminist co-mentoring" to challenge the "power differential of traditional mentoring" (McGuire & Reger, 2003, p. 2003). Yet, at the same time, we could not ignore the power imbalance between us that played an important and positive role in Jenni's dissertation process. As a nontenured faculty member, Cliff's role on Jenni's committee was to serve as a mentor in her research. This experiential imbalance framed our working relationship in the beginning. Jenni benefited from Cliff's scholarly experience and insights about the politics of the academy. But, soon, Cliff benefited from Jenni's feminist perspective and her insights and encouragement on how to share his emotions in his work. Therefore, Jenni became a mentor to Cliff. Sharing our critical incident with you here is both an academic exercise for Jenni, in which she learns from Cliff the art of academic publication, plus an opportunity for Cliff to practice vulnerability as strength. In doing both we hope to play a positive role in promoting a "feminine-friendly" academy.

IMPLICATIONS OF CO-MENTORING

Earlier we suggested a feminist framework for dissertation research, enacted through a co-mentoring relationship. We agree with postmodern conceptualizations that power is not something that can be eliminated in relationships. Instead it constitutes and constructs relationships. Therefore, co-mentoring not only acknowledges the importance of the formal mentor's power, but also strategically and intentionally mobilizes the power of the mentee. In a co-mentoring relationship, the faculty member and graduate student agree to switch roles by asking what the graduate student has to teach the faculty member. In this way the relationship approximates equality in a back-and-forth privileging of the faculty and graduate students' experiences. This is not a model solely applicable to the "feminist-friendly" department. It is, rather, a model we believe can be practiced in a variety of academic disciplines under the philosophy that good dissertation supervision necessitates an open and collaborative mentor–mentee relationship. We believe that inadvertently in some disciplines and intentionally in others, the co-mentoring relationship undercuts the masculine academic *habitus* by encouraging collaboration, sharing of emotions, and engaging professional vulnerability in dissertation research mentoring.

CONCLUSION

Our discussion above explains how what began as a strained conversation became a critical incident, an analyzable narrative revealing avenues of replication and resistance of the masculine academic *habitus*. Coming together and analyzing our conversation was not just a form of resistance that yielded a feminist framework through co-mentoring for dissertation research, it importantly brought us closer through listening and engaging with one another's thoughts and ideas. This article was a collaboration by the standards of our new framework in that we discussed our emotions, aired our vulnerabilities, and offered hope for equitable collaborations, through co-mentoring, across gender and the faculty–graduate student divide.

Yet our collaboration was not without tension. For example, Jenni continued to want to "lay it all out there," while Cliff argued "excessive disclosure" was unnecessary and could undermine the strength and reception of the article's arguments. In the end, co-mentorship allowed Jenni to assist Cliff in practicing vulnerability, and our final writing and editing provided us with a work product that acknowledged our respective needs and interests. Guided by our new framework, the underlying tensions did not disappear; rather we had found a way to acknowledge them that directed us toward our goal—practicing our work in a co-mentoring relationship where we supported each other in our work to resist the academic masculine *habitus*. This resistance opened up a space for us to think and talk differently about the limits and purposes of self-disclosure.

In this article we described a different kind of successful academic: one who sees the emotions in reason and the reason in emotions, the strength in vulnerability and the vulnerability in strength, and works for gender equity in the academy. This academic is critically resistive because s/he refuses to inhabit either end of the academic *habitus's* masculine/feminine binary, but adopts a "self-reflective" both/and position (Hoy, 2005, p. 136). But our analysis is limited by its focus on how emotionality and vulnerability are (not) permitted by the academic *habitus*. Our different kind of successful academic is one example of how this resistance may occur. We acknowledge many resistive academics can be found in higher education, already making significant contributions by challenging the masculine *habitus*. Our hope is this work opens up similar spaces for faculty and graduate students to reflect on and construct alternative frameworks for the successful and resistive academic.

REFERENCES

Bensimon, E. M., & Marshall, C. (2003). Like it or not: Feminist critical policy analysis matters. *Journal of Higher Education, 74*(3). 337–349.

Boler, M. (1999). *Feeling power: Emotions and education*. New York: Routledge.

Bourdieu, P. (1977). *Outline of a theory of practice*. New York: Cambridge University Press.

Bourdieu, P. (1990). *The logic of practice*. Stanford, CA: Stanford University Press.

Bourdieu, P. (2001). *Masculine domination*. Stanford, CA: Stanford University Press.

Bourdieu, P., & Wacquant, L. J. D. (1992). *An invitation to reflexive sociology*. Chicago: The University of Chicago Press.

Castellanos, J., Gloria, A. M., & Kamimura, M. (Eds.). (2006). The Latina/o pathway to the Ph.D.: Abriendo caminos. Sterling, VA: Stylus Publishers.

Chapman, V-L., & Sork, T. J. (2001). Confessing regulation or telling secrets? Opening up the conversation on graduate supervision. *Adult Education Quarterly, 51,* 94–107.

Ellis, C. (1991). Emotional sociology. In N. K. Denzin (Ed.), *Studies in symbolic interaction* (vol. 12, pp. 123–145). Greenwich, CT: JAI Press.

Ellis, C., & Berger, L. (2003). Their story/my story/our story. In J. F. Gubrium & J. A. Holstein (Eds.), *Postmodern interviewing* (pp. 157–183). Thousand Oaks, CA: Sage Publications.

Farmer, V. L. (2003) (Ed.). *The Black student's guide to graduate and professional school success.* Westport, CN: Greenwood Press.

Fitzpatrick, J. (1998). *Secrets for a successful dissertation.* Thousand Oaks, CA: Sage Publications.

Graves, N., & Varma, V. (Eds.). (1997). *Working for a doctorate: A guide for the humanities and social sciences.* New York: Routledge.

Hesse-Biber, S. N., & Leckenby, D. (2004). How feminists practice social research. In S. N. Hesse-Biber & M. L. Yaiser (Eds.), *Feminist perspectives on social research* (pp. 209–226). New York: Oxford University Press.

Hesse-Biber, S. N., Leavy, P., & Yaiser, M. L. (2004). Feminist approaches to research as a *process*: Reconceptualizing epistemology, methodology, and method. In S. N. Hesse-Biber & M. L. Yaiser (Eds.), *Feminist perspectives on social research* (pp. 3–26). New York: Oxford University Press.

Hoy, D. C. (2004). *Critical resistance: From poststructuralism to post-critique.* Cambridge, MA: MIT Press.

Jamieson, K. H. (1995). *Beyond the double bind: Women and leadership.* New York: Oxford University Press.

Leonard, D. (2001). *A woman's guide to doctoral studies.* Philadelphia: Open University Press.

Lorde, A. (1984). *Sister outsider: Essays & speeches.* Trumansburg, NY: The Crossing Press.

Martin, J. R. (2000). *Coming of age in academe: Rekindling women's hopes and reforming the academy.* New York: Routledge.

McKenna, K. (1991). Subjects of discourse: Learning the language that counts. In H. Bannerji, L. Carty, K. Delhi, S, Heald, & K. McKenna (Eds.), *Unsettling relations: The university as a site of feminist struggles* (pp. 109–128). Boston: South End Press.

Morley, L. (1999). *Organising feminisms: The micropolitics of the academy.* New York: St. Martin's Press.

Ng, R. (2000). A woman out of control: Deconstructing sexism and racism in the university. In J. Glazer Raymo, B. K. Townsend, & B. Ropers-Huilman (Eds.), *Women in higher education: A feminist perspective* (pp. 360–370). Boston: Pearson Custom.

Phillips, E. M., & Pugh, D. S. (2005). *How to get a PhD: A handbook for students and their supervisors*. Philadelphia: Open University Press.

Reay, D. (2004). Cultural capitalists and the academic habitus: Classed and gendered labour in UK higher education. *Women's Studies International Forum, 27,* 31–39.

Reay, D., & Ball, S. (2000). Essentials of female management: Women's ways of working in the education marketplace? *Education Management and Administration, 28,* 145–159.

Richardson, L. (2000). Skirting a pleated text: De-disciplining an academic life. In E. A. St. Pierre & W. S. Pillow (Eds.), *Working the ruins: Feminist poststructural theory and methods in education* (pp. 153–163). New York: Routledge.

Swartz, D. (1997). *Culture & power: The sociology of Pierre Bourdieu*. Chicago: University of Chicago Press

Tierney, W. G. (1997). *Academic outlaws: Queer theory and cultural studies in the academy.* Thousand Oaks, CA: Sage Publications.

Tierney, W. G., & Bensimon, E. M. (2000). (EN)Gender(ING) socialization. In J. Glazer Raymo, B. K. Townsend, & B. Ropers-Huilman (Eds.), *Women in higher education: A feminist perspective* (pp. 309–325). Boston: Pearson Custom.

Tillmann-Healy, L. M. (2001). *Between gay and straight: Understanding friendship across sexual orientation*. Walnut Creek, CA: AltaMira Press.

Tinkler, P., & Jackson, C. (2004). *The doctoral examination process: A handbook for students, examiners, and supervisors*. Philadelphia: Open University Press.

American Indian Women in Academia: The Joys and Challenges

Mary Jo Tippeconnic Fox
Associate Professor
The University of Arizona
Tucson, Arizona

This study explores the joys and challenges of being a professor based upon the personal experiences of 10 American Indian women in public Research I universities. Since the literature is sparse on the experiences of Native women in the academy, this study provides insight, especially to American Indian women aspiring to such careers, and for administrators and policy makers encouraging diversity on their campuses. The American Indian female professors in this study have both satisfying and challenging experiences at their universities. Not one of the women regrets her decision to pursue a career as a professor, but their journey is not easy. They enjoy academic freedom and autonomy; their research agendas, teaching, and working with students; the flexibility of the job; collegiality; support of mentors and colleagues; and service opportunities, especially with tribal communities. However, several of these Native women express feelings of isolation as the only person of color in their department, being treated as "tokens," feeling their research is undervalued, struggling to find mentors, trying to balance demands, having to go outside their departments for intellectual support, and experiencing racial/ethnic and gender bias. The findings of this study demonstrate that further analysis of the experiences of American Indian female faculty in mainstream public Research I institutions is needed to underscore the advantages of this career path and to address the challenges voiced by the respondents.

INTRODUCTION

"Tunetskuh Keta Naraakauparu," in the Comanche language means "Keep going . . . don't give up." This is the message for American Indian women pursuing a career in higher education as a professor. Native women on tenure track appointments have both satisfying and challenging experiences at their colleges and universities. However, for many of the women, the rewards outweigh the demands, and they have fulfilling careers. This study explores the joys and challenges of being a professor based upon the personal experiences of American Indian women faculty in the academy. Since there is a lack of literature addressing this topic (Tippeconnic & McKinney, 2003), this study provides insight for American Indian women aspiring to such careers, and for administrators and policy makers encouraging diversity on their campuses.

This article begins with an overview of the enrollment and graduation rates of American Indian women in higher education, the number of tribal women in faculty ranks in the academy, and a brief look at the literature. Next, the findings from the study are presented, concluding with a discussion and recommendations.

The views expressed by the American Indian women in this study may not appear dissimilar from other ethnic women professors. In fact, many of the same issues are expressed by minority women professors in Turner (2002) and by minority faculty of both genders in Turner and Myers (2000). By giving Native women faculty a voice, it is clear that a degree of uniqueness lays within their tribal values, traditions, and world view that can influence their teaching, research, and service. How advantageous these tribal perspectives are in academe is questionable and needs study.

ENROLLMENT AND GRADUATION OF AMERICAN INDIAN WOMEN IN HIGHER EDUCATION

According to the National Center for Educational Statistics (NCES, 2005), the enrollment of American Indians/Alaskan Natives in colleges and universities more than doubled in the last 25 years. American Indian/Alaskan Native student enrollment grew from 76,100 in 1976 to 165,900 in 2002, and accounted for 1% of the total enrollment of students. In 1976, there was near parity between male and female enrollments, 38,500 and

37,600 respectively; but by 2002, there were 100,200 American Indian/ Alaskan Native females compared to 65,700 males enrolled in colleges and universities. In 2002, American Indian/Alaskan Native student enrollment in higher education was 60% female and 40% male.

This trend is also reflected in degrees conferred. Of the 20,892 degrees conferred to American Indians/Alaskan Natives in 2002–03, women earned 13,022, degrees and men 7,870. In 2002–03 at the graduate level 1,819 females earned masters, 119 doctorates, and 293 first-professional degrees. The number of degrees awarded by colleges and universities to American Indians/Alaskan Natives more than doubled between 1976–77 and 2002–03 (NCES, 2005). The reason for more American Indian/Alaskan Native women than men entering and graduating from higher education needs examination. This trend may indicate academic or socioeconomic problems for males at the elementary and secondary levels that need to be addressed.

Although, the number of American Indians/Alaskan Natives earning doctorates and professional degrees is small compared to the general population, the numbers are increasing. There are more American Indian women seeking degrees than men. It is not a reach to assume that some of these American Indian women will be seeking careers in the academy as faculty members.

AMERICAN INDIAN FACULTY IN THE ACADEMY

From 1983–93, full-time faculty positions held by American Indians grew by 53%, and most of this growth was due to women. During this time, the number of full-time faculty increased 112% for American Indian women and 30% for men. In 1993, American Indian/Alaskan Native full-time faculty was 38% female (Pavel et al., 1998). In fall 2003, the number of American Indians in faculty positions (instruction and research) in degree-granting institutions was 8,495; and of this number, 2,923 were female and 5,572 male (NCES, 2005).

In fall 2003, most American Indian faculty members worked in public 4-year institutions (2,681) compared to 893 in private 4-year institutions. In the public 2-year institutions there were 2,269 American Indians/ Alaskan Natives compared to 142 in private 2-year institutions in fall 2003. There was more part-time faculty (2,978) than full-time (2,649) in fall 2003 (NCES, 2005). American Indian/Alaskan Native professors are concentrated in institutions in states with large populations of American Indians such as Arizona and Oklahoma (Pavel et al., 1998).

In 2004–05 at the tribal colleges, approximately 778 persons were employed in the faculty ranks (full-time), with 219 being American Indians/Alaskan Natives, 97 female and 122 male (AIHEC, 2006).

Only 38% of full-time American Indian/Alaskan Native faculty had tenure in 1993, and they are the least likely to have tenure of any racial–ethnic group in colleges and universities (Pavel et al., 1998).

THE AMERICAN INDIAN PROFESSORIATE

The literature on the American Indian professoriate is sparse and does not speak specifically to Native women except for a few scattered examples. The lack of information on this topic may be related to the small number of Native professors in higher education in comparison to other groups. This is often cited as the reason American Indians are left out of studies and reports (Turner & Myers, 2000), and their issues are collapsed into the general category of minority.

Success in mainstream 4-year institutions means earning tenure, which is a major concern for American Indian professors since they are the ethnic group least likely to achieve it (Pavel et al., 1998). One possible reason according to Tippeconnic and McKinney (2003, p. 242) is the lack of congruence between what American Indian faculty want to do and what the institution expects. This difference may be so great that it jeopardizes tenure. Another fear of minority professors is the possibility of being denied tenure due to race or ethnicity, according to Turner and Myers (2000).

In spring 1992, Stein (1996) surveyed American Indian faculty members (22 responded out of 30) to collect information on how and whether American Indian academics survive in 4-year institutions. Stein (1996) found it difficult for American Indian professors to overcome the perceptions of having inferior qualifications and being hired only because of their minority status. These perceptions are especially damaging for Native women because of the additional factor of their gender. To overcome these perceptions, American Indian professors have to work harder to prove they are worthy scholars at White institutions. As for women of color, Hu-DeHart (2000, p. 30) refers to them as "two-fers" (women and minorities) and believes they present "surplus visibility" for the institution and its committees that can be used to the woman's advantage in some situations.

One American Indian woman professor considers being hired only because of being a "two-fer" as a myth, but she acknowledges her gender gave her an advantage since only females were interviewed for her position (Stein, 1996).

A major concern for American Indian professors according to Stein (1996) and Tippeconnic and McKinney (2003) is the lack of support for research efforts, and the devaluing of their research, especially if it deals with Indian issues. Turner and Myers (2000) found that the talents and contributions of minority faculty including American Indians are devalued or undervalued, and the racial and ethnic bias carries over to the tenure and promotion process. Pepion (1994) also found nonminority faculty downplay or deny unique scholarly contributions of minority faculty and refer to them in a collegial and social context rather than a scholarly or intellectual context.

Mentoring works toward retaining and developing American Indian faculty professionally in higher education (Stein, 1996). However on many campuses there is a lack of American Indians to serve as mentors (Tippeconnic & McKinney, 2003). Stein (1996) found only 50% of the American Indian faculty surveyed in his study had mentors. A Native woman scholar highlights the importance of mentors:

> Some of the most basic advice from my mentor regarding surviving and thriving in the academy was know the campus, know who's who, understand the governance, know how the system works, find your allies (sometimes in seemingly unlikely places—be open to seeing). Know your rights. Choose your battles, and only go to battle when you know you are going to win. (In other words, think it out. Prepare. Line everything up. Think ahead. Make the system work for you.) (Hernandez-Avila, 2003, p. 242)

Teaching is rewarding for American Indian faculty, personally and professionally; but at the same time teaching can be demanding (Stein, 1996), especially when students are not interested in the Native perspective or exhibit racist attitudes that are reflected in evaluations (Tippeconnic & McKinney, 2003). As Hernandez-Avila (2003, p. 246) states: "Some (students) even come into our classrooms to counter us and at the same time save us." Another down side to teaching for American Indian professors (Stein, 1996) is carrying a heavier teaching load as institutions diversify their curriculum, being asked to develop new courses, or taking on large class enrollments.

Working with American Indian students as mentors, advisors as well as teachers can take an inordinate amount of time, but most American Indian faculty feel it's important. Even though, the institution may hold Native professors responsible for American Indian student success or failure; and other staff, faculty, and administrators may feel they are relieved of their responsibility to serve these students (Stein, 1996). An added benefit of retaining American Indian faculty is the likelihood of more American Indian students attending the institution due to the presence of Natives professors (Tippeconnic Fox, 2005).

Climate and politics of a university and department are important to the success of American Indian professors. The support of department colleagues is essential for gaining promotion and tenure; and department heads, senior faculty, and staff can help American Indian professors acclimate to the academic environment. Hu-DeHart (2000) stresses the importance of participating as fully as possible for minority female professors; but in bad climates where politics abound, document situations and keep good records—they may be handy in case of appeals or justifications for transfer to another program. As the American Indian female scholar, Hernandez-Avila (2003, p. 240) says: "I have been knocked down many a time. . . . Sometimes I have been brought down by my peers, by Native scholars themselves."

Service gives "American Indian faculty their greatest joy and greatest headaches," according to Stein (1996, p. 393); and it is the most demanding responsibility of faculty, though the least valued. Since there are few American Indian professors in mainstream institutions, they are asked to serve on many committees, especially with diversity efforts. There is pressure to be the "Indian expert" on campus (Kidwell, 1991). Service can assume many hours if limits are not imposed, and it takes the faculty person away from research and teaching. This is especially difficult for American Indian faculty who want to maintain ties to their own tribal communities by providing assistance and service, which may not be valued in their institutions in the promotion and tenure process (Tippeconnic & McKinney, 2003). As Turner (2002, p. 82) states: "Junior faculty members are particularly at risk. Institutional reward systems can deny tenure and security of employment to those who spend more time on service than on research and scholarship, even when the service is assigned to meet institutional needs."

In an essay on American Indian women in the academy, Cook-Lynn (1996) expresses her concern about the lack of connection to tribal legacies when Native women are isolated from tribal communities, which is often the case in mainstream institutions where the philosophy and expectations are different. How Native professors maintain this connection to community and reinforce their identity as a tribal member is challenging when demands of higher education keep them separated from their culture and traditions.

The data focusing on American Indian women's experiences as professors is almost nonexistent, but their inclusion in studies on American Indian professors and minority faculty does provide some helpful insight into issues affecting them.

METHODOLOGY

Data were collected through a series of informal discussions with American Indian female professors in person or through e-mail. These exchanges gave a select number of American Indian women the opportunity to express their views about their particular experiences in academe.

The sample consists of 10 American Indian female professors, eight from campuses in the southwest, one from a Big Ten university, and one from a Big Twelve institution. All the respondents are on faculty at four major public Research I institutions, and they are citizens of eight different tribal nations. The American Indian female professors have tenure track appointments; two have tenure at the associate level, two are full professors, and six are working toward tenure at the assistant level.

The identity of each professor and her institution is confidential to create a comfortable and safe environment for sharing. This is important because the number of American Indian women in the professoriate is small, and giving names of institutions might immediately identify an individual. Five of the women have appointments in American Indian studies, two in education, one in art, one in psychology, and one in library science.

Each American Indian woman was asked two open-ended questions: (1) What are the joys of being a professor, and (2) What are the challenges of being a professor? The project was explained, individuals agreed to participate, and the women given the opportunity to respond freely from their personal perspective. The data were collected in discussions, not formal interviews. Six were held in person and four were conducted through e-mail, with two women giving additional e-mail comments after the initial contact.

The responses to the questions were analyzed and arranged into common themes under the general headings of joys and challenges and further examined under the categories of teaching, research, and service, which are the primary responsibilities of Research I university faculty.

The small sample size makes the results of this study limited, but it is the start of a dialogue that needs to take place. The American Indian female professors in this study are acquaintances of the author, and they were asked to participate based upon their availability and willingness to participate. All the women just happen to be at public Research I institutions.

FINDINGS

The findings from the study are presented in two general headings: (1) The Joys of Being a Professor, and (2) the Challenges of Being a Professor. The themes emerging from the study at times overlap, and some themes such as teaching have rewards as well as demands. Only the most frequently mentioned themes are listed under each category using personal comments (voices) of American Indian female professors to illustrate the points.

The Joys of Being a Professor

Academic Freedom/Scholarship

"The freedom to have a romance with ideas" (Respondent 2, 2006) is how one American Indian female professor expresses her joy of having academic freedom and autonomy. The Native women in the study appreciate the opportunity to pursue interests (ideas) and to follow intellectual passions: to think, explore, analyze, and research ideas and concepts; to discover new knowledge, topics, and the ability to share with society through publications and presentations. The ability to engage in research, teaching, and service in areas they are passionate about.

The chance to have intellectual pursuits and exchanges with colleagues in and outside their discipline, which transcends ideas and boundaries to learn and discover, is exciting for the American Indian female professors. "The joy or satisfaction of being a professor is that you are around very intelligent people where ideas are exchanged, debated and defended" (Respondent 10, 2007). Pursuing research agendas they are passionate about gives these women satisfaction. A female professor in American Indian studies whose research focuses on American Indian women feminism and Native higher education is able to cross into women's studies, higher education, and American Indian studies. As she states: "And best of all, I get paid to do this, to pursue my passions" (Respondent 7, 2006). A respondent says as she works toward tenure, "It brings me great joy to look at my vita and my promotion and tenure dossier and see evidence of the work that I have done, both individually and collaboratively over my first three years" (Respondent 3, 2006).

The American Indian women in the study enjoy writing and publishing. Their challenge is having enough time to devote to research and publishing, especially when working toward tenure. One Native female associate professor in American Indian studies says: "I got advice from a colleague when I first arrived on campus to publish in both American Indian studies journals as well as mainstream journals" (Respondent 2). She believes this advice helped her earn tenure.

Teaching

It is the consensus of all 10 American Indian female professors in this study that teaching is rewarding but demanding at the same time. They express this satisfaction in various ways. One professor says: "When I look out at the sea of faces, I love those moments when I can see that the students are all engaged, that I've got them interested and excited by the material" (Respondent 8, 2007). "Most students are still a joy to teach and to know. They are bright and have the potential for great careers" (Respondent 10, 2007). "Having a good discussion or lecture can make my day. There is nothing better than having a good class; it lifts my spirits" (Respondent 7, 2006). The chance to teach and impact future generations is gratifying to these women. Several of the women say that at the end of each semester, they thank the students in their classes for teaching them new things. As a Native woman professor says:

> For me, the best class is one in which I do little lecturing, but come out of the class feeling as if I have learned more from my students than they have learned from me. Each semester, my students challenge me to think critically about the scholarship that I do and its impact on the field, at both local and national levels. (Respondent 3, 2006)

An additional reward of teaching mentioned by the respondents is the freedom to plan and develop classes, choose materials (including texts), and create a classroom climate conducive to learning.

> No one is standing over me telling me how to teach. Creating a classroom climate where respect is shown and ideas flow freely is exciting. Of course, there are student evaluations, which judge my performance in the classroom. (Respondent 7, 2006)

Another satisfying element of teaching is working with students in the capacity of advising, mentoring, conducting research in labs, and directing independent studies. These associations with students can be joyful and last a lifetime. For many of the American Indian female professors, this aspect of their job is important because they are able to assist the next generation. This can vary from just listening to a student, editing a student's work, writing references, or working with students in a research laboratory. "I love seeing students grow and learn as individuals, and I especially enjoy watching them make the next step in their life" (Respondent 8, 2007). Native women take their teaching responsibilities seriously, which is exemplified by an assistant professor in American Indian studies:

> For many of these non-native students, my class may be the only exposure they will ever have to American Indian history, politics, culture, economics, spiritually, and literature. . . . I can offer American Indian students a broader perspective of what it means to be an American Indian. (Respondent 1, 2006)

Teaching and mentoring are rewarding but they can also present challenges. One assistant professor says: "At some time or another, there will be racist remarks directed against us, and even if it is only an overheard conversation between thoughtless students, it will hurt. There may be overt discrimination, but more likely subtle, not easily pointed out, not easily eradicated" (Respondent 1, 2006). Another professor (Respondent 10, 2007) says: "I have found that in the past 5 years or so it seems to me students are changing. Now they are so 'empowered' and such a sense of 'entitlement' that they have become demanding and less willing to commit to what I call scholarship."

Flexibility of Time

The management of time (flexibility) is important to American Indian female professors in this study. They stress the importance of teaching classes, having office hours, working with students, and serving on committees; but this is not necessarily an 8 to 5 job. Professors can control much of their time, which often means working more than 40 hours a week; but the flexibility is a real luxury as they pursue their research agenda (Respondent 5, 2006). "I love that being a professor provides the flexibility to choose for myself how I will dedicate my research time. If this were not the case, I would not be a faculty member—I would have gone home to work in my community" (Respondent 8, 2007). The option to work in different environments at different times encourages scholarship for these women. For one person, early in the mornings or late at nights in her home office, when no one disturbs her but her cat, is a productive time to work. Another respondent says: "I get up and start writing and the day is gone before I realize I am still in my pajamas" (Respondent 2, 2006). Travel for research and professional growth is another enjoyable experience mentioned by the women (Respondent 4, 2006; Respondent 5, 2006). For the majority of the women respondents, the connection to the real world is very important, and this real world is usually tribal communities, which they care passionately about (Respondent 8, 2007).

Regardless of where and when these women chose to work, they feel they must be productive especially if working toward promotion and tenure.

Collegiality: Networking with Colleagues

Establishing rapport and working collaboratively with people in your field and other disciplines is rewarding for American Indian women in academe. It is their chance to learn from each other and to collaborate on department, college and campus committees, and projects. "I really like learning and having to stretch my mind. I am constantly learning and having to think. I learn from faculty and students as well as the constant reading of the literature and review of research that is on-going all the time—my own and others" (Respondent 10, 2007). These associations lead to collaborative efforts including research projects, co-authoring articles, team teaching as well as trying to make positive statements on campus for Native women professors. "It keeps me motivated and excited about my work," according to one faculty person (Respondent 4, 2006). One respondent (7, 2006) relates how she is working with a colleague who focuses on American Indian law and policy. Her focus is on gender issues. They plan to write a book on American Indian women leadership. This partnership is an opportunity to present their research, utilizing different perspectives, and to disseminate combined work through publication. Both women are excited about the project.

A Supportive Climate

If the fit is right, it can be a joy to wake up every morning and go to work according to the American Indian female professors in the sample. If the climate in the department is positive and the rapport with colleagues is good, especially with a department head that is supportive, being a professor is rewarding. "I like the many committee meetings; the decision making role that faculty have regarding curriculum, policies, and department mission and goals. I like the opportunity afforded by my position to make a difference in the profession and in student lives" (Respondent 10, 2007).

Challenges of Being a Professor

Lack of Mentors for American Indian Female Professors

From the various discussions, it was the consensus of the 10 American Indian women that a mentor is a must. This person does not have to be of the same ethnic group, but it helps when American Indians are available. Some departments assign a mentor, some colleges have support groups to work with new junior faculty, and there are organizations that provide mentoring support. At one institution, a minority women faculty association is available for mentoring. A junior faculty member experiencing feelings of being "different" and like a "struggler" gives credit to her mentors for helping her adjust to her job and university:

> Fortunately, I had a wonderful graduate school mentor who listened and legitimated my concerns, and who kept pointing out to me that these people were seeing me through the lens of the stereotype that junior faculty of color could not do well in a mainstream research university. She kept assuring me that if I kept pushing forward, I would prove them wrong. I also picked a senior faculty member who turned out to be very forward thinking about mentoring. She acknowledged and valued my differences and was instrumental in helping me carve out my own place in the department and in the university. (Respondent 8, 2007)

The Native women in this study contribute much of their success to good mentoring. One assistant professor says of her mentor (a Native male professor):

> He exemplifies true mentoring. He provides a safe place where I can go to vent when the challenges of becoming a professor seem overwhelming,

> and he has a wealth of knowledge of the field as well as of the academy, which few people have access to. And he makes me laugh, which is critical to one's well being. (Respondent 3, 2006)

Another respondent talks about her mentor as another Native woman professor in her department, who is willing to help with insight and advice:

> She reads and edits (critiques) my writings, she collaborates on projects, she even cotaught with me, and introduced me to other colleagues in the field for networking, which has led to more collaborative work. She is willing to share her secrets for success in academia. Giving helpful hints such as write journal articles that can be compiled into a book. Another mentor is my dissertation director from my doctoral program, who still calls or visits me. (Respondent 7, 2006)

The advice from all the women (Respondents 1–10) was to seek a mentor if one is not assigned. Someone you feel comfortable with; someone you feel safe expressing your feelings and opinions. Someone you respect and someone to laugh with you. The system is unfamiliar to most junior faculty, and it is helpful to have someone to guide you. The women stressed once tenured, you need to pay back by mentoring junior faculty.

Department Politics, Culture, and Support

Department politics and culture can be disruptive to the success of American Indian women faculty. Some of the American Indian female professors talk about their firsthand experience with vicious department politics (Respondent 6, 2006; Respondent 7, 2006). "Jealously, competition, favoritism, and other forms of preferential treatment all play a part in academia. And, of course, universities are full of people with huge egos—it goes with the territory" (Respondent 10, 2007). The women professors in this study feel it is important for junior faculty to learn about the culture and politics of their department and campus. They need to understand what is going on in order to maneuver successfully within the system. If the department has problems or is divided, one needs to display collegiality but try to mind your own business, if possible. Work with the department head or senior faculty members. "Concentrate on getting tenure and let your work speak for itself. If you must speak up, think about it carefully and try not to burn bridges. Remember, your peers review your tenure package" (Respondent 7, 2006).

Lack of support from department heads is an unfortunate situation for some of the Native women in this study. As one American Indian woman professor relates, she recently had a visit from an assistant professor who feels her department head is targeting her. She feels no support and is fearful to the point of not saying anything (Respondent 1, 2006). These situations are difficult, and there are no easy solutions. When departments experience difficulties, it can literally tear the program apart and leave faculty, staff, and students in dismay with some choosing to leave.

Isolation is a real issue for some American Indian female professors in mainstream institutions as expressed by an assistant professor in psychology:

> I think the most difficult part of being a professor has been feeling like a token (the only) in my department. I believe my colleagues care about diversity, and in particular increasing diversity among the faculty, but their efforts fall short and they see this as being about lack of qualified candidates rather than as a consequence of their potentially biased evaluation (i.e., they don't know how to evaluate the work) of faculty of color. Since joining the faculty, I have witnessed firsthand the code words and the attitudes that keep our faculty homogenous looking (i.e., aside from me, the last six hires have been White males). This reality makes me feel lonely and sad inside. I long for colleagues with whom I can share my experiences, but without having to provide "how to" lessons for understanding. I could never think of a place like this as my long-term professional home—I always feel like I'm just visiting, but trying to make a few changes during my stay. (Respondent 8, 2007)

The lack of intellectual environment has been a struggle for one respondent:

> As a junior scholar, I still have much to learn, but given the lack of diversity in the department, I've had to look elsewhere for varied intellectual perspectives. Many of my ideas I'm interested in stray from these mainstream paths, but without others who see the path, I get mixed messages about whether it's "safe" or too "risky" for me, as a junior scholar to go down that path. In my short tenure in the academy, I've had to look outside my department and university for a community of scholars with whom I can share and develop my work. (Respondent 8, 2007)

Service in Perspective

To American Indian female professors, service to the university and community is a challenging issue. The women are serving on many committees, especially those that focus on diversity. The message from the tribal women is not to let service commitments get in the way of your scholarship and teaching. Accept a few meaningful assignments, but do not be overwhelmed by them. Even though universities say more weight is given to service in promotion and tenure, publishing is still the most important. A balance between teaching, research, and service is critical for success in academe. An American Indian female professor (Respondent 7, 2006) relates: “My mentor advises me to limit my service to one university committee, one department committee, and one outside committee.” Another respondent says: “A key to success is not overextending yourself when you already have a full plate. It is okay to say no” (Respondent 2, 2006). This is a challenge for one American Indian woman professor in Native studies who states: “I feel a connection to community (obligation); it is essential, keeps me rooted and grounded, and gives me creditability. Plus, I hope my research will have some practicality” (Respondent 1, 2006).

Balancing Professional and Personal Lives

Balancing professional and personal demands is difficult for the women in this study, especially if they are working toward tenure. As one American Indian female professor states: “Since I love my work, it is difficult to create and sustain a separation between work and home. My work is always with me and it is not easy to turn it off. It is hard to relax and not think about work, especially when you are working toward tenure” (Respondent 3, 2006). The demands of work are hard to leave when there are publications deadlines to meet, and students or colleagues live and shop in the same area as you. One professor attempts to devote her weekends to her family, and she lets her colleagues know that weekends are family time. This usually works for her, but she also has an understanding husband who is willing to care for the children or do other tasks (Respondent 7, 2006). Another professor says: “As a Native woman, balancing family and community obligations with work obligations is difficult. But I’ve figured out ways to merge these worlds. Giving back to my community is a deeply held value; and when we make progress in the community, it gives me great joy and satisfaction” (Respondent 8, 2007). Balancing the demands of work, home, and community can be stressful. The support from family, friends, and colleagues helps the women in this study maintain harmony. The Native women professors have no easy answers for balancing professional and personal lives, but they feel the pressure lets up once you achieve promotion and tenure. "I'm looking forward to the spring of 2009 when the promotion and tenure decision has been made and I can breathe a little more easily" (Respondent 3, 2006).

Maintaining Strength and Motivation

The Native women professors feel their tribal identity provides them with the strength and motivation (spiritually and physically) to meet the challenges and embrace the rewards of being a faculty member in academe. Community and family are a source of strength for these women, and they have come to rely on it. It helps them deal with the feelings of isolation (being one of a few American Indian faculty members on campus), the demands of the job, and the physical and psychological distance from their tribal communities. "Keeping up with everything—doing a good job of teaching while conducting research and getting it published—is a challenge" (Respondent 10, 2007). The importance of community is expressed by one assistant professor:

> For me, it is critical that my work not only meet the demands of promotion and tenure, but that it also have real utility for my home community, which I define broadly not only as my local, tribal community, but the larger field of Indian education. It is what keeps me rooted and grounded and what really excites me and challenges me to do good work. (Respondent 3, 2006)

DISCUSSION AND CONCLUSION

This article paints a realistic picture of the joys and challenges of being a professor based upon the personal experiences of a select group of American Indian female professors in public Research I universities. Not one of the women regrets her decision to pursue a career as a professor, but their journey is not easy. They enjoy academic freedom and autonomy, their research agendas, teaching and working with students, the flexibility of the job, collegiality, support of mentors and colleagues, and service opportunities, especially with tribal communities. As one full professor says: "A graduate dean once told me that being a professor in a university is the 'Cadillac of professions.' I agree with this" (Respondent 10, 2007).

However, several Native women faculty in this study express feelings of isolation as the only person of color in their department, being treated as "tokens," feeling their research is undervalued, struggling to find mentors, trying to balance demands, having to go outside their department for intellectual support, and experiencing racial/ethnic and gender bias.

The findings of this study demonstrate that further analysis of the experiences of American Indian female faculty in mainstream public Research I institutions is needed to underscore the advantages of this career path and to address the challenges voiced by the respondents.

RECOMMENDATIONS

Based upon the findings, literature, and personal insight on the joys and challenges of being a professor, the following recommendations are presented for discussion:

1. **Supportive Environments:** Universities and departments need to provide supportive environments for American Indian female professors to develop professionally—creating a climate where diversity, including tribal identity, is truly appreciated in action not just in words. This means the commitment of resources for program efforts to retain and develop Native women professors, including support for research. Guidance needs to be given to department heads and faculty on how to assist and support diverse colleagues including Native women. Some workable strategies are assigning mentors, encouraging a productive research agenda, and helping Native women faculty to balance teaching, service, and scholarship. As the women in this study articulated there are still challenges for mainstream institutions to address if they are serious about inclusion. Also, it should not be assumed that an American Indian female professor is in a supportive environment in an ethnic studies program. Native studies, like any other department, can have unsupportive heads and unhealthy climates as indicated by some of this study's respondents.

2. **Networking:** American Indian female professors need to develop a support network of Native or helpful nonnative scholars who are willing to provide input on scholarship and research. This will help eliminate the feelings of intellectual isolation some Native women professors are experiencing, and it is a constructive way for department heads and

colleagues to support the scholarship of these women.

3. **Time and Priorities:** Managing time and setting priorities are important skills for American Indian female professors trying to balance the demands of their job, family, and community. Sharing workable strategies to accomplish this is one positive approach that mentors, department heads, and colleagues can use to help these women thrive in mainstream universities.

4. **Policy:** Policy makers and leaders of mainstream public Research I universities should continuously evaluate how they do business to better serve the diverse populations of students, faculty, and staff of the 21st century. Communication and collaboration needs to occur between all stakeholders in the university, including American Indian female professors, on a regular basis to create a supportive and inclusive climate.

American Indian women professors in mainstream public Research I institutions experience a combination of rewards and challenges, and it is essential for them to find a balance without sacrificing their tribal identity. One American Indian female professor speaks for many of the women in this study when she states:

> Being a minority professor in the White-dominated academy is both an act of resistance and an act of reconciliation. In a positive sense of the reconciliation, we build bridges between the walls that separate people and cultures through teaching, mentoring, writing, and publishing. If we cannot build bridges, in the positive sense, then we must perform acts of resistance and tunnel underneath those walls. (Respondent 1, 2006)

"Tunetskuh Keta Naraakauparu." "Keep going . . . don't give up."

REFERENCES

American Indian Higher Education Consortium. (2006). *AIHEC AIMS Fact Book 2005 Tribal Colleges and Universities Report* (124–134). Retrieved August 8, 2007, from http://www.aihec.org

Cook-Lynn, E. (1996). The American Indian Woman in the Ivory Tower. In *Why I can't read Wallace Stegner and other essays* (pp. 99–109). Madison,

WI: The University of Wisconsin Press.

Hernandez-Avila, I. (2003). Thoughts on Surviving as Native Scholars in the Academy. *The American Indian Quarterly*, 27 (1 & 2, pp. 240–248). Retrieved November 11, 2006, from http://muse, jhu, and edu/journals/amerian_indian_quarterly/v027/27.1hernandes- avila.html

Hu-DeHart, E., Office Politics and Department Culture. (2000). In M. Garcia (Ed.), *Succeeding in an academic career: A guide for faculty of color* (pp. 27–38). Westport, CT: Greenwood Press.

Kidwell, C. S. (1991). Indian Professionals in Academe: Demands and Burnout. In *Opening the Montana pipeline, American Indian higher education in the nineties* (pp. 85-92). Sacramento, CA: Tribal College Press.

National Center for Educational Statistics. (2005, August). *Status and trends in the education of American Indians and Alaskan Native.* Retrieved January 15, 2007, from http://nces.ed.gov/pubs2005/Nativetrends/index.asp

Olsen, D., Maple, S. A. & Stage, F. K. (1995). Women and Minority Faculty Job Satisfaction: Professional Role Interests, Professional Satisfaction, and Institutional Fit. *The Journal of Higher Education, 66*(3), 267–93. Retrieved June 15, 2007, from JSTOR database: http://www.jstor.org

Pavel, D. M., Skinner, R. R., Farris, E., Cahalan, M., Tippeconnic, J., & Stein, W. (1998). American Indians and Alaskan Native in Postsecondary Education. *Educational Statistics Quarterly, 1*(1). Retrieved January 15, 2007, from http://nces.ed.gov/programs/quarterly/vol_1/1_1/5-esq11-a.asp

Pepion, K. (1993). *Ideologies of Excellence: Issues in the Evaluation, Promotion and Tenure of Minority Faculty.* Unpublished doctoral dissertation. The University of Arizona, Tucson.

Stein, W. (1996). The Survival of American Indian Faculty. In C. S. V. Turner, M. Garcia, A. Nora, & L. I. Rendon (Eds.), *Racial and ethnic diversity in higher education,* ASHE reader series (pp. 390–97). Boston: Peason Custom Publishing.

Tippeconnic Fox, M. J. (2005, spring). Voices from Within: Native American Faculty and Staff on Campus. In M. J. Tippeconnic Fox, S. C. Lowe, & G. S. McClellan, *Serving Native American students*, New Directions for Student Services (vol. 109, pp. 49–59).

Tippeconnic, J. W., & McKinney, S. (2003). Native Faculty: Scholarship and Development. In M. K. P. Benham & W. J. Stein (Eds.), *The*

Renaissance of American Indian Higher Education Capturing the Dream (pp. 241–255). Mahwah, NJ: Lawrence Erlbaum Associates, Publishers.

Turner, C. S. V. (2002). Women of Color in Academe Living with Multiple Marginality. *The Journal of Higher Education, 73*(1), 74–93.

Turner, C. S. V., & Myers, S. L. Jr. (2000). *Faculty of color in academe bittersweet success.* Boston: Allyn and Bacon.

Program Descriptions

Virtual Women's Center

Karyn Benner — Ferris State University, Michigan

The Virtual Women's Center at Ferris State University is an online Web-resource for women on our campus and in our community. Its mission is as follows: "The mission of the Virtual Women's Center at Ferris State University is to provide a Web site that organizes and presents information about local, state and national resources for women and men both on and off campus. Our mission is to engage the public in important topics related to college success, health, financial, safety and family issues."

Knowing that the national college campus gender landscape has changed dramatically in the last 10 to 20 years, the faculty and staff at the Ferris State University felt the students' needs were not being met effectively. Now, women comprise the majority of students in college campuses across the nation; currently, 51 to 56% of students are women (Touchton & Davis, 1991). Across the state of Michigan, this trend has held true. Out of our 15 publicly funded 4-year institutions, 12 institutions have seen a polar switch from a predominately male to a predominately female campus makeup (State of MI, 2006). On our campus, we are slowly seeing an increase of female students. In 2000, our total enrollment was 9,847. Of those, 4,411 (45%) were female; 5436 (55%) were male. In 2006, our total enrollment increased to 12,575 students. Of those, 6,068 (48%) were female; 6,507 were male (52%). In addition to the increase in female students, we noticed the needs of our female students were not being met; or, if their needs were being met, the resources were not easily accessible. Furthermore, there was little collaboration between various women's groups (i.e., student organizations, professional organizations, campus departments, and community agencies).

In lieu of a physical space to house such an office or center, the Virtual Women's Center was created. Through this center, we are able to offer various events and activities pertaining to women, along with necessary resources for promoting, developing, and mentoring our students and the women in the larger community. Since its launch in November 2005, the Web site has been extremely successful. We receive an average of 25 hits per day. We have participated in recruiting initiatives at women's expos throughout the state and provided programming for activities (e.g., Love Your Body Day, Sexual Assault Awareness Month, Women's History Month, MLK Week). The best part about this project has been the fact that we were able to do everything "virtually" for free.

Contact: Karyn Benner bennerk@ferris.edu (231) 591-5042

Pilot Women's Empowerment Program

Claudia F. Curry — Community College of Philadelphia, Pennsylvania

The Pilot Women's Empowerment Program at Community College of Philadelphia emerged during a practicum research study that I conducted in spring 2004. The study examined the *Impact of a Pilot Women's Empowerment Program on Female College Students.* The purpose of the program was to support the personal, social, academic, and leadership development of women students enrolled at an urban community college and who represent diverse backgrounds. The pilot emerged because of the demand for programs and services designed to meet the developmental needs of women students who were struggling with issues that affected their ability to persist academically.

The program was designed to support women students in making life choices and creating desired lives. It was also designed to assist the participants in recognizing and changing behavior patterns, improving communication with family members, and developing a sense of self-empowerment and responsibility that would positively influence their personal and academic growth and development. Through a structured curriculum, the program examined each student's perspective on the meaning of empowerment and assisted in developing strategies for confronting issues and making life changes through skills building workshops and activities.

A primary goal of the Pilot Women's Empowerment Program was to serve as an innovative educational vehicle designed to equip women students from diverse backgrounds with the tools to empower themselves. In doing so, the students were encouraged to use those tools to prioritize their options; make appropriate choices for their lives and families; and to enhance their personal, social, professional, and academic pursuits.

The Pilot Women's Empowerment Program employed a curriculum that reflected on current issues and themes that focused on empowerment and leadership development. Seven informal sessions were held over a 7-week period. The curriculum included interactive workshops, homework assignments, and journaling designed to enhance each student's awareness about the concept of empowerment. The program provided students with skill-building opportunities that assisted their efforts to make positive life changes. The program incorporated the participation of faculty members and colleagues who are skilled at designing and facilitating workshops.

Planned outcomes of this educational program helped participants recognize and change negative behavior patterns, identify the relationship between empowerment and the freedom of choice, improve communications with their families, develop a sense of self-empowerment and responsibility that will ultimately impact their overall growth and development, and identify and enhance their leadership skills.

The program was positioned as a prime source of guaranteed intensive skills development, problem solving, consciousness-raising, and hands-on experiential learning designed to empower the lives of each student who participated in the program. This model offered an innovative approach that challenged women students who participated in my study to consider and prioritize their options, exercise their freedom of choice, and create their lives as they wanted them to be. It was a vehicle for providing a safe environment where the students could be educated about the concept of empowerment in a structured setting. It was perhaps a unique strategy for providing empowerment training on a college campus.

Contact: Claudia F. Curry drclaudiacurry@earthlink.net

Professional Peer Clinical Supervision: A Model for the Professional Development of Counselor Educators

Jody B. Gallagher — Edinboro University of Pennsylvania

The proposed model evolved when three female student affairs professionals collaborated to improve their counseling skills through a peer professional development approach using team supervision. The structure of the team supervision consisted of the following:

- weekly meetings on campus;
- individual presentation of a case/tape for discussion (not a turn-taking expectation, all came prepared to present a case);
- quarterly goal setting and evaluation (added structure and accountability);
- self-reflection, using a self-critique worksheet;
- consistent homework assignments (increased accountability and encouraged completion of professional development activities); and
- evaluation (consisted of self, peer, and supervisor input).

The group utilized an integrated developmental model of supervision that contributed to each member's professional development in the following ways: Individual Professional Clinical Development (e.g., improved clinical supervision skills and enhanced self-evaluation), Professional Peer Group Relationships (e.g., broadened ethical decision making perspectives), and University Environmental Impact (e.g., improved supervision skills and integration of policy issues and programs).

This model proved extremely beneficial to the participants. Although this model can be applied to other female practitioners, it should not be assumed that this is a "one-size-fits-all model." A variety of practical considerations need to be addressed when entering into a professional peer group supervision relationship. If these considerations are addressed, this model may offer many advantages for a variety of female practitioners in higher education.

The following are among the practical implementation considerations:

- The model is not recommended for beginning professionals.
- All group members must view the process as a professional commitment.

- Regular meeting times and confidential meeting places should be established in advance.
- The use of specific tools, forms, and techniques during sessions increases accountability and focus.

Benefits of utilizing the team approach to supervision include the following:

- Each member of the team can alternate between supervisor and supervisee roles, thus enabling each participant to view the process through different lenses.
- Some issues transcend members' professional boundaries.
- Members have the opportunity to share varying viewpoints on solutions and approaches to issues.

A variety of professional accomplishments resulted from the support and encouragement generated among colleagues through the team supervision

The Collaborative Professional Peer Clinical Supervision Model was developed after critical reflection and analysis of the aforementioned outcomes and benefits and the process itself (see Figure 1). The model consists of three inner circles that represent the peer female professionals who comprise the team. The two-way arrows represent the ability of each team member to assume supervisor or supervisee roles at varying points in the professional development process. Finally, the three concentric, outer circles represent the three levels that can potentially be positively impacted as a result of the collaborative supervision process: Individual Professional Clinical Development (IPCD), Professional Peer Group Relationships (PPGR), and University Environmental Impact (UEI). This model can serve as the basis for other female professionals working within higher education to develop their own professional peer supervision team.

Contact: Jody Gallagher jgallagher@edinboro.edu (814) 732-1269

Figure 1. Collaborative professional peer clinical supervision model.

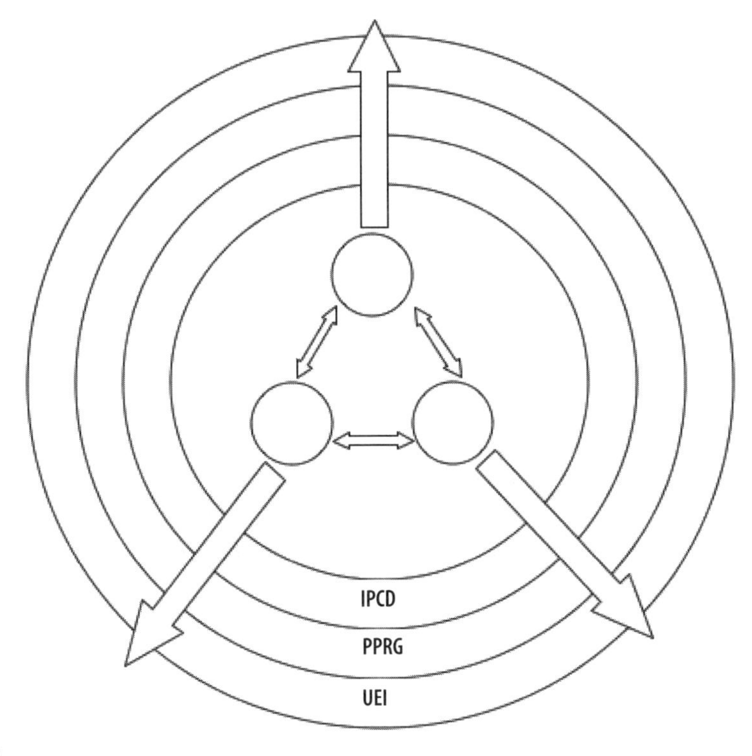

Key
IPCD=Individual Professional Clinical Development
PPGR=Professional Peer Group Relationships
UEI=University Environmental Impact

Benefiting Female Students in Science, Math, and Engineering: Establishing a WISE (Women in Science and Engineering) Learning Community

Laurie A. Witucki, Diana G. Pace, Kathleen M. Blumreich —
Grand Valley State University, Michigan

At Grand Valley State University (a 4-year public institution in Michigan with an enrollment of 23,000 students), a science faculty member and a student affairs administrator came together to plan a living–learning community for first-year female students in science and engineering. The rationale for the learning community included the successful track record for the learning community's concept nationally (i.e., evidence of increased retention and student engagement), support for female students in nontraditional majors, and greater academic support and contact between students and faculty. A planning committee consisting of the dean of students, the dean of the College of Engineering, the dean of the College of Liberal Arts and Sciences, the housing director, and the original science faculty member and student affairs administrator established the learning community, called WISE (Women in Science and Engineering). An existing on-campus living center with room for 46 students was chosen based on its proximity to campus science classrooms and labs and subsequently renovated (new paint, addition of a tutoring center/study room and a computer lab, a faculty office, and new artwork with a science emphasis). The faculty member received one-course release time to be the director of the program. Students were accepted based on their stated preference of a major. Among the first year group of students were 4 math majors, 5 engineering majors, 10 science majors (including biology, chemistry, computer science, and related majors), 15 medical health profession majors, 7 biomedical health science majors, and 5 undeclared majors.

A range of academic support and programming activities were provided for the students including a field trip on a research boat on Lake Michigan with biology and environmental science faculty and staff, lectures by faculty, academic tutoring in key science and math classes, a book club to discuss women Nobel Prize winners in science, and various social and service learning activities. Faculty in the sciences, math, and engineering were invited to participate in the learning community; and several held advising hours and attended various social events. The housing staff chose a WISE RA who was a health sciences major and provided staffing assistance

Early assessment of the program suggests that the students are doing as well as, or slightly better academically, than non-WISE first-year female students; and that retention is expected to be higher compared to all first-year students. Students reported liking the program. One mechanical engineering resident said, "The WISE program is very helpful because you can relate to the other students and to the faculty since you have something in common." Those involved in planning the program agreed that it was a successful endeavor and that the benefits included creation of a positive community of female students living and studying together, taking classes together, working problems together at the white boards throughout the living center, and using the computer labs with specific software installed for math and engineering on the computers.

Plans for the second year of the program include eight peer mentors who will live in the building. They were selected from interested first-year WISE students and will assist the new WISE first-year students in their academic and social adjustment.

Contact: Laurie A. Witucki witckil@gvsu.edu (616) 331-2986

Mentoring-for-Leadership Lunch Series for Women SEM Faculty

Joyce Yen — University of Washington

In 2001, the University of Washington (UW) was one of nine institutions to receive a National Science Foundation ADVANCE Institutional Transformation award to increase the participation and advancement of women faculty in academic science, engineering, and mathematics (SEM) careers. As part of the ADVANCE award, UW created the Center for Institutional Change (CIC) to implement programs designed to eliminate existing barriers and to precipitate cultural change at both the departmental and institutional levels (www.engr.washington.edu/advance).

One of the CIC's signature programs is the Mentoring-for-Leadership lunch series (http://www.engr.washington.edu/advance/mentoring/leadership_lunch.html). This program is a monthly 1.5-hour lunch gathering for SEM women faculty. Each month, a different woman leader discusses her career trajectory and the benefits and challenges of holding a position of leadership. Between May 2003 and December 2006, 44 women leaders (including 24 UW leaders) have spoken at the lunches. Sixty-five percent of the speakers have been at the associate dean level or higher. Forty-nine percent of the 100+ participants have attended three or more events.

The informal nature of the program facilitates open discussion. Participants and the speaker socialize and eat for the first 20–30 minutes. Then the speaker makes approximately 20 minutes of remarks on her personal experiences and thoughts on being in a position of leadership. Speakers have told their personal history, summarized career obstacles and how they overcame them, discussed success strategies, described what surprises they found when moving into academic leadership or the challenges encountered, explained how and why they made the decision to take on a leadership position, and shared work/life and research/ administration balancing strategies. The event concludes with a general question and answer session.

This program encourages SEM women faculty to consider leadership and exposes them to different career paths. Moreover, the program allows women to identify with other women's successes and provides tools and incentives for women to advance in their careers. Additional program benefits include cross-unit networking and community building. Participants have reported satisfaction with this mentoring model and positive personal and professional development as a result of participating. Results of a recent survey administered to past participants overwhelmingly indicated participation in the lunches has positively influenced their understanding of leadership, perceptions of being in a position of leadership, and thoughts about pursuing leadership. Moreover, survey results indicated participation has strongly increased participants' awareness of diverse paths to leadership and various leadership styles. Virtually all survey respondents recommended this program be adopted at other institutions.

The Mentoring-for-Leadership lunch series is a low-cost, high-impact program that facilitates networking, sharing of experiences, and building a culture of leadership. This format need not be limited to leadership development, but it could address many issues related to faculty success. This simple, effective, and easy-to-replicate mentoring strategy has created an ongoing forum that has influenced women faculty to consider and pursue positions of leadership and helps them reduce isolation, increase understanding of structural barriers and how to confront/navigate them, and develop allies that can bolster career advancement.

Contact: Joyce W. Yen joyceyen@u.washington.edu

Book Reviews

The Balancing Act: Gender Perspectives in Faculty Roles and Work Lives

by Susan J. Bracken, Jeanie K. Allen, & Diane R. Dean (Eds.). Sterling, VA: Stylus, 2006. 208 pgs. ISBN-13: 978-1579221492 (hardcover)

Reviewed by Jennifer O. Duffy — Suffolk University, Massachusetts

---

As part of a book series on "Women in Academe," this volume addresses work/family issues for female and male faculty and also examines gendered aspects of academic life. The editors began this project as an extension of their advocacy work for women in higher education with the former American Association for Higher Education's Women's Caucus. Together, they collected scholarship from current research focused on improving the academic environment for women faculty and particularly working mothers. The book not only acknowledges the impressive progress that women have made in achieving equity to their male counterparts in the academy, but also calls attention to the remaining gender gaps. The purpose of this book is to use the latest research to inform policy and programs that act as solutions to retaining female faculty.

Stated otherwise, a central theme of the edited book looks at how institutions can enact policies that support women in developing both productive work lives and satisfying personal lives.

This book contributes to knowledge and practice by highlighting new research that examines the changing nature of how professors balance their professional responsibilities and personal lives. More specifically, current challenges for female faculty and institutional strategies used to help women overcome the demands of academic life are discussed. The book argues that family-friendly academic campuses are necessary not only to the achievement of gender equity, but also in response to the increasing number of women entering higher education as a profession. Institutions that understand the need to revamp the career structure with more flexibility and accommodations for working mothers will ultimately benefit from a competitive advantage in recruitment and retention of female faculty.

Particular strengths of this work include its recognition that the 21st century university and college system includes a diverse group of faculty members in a range of appointment types at myriad of institutions, all with distinctive career needs and interests. Furthermore, this book contains a unique perspective in its incorporation of how both men and women manage work and personal roles. Even more, the book explores the exceptional, and rarely examined, difficulties of dual academic couples in pursuing their individual careers.

The six chapters are tied together by the pivotal idea that policies supporting the diverse needs of faculty serve the overall interests and missions of institutions. The collective work argues that faculty satisfaction and productivity is enriched when the faculty work/life balance is an institutional priority: "The academy will be stronger in the coming years if the new faculty are knowledgeable about options, policies, and strategies that help individuals create successful and productive careers and meaningful personal lives" (p. 156).

Moreover, the scholarship reveals the complexity of demands related to parenting and academic work. The book is based on the plethora of research showing that such challenges are exaggerated for female faculty who report a significant higher number of domestic and caregiving activities in comparison to their male counterparts. The weighted responsibility adds pressure to female faculty building their careers who attend conferences away from home and other time-intensive responsibilities required for tenure such as writing and publishing. Furthermore, female faculty try to minimize the negative aspects of parental responsibilities by timing childbirth in the summer and taking minimal maternity leaves in an effort to appear committed to their careers. The sum result is twofold. First, women enter academic careers at a rate proportionally lower than their degree attainment. Second, women do not achieve tenure and promotions at the same rate as men.

Chapter one entitled "Babies Matter: Pushing the Gender Equity Revolution Forward" by Mason, Goulden, and Wolfinger highlights the University of California's (UC) developmental efforts to enhance faculty's family-friendly resources and services. UC's policies have been cited as an institutional "best practice" and serve as a model for other campuses looking to improve the career and family lives of professors. The chapter by Colbeck, "How Female and Male Faculty with Families Manage Work and Personal Roles," looks at the relationship between satisfaction levels and role integration of family and academic work for men and women. Wolf-Wendel and Ward's chapter, "Faculty Work and Family Life," compares how liberal arts, community colleges, comprehensive and research institutions treat junior faculty women with young children.

Creamer's chapter, "Policies that Part," promotes a culture shift in higher education for the early careers of dual academic couples by rewarding teamwork to maximize productivity. Neumann, LaPointe Terosky, and Schell's chapter, "Agents of Learning," focuses on how tenured professors can "respond strategically to increased demands, in the form of work and learning, can invent useful ways to manage expanding work expectations, increasing calls to learn new work, and growing desires to continue their scholarly learning" (p. 92). The final chapter by Hart entitled "Faculty Change Initiatives" presents a case study on a particular campus where faculty advocated for the establishment of a more diverse, hospitable, and fair campus climate. Other campuses working toward change can learn from the mistakes and successes of this study.

The Balancing Act is a valuable read for all academics interested in improving the quality of the work/life balance. As a junior faculty member currently on maternity leave, I found this read quite informative and applicable. I would recommend this book for any pregnant professor in a tenure track position who is contemplating her options for leave after childbirth. For all women, this edited book offers creative solutions to diminishing the combative and simultaneous pressures of tenure and childbearing. For administrators and campus leaders, the work also suggests institutional policies that can help retain women faculty throughout the pre- and post-tenure process. Overall, the book accomplishes its goal of raising the attention of institutions with the message that in order for gender equity to move forward and talented female faculty be retained, family-friendly initiatives are of extreme importance.

The Doctor's Complete College Girls' Health Guide: From Sex to Drugs to the Freshmen Fifteen

by Jennifer Wider, M.D. (Ed.). Bantam Books, 2006. 368 pp.
ISBN-10: 0553383426 (paperback)

Reviewed by M.E. Yeager — Kansas State University

This book is important because it discusses many important topics pertaining to a young woman's health. These topics include birth control, date rape and sexual assault, alcoholism, tobacco, drug use, eating disorders, depression, anxiety, stress management, studying abroad, spring break, diet, and fitness. Topics that are relatively new, such as tattoos and body piercing, are covered as well. Wider includes a section entitled "Head to Toe Health" that serves as a question-and-answer section. For example, one problem is "Things that Make You Tired." This problem is followed by a detailed list of potential causes. These consist of mononucleosis, anemia, chronic fatigue syndrome, and thyroid problems. This book is easy to read, contains practical information, and may be useful to college students and their advisors.

Dr. Jennifer Wider establishes her credibility with young women between the ages of 18 and 24 in multiple ways. She shares stories from her college experience, examples from interviews with many college-age women, and practical medical advice. Wider connects with her target audience by using a light, humorous, and easy-to-understand style. When discussing birth control options, she suggests, "Just pretend you're a contestant on the *Dating Game.* But while choosing, keep in mind that none of these protects you against disease." Dr. Wider labels each method, for example "Bachelor #1, The Pill," and explains how each method works, its advantages, and disadvantages.

Wider uses a case study format to help readers learn from recognizable situations that are fairly common during the college years. Her example of tattoos is typical. "Schyler's entire basketball team is getting the school's mascot tattooed on their ankles. Most of her teammates are excited to do it, but Schyler has some reservations. She's heard that tattooing can cause serious infections, and she knows that if her parents found out, they'd kill her. Her best friend told her that she's overreacting, but she's still nervous." Dr. Wider follows each case study with questions and answers such as

"How is a tattoo made?," "Is it a big deal?," "Is it dangerous?," and other issues such as "I hate it—get it off now!"

The text is appropriate for those interested in women in higher education settings. The survival guide format is a strength that allows one to deal with women's issues and health problems from both personal and counseling perspectives. Freshmen college women are most likely to benefit from this text. This book offers helpful hints and contributes to a field that has not been presented in a readable tool-box format. A second audience consists of higher education professionals. Those who counsel young women can confidently give them this practical guide.

Many of the same issues are covered in more formal medical texts and professional journals, but there is not much practical information there that is geared toward young college-age women and written in an appealing voice. Wider's style is easy to understand and relate to.

Despite its positive qualities, an occasional reader might be put-off by Wider's light style, which is manifest throughout the text, and consequently might not take her seriously. For instance, a game show format in the section on STDs includes "Guess the STD." For herpes Dr. Wider uses the clue "it rhymes with slurpies." This light approach might hold the interest of a young adult, while seeming inappropriate to a more wizened audience.

Dr. Wider offers practical advice about many problems, their prevention, symptoms, and remedies throughout the book. However, the reviewer notes that with complex problems, such as acne, that have multiple causes and many potential remedies, she only offers general information. In the case of acne, since she is lacking adequate diagnostic information about individual cases, she does not make blanket suggestions about commonly used prescription medicines such as sulfur drugs, tetracycline, and accutane. In this example, a quick search on the Internet might suggest whether these medicines are appropriate for a given individual.

The book is a significant contribution as a practical reference for higher education students and professionals alike. The reviewer would recommend this text as mandatory reading in a Freshmen Year Experience seminar where students are learning about college life and how to handle themselves. Is there a similar book for college men?

"Strangers" of the Academy: Asian Women Scholars in Higher Education

by Guofang Li & Gulbahar Beckett (Eds.). Sterling, VA: Stylus, 2006. 304 pp. ISBN-10 1579221211 (paperback)

Reviewed by Yuanting Zhang — Bowling Green State University, Ohio

"Strangers" of the Academy: Asian Women Scholars in Higher Education is about the empowerment of Asian women scholars—about their lived experience and their feelings of frustration, estrangement, and "otherness" in Western academia, which is predominantly a White male institution. This timely collection of essays from scholars in diverse disciplines details counterstrategies against the hegemony of the institution and celebrates the powerful vehicle of a collective voice. In their introduction, Guofang Li, a first-generation immigrant scholar in the field of education, and Gulbahar Beckett, also a professor in education, summarize overarching themes key to understanding the experience of Asian female scholars in the American academy. Among them are the double-edged sword of being female and a "model minority" and professional barriers, from linguistic obstacles to the construction of cultural and professional identities.

In part one, "Asian Female Scholars in Context," the first two essays by Hune and Lee situate Asian women in the American academy by analyzing nationally representative data from the 1980s and 1990s. Hune addresses the increased proportion of Asian/Pacific Islander American (APA) women possessing doctorates as demographics shift, though these women still have the lowest tenure rates among all gendered minority subgroups and lag behind their Asian male counterparts at the doctorate, full-time faculty, and higher administrative levels. Lee focuses on the gap between Asian males and females in SME (science, mathematics, and engineering) and how it is much skewed at the postgraduate level, indicating the intersection of culture and gender as well as other social forces. In the third essay, Lin et al. use key excerpts from narratives of five Asian female scholars to illustrate the systematic marginalization they face in the second- and foreign-language education field, which is usually the hardest battleground for Asian female professionals. Their authority seems to be shattered from all directions within academia and voices against this systematic marginalization can also be stifled.

Part two, "Teaching, Mentoring, Advising, and Securing Tenure," addresses the triple jeopardies of being a woman, minority, and foreigner in the fight against the *native fallacy;* or the view that native speakers are the ideal teachers, including some harsh resistance from their female Asian graduate students. Samimy writes about the importance of having mentors; though as Hune mentioned earlier in the book, on the whole, Asian women lack support in advising and guidance through their doctoral programs and academic careers. Liang, Loo, and Ho offer practical counterstrategies and positive ways of approaching teaching in a nonnative tongue.

Essays in part three, "Gaining Voice, Forming Identity," continue the narratives while calling for alliance among underprivileged groups for "counter-hegemonic" pedagogy. Nina Asher and Eunai Kim Shrake both encourage unmasking the prescribed, inferior position of Asian women and deconstructing "model minority" stereotypes, which have been used by the dominant group as a "hegemonic device" in the politics of divide and rule.

The final section, "Building Bridges, Building the Future," offers reflections of overcoming differences by practicing global pedagogy as world citizens. Rong and Preissle present an exemplary case for cross-cultural mentoring by describing their transforming relations from mentor-mentee to equal colleagues and mutually beneficial professional collaborators. They stress that equality and mutual respect are keys for successful cross-cultural mentoring.

The strengths of the book include its readability and the underlying tone of empowerment for Asian female scholars, which as Li and Beckett claim, is critical for them to survive and thrive. The book clearly demonstrates that discrimination does not happen in isolated acts, but is produced systematically in a racialized and gendered society, and confrontation is the necessary first step to solve the problem. Also, the book helps fill the gap in research on Asian/Asian American women in higher education and does an excellent job in providing many persuasive examples of challenging model minority discourse.

Different from other macro-analyses on minority female faculty, this book is unique as it honors Asian female faculty's real voices. The similarities of this book with another book in the field, *Women Faculty of Color in the White Classroom,* edited by Lucila Vargas, lie in that both use autoethnographic approaches or standpoint epistemologies by situating chapter authors in a context of interplay with their race/ethnicity, class, and nation. However, Vargas does a more effective job eliminating the confounding factors such as years of teaching and types of colleges.

Due to its autoethnographic style, some parts of the book are inevitably repetitive. Furthermore, it lacks a compelling macro-perspective on why large numbers of highly educated Asian immigrants choose to stay in Western academia and under what situations they are most likely to be hired. Moreover, the dearth of narratives from women in the natural sciences makes the conclusions less generalizable. Shirley Geok-Lin Lim points out in the book's foreword another limitation of the text: The term "Asian woman scholar" is slippery as it does not distinguish between Asian immigrants and Asian Americans. Perhaps the book would benefit from a separation of the two groups, which have similar but also different issues in their academic struggles. I also second Lim's critique that the book only includes success stories; and further, there is an overrepresentation of female faculty members from China.

Despite these shortcomings, as a scholar from China, trained in the United States and deciding whether to enter the North American academy, I found this book an eye-opener for Asian women, including Asian female graduate students, postdoctoral fellows, and Asian faculty, who are either in or are contemplating joining the academy. Also, this book is definitely a useful resource for North American faculty and administrators, so they can better understand their international minority students, colleagues, and employees.

By sharing stories, minority female faculty members can join in the collaborative journey toward a "counter-hegemonic" pedagogy. Many are struggling from overt discrimination to the "glass-ceiling" effect, and the reason most are not fighting is because they know the costs will be huge. Though implicitly, this book provides a realistic picture about working in the United States, a picture that can better mentally prepare the overseas Asian female students who dream about their American pilgrimages.

Removing Barriers: Women in Academic Science, Technology, Engineering, and Mathematics

by Jill M. Bystydzienski & Sharon R. Bird (Eds). Bloomingdale, IN: Indiana University Press, 2006. 347 pp. ISBN-10 0253218179 (paperback)

Reviewed by Shaki Asgari — Fordham University, New York

Over the past 25 years, there have been some improvements in the status of women and minorities in higher education. According to the U.S. Department of Education, women have begun to outnumber men in college graduation rates and the proportion of full-time female faculty increased by 3% between 1992 and 1998 across all types of postsecondary institutions. However, there is an unequal distribution of men and women across all levels of higher education and at all types of institutions. Specifically, the overall college graduation rates do not directly translate into earned undergraduate and graduate degrees by women in physical sciences, engineering, and computer technology. In 1996, for example, women earned the majority of graduate degrees in education and health, whereas men earned the majority of graduate degrees in computer science and engineering. In addition, women continue to represent a small proportion of faculty members in science and technology programs, especially in more prestigious research institutions.

What are the barriers that contribute to the low numbers of women in STEM (science, technology, engineering, and mathematics) fields? What are the experiences of women who participate in science and technology fields as college students or faculty members? What strategies are in place or can be developed to help recruitment, retention, and success of young girls and women in scientific fields? These are some of the questions addressed by Iowa State University colleagues Jill M. Bystydzienski, director of the Women's Studies Program and professor of sociology, and Sharon R. Bird, associate professor of sociology and an affiliate of the Women's Studies Program, in their edited book *Removing Barriers: Women in Academic Science, Technology, Engineering, and Mathematics.*

A noteworthy strength of this volume is the diversity of perspectives presented by a group of social, natural, and physical scientists, each of whom provides a unique analysis of the barriers faced by women including African American (and African) women in STEM fields. Another equally important feature of this book is the contributors' pragmatic recommendations for removing barriers that contribute to the low numbers of women in science and technology.

The volume begins with the editors' well-written and thorough introduction, which summarizes the main topics in a precise and easy-to-follow manner. What follows is a collection of 17 chapters organized into four parts. Part one is a historical account of women's struggle for equity from their early ingenious efforts to gain recognition in science to their systematic activism and research in years to come.

In part two, the authors discuss a recent shift in research efforts that addresses the need to look beyond individual and personal choices to include efforts that can identify systematic cultural and institutional barriers to full participation of women in STEM fields. This section can help educators and mentors develop a better appreciation for positive and negative influences of their actions on students' motivation to pursue scientific careers.

I particularly liked part two's focus on frustrations experienced by women graduate students and STEM faculty who, despite their efforts to remain in science programs or survive the so called "leaky pipeline," still find themselves faced with an unfavorable academic climate. Lack of female mentors and role models as well as professors' reluctance to tap into their network to secure challenging research, jobs, or postdoctoral fellowships for their female students are discussed as some of the factors that continue to alienate women in graduate school. In this part, authors also elaborate on difficulties faced by STEM women faculty, for whom academic tenure often coincides with their child-bearing years—which along with a combination of other factors including decreased lab space, inadequate resources, lower salaries, and fewer prestigious opportunities make early stages of an academic career particularly difficult.

Part three of this volume presents a feminist analysis of the interaction between societal values and conceptions of knowledge. The authors argue that gender has thus far played a central role in the process of inquiry and practice of science. They argue that sexist language and methodology perpetuate gender divides and systematically excludes women and minorities from full engagement in science.

Part four provides constructive suggestions for removing cultural and institutional barriers toward advancement of women in science and technology. What seems to resonate among the potential solutions is creation of an environment in which women can become a part of their academic culture, feel a sense of belonging, and be confident in taking ownership of what their program and field has to offer. Graduate programs can demonstrate their interest and investment in success of all students by providing information, guidance, and opportunities to interact with faculty on an ongoing basis.

Institutional leaders can especially benefit from the recommendations presented in this section by evaluating their existing policies and practices that pertain to women's participation, hiring, and promotion in science programs. Institutions can make serious attempts to recruit and promote women faculty by offering attractive salaries, start-up funds, adequate resources, laboratory space, and dual-career hiring. Institutional leaders can promote policies to stop the tenure clock during child-bearing years and protect pregnant faculty in hiring, promotion, and tenure.

In addition to extensive index, footnotes, and references, this volume includes an overview of research and data from a variety of independent sources that can be of particular use to readers interested in enhancing their understanding of the current research trends in the status of women in higher education.

Although this book is not an introductory text, some chapters can be assigned readings in undergraduate classes in science and gender studies. I also think reading first-person accounts of survival strategies used by women and minorities presented in this volume can be a source of inspiration for graduate students and junior faculty.

This volume may be of less relevance to readers interested in a specific take on the status of women in higher education. In fact, the diversity of perspectives presents somewhat of a divergence from the general focus of the book. For example, a feminist interpretation of barriers and discussion of obstacles faced by African American or African women in STEM fields are topics that would require a more in-depth and focused analysis.

Overall, the text is an outstanding contribution to the field of higher education. I think graduate students, faculty, administrators, and all others interested in understanding the gender gap in STEM fields will both enjoy and benefit from reading this book. This volume can also provide faculty and institutional leaders with a better understanding of their instrumental role in paving the path to women's full participation in science programs.

College Girls: Bluestockings, Sex Kittens, and Coeds, Then and Now

by Lynn Peril. New York: W.W. Norton & Company, 2006.
352 pp. ISBN-10: 0393327159 (paperback)

Reviewed by Amy Thompson McCandless — College of Charleston, South Carolina

From the founding of the American republic, there has been considerable debate over the nature and role of education for women. Collegiate education, connected as it was to the preparation of men for the ministry and other professions, was particularly controversial. To many men, higher education for women was a waste of time and resources. At its best, it could enhance women's innate domestic and maternal talents and make them more attractive to future husbands; at its worst, it could ruin their health, corrupt their innocence, and coarsen their character. As Lynn Peril notes in her introduction to *College Girls*, perceptions of the educated woman were conflicted from the beginning. Despite the Enlightenment emphasis on human reason, intellectual women were seen as unnatural. "The bluestocking was the most widely known (and reviled) stereotype associated with the early college girl" (p. 31). Although the term originated from an invitation to a guest to come dressed informally, in "your blue stockings," its association with the assertive women of the eighteenth-century literary salon led to a denigration of bluestockings as those who "unsex and degrade themselves, by their boisterous assumption of man's prerogatives and responsibilities" (p. 29). There were exceptions to these negative characterizations—those women whose feminine personalities and appearances remained unsullied by their studies. Alfred, Lord Tennyson wrote admiringly of the "sweet girl-graduates in their golden hair" (p. 31). The bluestockings were doomed to spinsterhood, while the sweet girl-graduates were destined for marriage and motherhood. Drawing on images of college women from popular culture, Peril provides a satiric history of "Bluestockings, Sex Kittens, and Coeds, Then and Now."

Lynn Peril is best known as the author, editor, and publisher of the zine, *Mystery Date: One Gal's Guide to Good Stuff.* As she explains in the introduction to Mystery Date online, "Mystery Date is a fanzine devoted to my obsession with used books—particularly old sex and dating manuals, etiquette and self-help books, and health, beauty and fashion guides" (http://members.tripod.com/~Mystery_Date/introduction.html). Her first book, *Pink Think* (2002), employed such sources to illustrate "how media messages have long endeavored to shape women's behavior and self-image, with varying degrees of success." These materials are also integral to Peril's analysis of images of the American college "girl" throughout the centuries. She consults academic studies of women's higher education as well as popular culture, but her primary sources are drawn from "prescriptive literature, fiction, popular works of sociology and guidance, girlie magazines and pulp fiction, as well as student handbooks and the like—a constellation of sources that make up the constant, under-the-conscious-radar flow of ideas that academics refer to as discourse" (pp. 11–12).

Vignettes and photographs from these sources are scattered throughout the chapters, supporting Peril's contention that popular culture both shaped and was shaped by women's educational experiences. This interaction of the collegiate and the noncollegiate can be seen in fashion. "By giving consumer items names like 'campus' or 'coed,' manufacturers hoped that nonstudents would associate the college girl's youth and freshness—or her sexuality—with such products, and thereby profited from a national obsession with youth and youthfulness that continues to this day" (p. 116). Fictional accounts of campus life also reflected the mixed messages college women received about their sexuality. On the one hand, college was promoted as the ideal place either to meet a husband or to acquire those accomplishments that would attract a husband. On the other hand, these "sex kittens" were expected to remain chaste virgins.

Peril warns readers of the shortcomings of prescriptive sources, and she tries to balance the etiquette manuals for and fictional stories of college women with descriptive and historical materials. Still, it is the stereotypes of bluestockings, sex kittens, and coeds that dominate the narrative—the nonfictional as well as the fictional accounts of women's educational experiences. As Peril asserts, "certain attitudes about women and higher education crop up too frequently to be considered entirely quaint or anachronistic" (p. 12).

A variety of colleges are examined—women's colleges, denominational colleges, land grant universities, private institutions, historically black colleges—although most of the sources Peril consults focus on White, middle-class women. Peril does not ignore the impact the prevailing stereotypes have on non-White, working-class women, but because these women are not the main subjects of her sources, the distinctive experiences of the "other" are lost in a literature that privileges their White sisters.

College Girls is very different in tone and content from educational histories such as Barbara Miller Solomon's *In the Company of Educated Women* (1985), Christie Anne Farnham's *The Education of the Southern Bell* (1995), or Paula Fass' *The Damned and the Beautiful* (1978), although Peril cites all three. Rather, Peril's prose recalls the wit of Florence King and Molly Ivins. Commenting on Dr. Howard's 1911 warning that vigorous exercise could jar the womb loose from its moorings, Peril writes: "It was a frightening vision of the uterus broken loose from its strings like an out-of-control Macy's Parade balloon tangled in telephone wires on a windy day . . ." (p. 241). Peril's volume also contains a lot more on extracurricular activities than the standard institutional history. There are chapters on "The Collegiate Look," "In Loco Parentis and Other Campus Rules," "Fit in Mind and Body," "Sex Ed and Husband Hunting," and "Graduation and After." Peril also intersperses the narrative with reflections on her own undergraduate experience at the University of Wisconsin-Milwaukee and includes a copy of her student ID that showed her "wearing a purple thrift store T-shirt and black stovepipe jeans from Trash and Vaudeville . . . [and] sporting the shortest haircut I'd ever had, a buzz cut anomaly back in the days of Farrah feathering . . . " (p. 6).

Peril's chatty style of writing should appeal to undergraduate students and the general public, and her use of nontraditional sources would be a good introduction to material culture for a graduate class in the history of education or in women's studies. The outrageous contentions of some of her sources would certainly provoke discussion on the strengths and weaknesses of popular literature to an academic analysis of gender identities, roles, and relations.

Guidelines for Authors

The *Journal About Women in Higher Education* seeks scholarly essays and research-based manuscripts that illuminate important issues related to women in higher education and that make an original contribution to the knowledge base about these women. The *Journal* welcomes manuscripts that look at women in non-U.S. higher education settings as long as connections are drawn between the manuscript's topic and related studies about U.S. women.

Additionally, the *Journal* seeks book reviews and brief program descriptions. To submit a book review, please contact the editors for advance approval and guidelines. Books being reviewed must be on a topic relevant to women in higher education and have been published in 2007. Program description submissions should be 500-word descriptions highlighting an innovative program designed for women in higher education.

Style Guidelines

All manuscripts must follow American Psychological Association (APA) style. Depending upon the type of article, manuscripts should be at least 15 pages, and no more than 25 pages, double-spaced in 12-point Times New Roman font. Page length includes tables and figures, but does not include title page, abstract, or references.

Manuscript Review Process

Manuscripts are judged using a blind review process, each by at least two reviewers. The genre of the paper is taken into consideration when being critiqued. Criteria related to some modes of inquiry are noted below, but these are suggestive, not definitive or exhaustive.

- **Research Paper:** Consider the use of theory and the available literature; the design, sampling, and data gathering procedures; appropriateness of the method for the question; the treatment and interpretation of data; the importance of results; the practical and substantive implications of results.

- **Professional Practice Paper:** Consider the validity of the description of the problem and its context; the clarity of assumptions; the discussion of alternative solutions; the defense of the chosen course of action; practical or theoretical implications.
- **Best Practices Paper:** Consider the adequacy of the description of the practice or program, the uniqueness of the case, the method for gathering data about the program, the implications of the program for other colleges and universities.
- **Scholarly Essay:** Consider the importance of the problem, thoroughness of coverage of relevant literature, and logical development of the essay.
- **Literature Review:** Consider its scope, coherence, and impartiality; the development of meaningful insights for the practitioner; its suggestions for necessary scholarship.

Each manuscript is evaluated on the paper's form and content. Form includes writing style and readability, logical development, length, and relation of author's objectives to those appropriate for the genre. Content includes originality of topic or approach, significance of the subject, and significance to the readers.

The manuscripts published in the *Journal About Women in Higher Education* are selected by the editors in consultation with the reviewers.

How to Submit

To submit a manuscript, please send an electronic copy in Microsoft Word to jawhe@naspa.org, with "JAWHE Manuscript Submission" in the subject line. A title page, abstract, and author(s) biography (40 words maximum) should be included with the manuscript. Please include manuscript title; name and title of author(s); and submitting author's address, phone number, and e-mail address on the title page.

Submission Deadline

The *Journal About Women in Higher Education* is published annually in March. Manuscripts are due no later than March 15 for publication consideration. Visit www.naspa.org/jawhe for deadline information.